CONFUCIUS
THE ANALECTS

孔 夫 子 　 論 語

Kong　Fu　Zi　　Lun　Yu

CONFUCIUS
THE ANALECTS
Psychotherapeutic Commentaries

論 語

孔 夫 子

A WAYFARING COUNSELOR'S RENDERING
OF
THE COLLECTED SAYINGS OF KONG FU ZI

Raymond Bart Vespe

REGENT PRESS
Berkeley, California

Copyright © 2025 by Ray Vespe

Paperback
ISBN 13: 978-1-58790-703-6
ISBN 10:1-58790-703-8

E-book:
ISBN 13: 978-1-58790-704-3
ISBN 10: 1-58790-704-6

Library of Congress Cataloging-in-Publication Data: 2025012579

Manufactured in the United States of America

REGENT PRESS
www.regentpress.net
regentpress@mindspring.com

CONTENTS

水

DEDICATION

This rendition of *The Analects* of Confucius is dedicated to those human beings; 1) who only have superficially considered and prematurely discounted the teachings of Confucius as being patriarchal, misogynistic, authoritarian and rigidly moralistic; 2) who haven't dug a little deeper to discover some realities and truths about the person and life of the most influential human being in the history, culture and politics of the Chinese nation, its people and leaders and 3) who haven't seen any relevant or meaningful applications of the ethical wisdom and moral teachings of Confucius to themselves and to their lives, work and human relationships.

水

The Chinese character Shui/Shui - water, a stream of flowing water, river, liquid, fluid is a symbol for Confucianism. In ancient writing, the center stroke is a small stream, rivulet, brook and the side strokes are ripples, whirls, waves of water.

ACKNOWLEDGEMENT

Of the Spirit of Lao Tzu, the Buddha and Confucius; three wise, compassionate, generous and exceptional human beings who devoted themselves and their lives to teaching, awakening and healing our conflicted, suffering and morally disordered human world and who showed us Ways of being, living and relating more truly, freely, peacefully, intimately and happily.

Of former non- and anti-Confucian teachers and students who contributed to my avoiding exploring the teachings of Confucius until the present time when I'm now old enough to accept and appreciate them and to discover how much they reflect my own Way of being.

Of my ancient Italian-Sicilian ancestry from Emperor Vespasian (9-79 CE) and explorer Amerigo Vespucci (1454-1512 CE) to the memory of my grandparents, mother, father and brother and of my current family of three daughters, their husbands and their eight children, my grandchildren. You are the most meaning, fulfillment and happiness my heart can feel.

Of Mark Weiman of Regent Press for his continuing interest, support, encouragement, collaboration and skills in publishing all seven of my books.

水

PREAMBLE

It appears that the moral fabric of the country and the world is threadbare as a whole, (its multi-cultural infrastructure), fading in its colors (its richness of human diversity) and fraying at its edges (its global future vision). The world situation, international governmental policies and economic conditions appear to be moving in the direction of greater autocratic rather than democratic leadership, greater isolationism rather than globalism, greater hierarchically skewed distribution of wealth and resources and greater mobilization of the war-machine.

There appears to be a greater prevalence of humanitarian crises, domestic and foreign terrorism and existential threats to the lives, freedom, intimacy, peacefulness and happiness of human beings. The global world order, international stability, national security, harmonious and peaceful co-existence and the personal viability, vitality and vibrancy of humane human being, living and interrelating appear to be at a greater risk of decay, deteriorization, degeneration, disintegration and demise.

The 'business as usual' of everyday and ordinary human living does continue going on but often is only possible and actualized through the ignorance of, misinformation about, rationalizations of, distractions from and/or denial of the state of the larger cultural and social context and reality within which daily living is occurring.

Infants and young children naturally make differentiating discriminations of and preferential choices for things but not discriminating and prejudicial judgments about them. They don't begin their lives discriminating about the skin color, hair texture or bodily appearances of other infants and young children as a basis for accepting or rejecting and disliking or hating them.

Young children aren't concerned with such things. Any perceived differences don't make a difference and such things don't mean anything to them save for their own observations, interest, curiosity, inquisitiveness, questions and desire to learn about the 'whys' of things and to expand their knowledge about themselves, their parents, other children, their world and their lives.

In the process and vicissitudes of growing up, young children experience that their attitudes, feelings and behaviors create effects, results and consequences and can invoke admiration, pride and praise as well as disciplinary limitations, restrictions and punishments from parents. They begin to develop a conscious awareness, ethical sense and moral understanding of what are good and bad, right and wrong and proper and improper attitudes, feelings, thoughts, behaviors and choices which typically are those that either are or aren't okay, acceptable and allowable for their parents and other adults.

Unfortunately, these naturally alive, vibrant, open, dear and lovable young children concurrently develop a dualistic self-sense that also is either good or bad, right or wrong and proper or improper. In addition, in the process of acculturation and socialization; they may be painfully objectified, negatively judged, deeply shamed and physically, sexually, verbally, psychologically and/or emotionally abused by immature, insensitive, unwise, unskilled, wounded, borderline, narcissistic and dysfunctional parents and adults.

Young children also simultaneously develop a similar sense of what is or isn't okay, acceptable and allowable in the attitudes, feelings, thoughts and behaviors of their parents and the other children and adults in their lives. In their ego-formation and development, unconscious or conscious decisions are made as to whether or not to be; or to self-identify as being; a good, right and proper child or to be and to self-identify as their opposites. Hypocricies are noticed in parents, adults and other children whose self-identifications, words and behaviors are incongruent and children typically imitate how parents are and what they do rather than what they say.

With the possible exception of broccoli, resisting wiping runny noses, avoiding pain and the 'nos' of the 'terrible twos'; young children have to LEARN to make discriminating, negative and prejudicial judgments about; and to dislike, hate, avoid and reject other children.

They are TAUGHT to do so by parents, relatives, teachers and other adults in their lives who exemplify, model and TEACH objectifying and discriminating 'negative'; 1) definitions and descriptions of fellow human beings; 2) feelings and thoughts about them; 3) judgments and prejudices of them, 4) separation and alienation from them; 5) apprehension about and fear of them and 6) dislike and hatred of them.

Also, it is more the case that it is the supposedly 'adult' governing leaders, officials, politicians, generals, elite and their cohorts and accomplices of different nations who dislike and hate each other rather than do their many human citizens. Non-democratic international male 'leaders' establish, command and rule a patriarchically, hierarchically, autocratic, authoritarian, controlling and coercively-run country; 1) that re-creates and macroscopically institutionalizes the very worst attitudes, policies, dynamics, mechanisms, practices and conflicts of a dysfunctional 'family' non-unit and 2) that reflects their own likely histories of childhood rejection, abandonment, neglect, trauma, abuse, 'craziness', skewed ethics and warped morality, e.g., ones that rationalize and justify killing fellow human beings because of racial, ethnic, religious, ideological, cultural and political differences and fears and phobias about them.

For our world to be a more peaceful, evolved, intimate and better place to be and in which to live and reside; it is essential, necessary and appropriate that each one of us lives and shares; 1) an ethically grounded and fundamentally principled, 2) a morally cultivated and virtuously enacted and 3) an harmoniously developed and heart-centered humane life of goodness, rightness and properness.

Being and living so will naturally radiate concentrically from ourselves and our families to; 1) create a much-needed shared collective, multi-national and global moral awakening, renaissance and restoration of humane being and living, political order, social harmony and world stability and to 2) return us to the freedom, peacefulness, intimacy and happiness of a humane and cultured human life of goodness and rightness, dignity and respect, kindness and gentleness, civility and courtesy, loving and caring, gratitude and appreciation, generosity and forgiveness and other life-safeguarding, life-supporting, life-nourishing, life-sustaining, life-improving, life-refining and life-enhancing virtues.

In all places and situations, under all circumstances and conditions and with any and every human being; we need to be and to do our very best to feel, think, act and relate in ways that; 1) are ethically and morally both good and right, 2) are meaningfully and beneficially supporting, inspiring, encouraging, assisting, developing, improving, refining, optimizing, enhancing and uplifting ourselves and fellow human beings and 3) are positively influencing and vitally contributing to the harmonious ordering, regulating, unfolding and fulfilling of life events, human affairs, social relationships and our uniquely and truly individual conscious human being, experiencing, relating and living.

Here and now, we need to value being, cultivating, refining, living and sharing an ethical and moral Way of life as a reality in its own right, for its own sake and as an end in itself and not as a means to insure forgiveness, exoneration, expiation, absolution, deliverance, redemption, salvation and freedom from damnation in another life. However, should there be another life after death; being an ethical, moral and humane human being in this life will likely make the next one more enjoyable.

First...open your heart, eyes and hands and then...open your mouth.

水

PROLOGUE

My personal, academic, professional and practical interest is in the wisdom of 'The East', specifically the Asian spiritual traditions of Taoism and Buddhism during c. 500s BCE; The Golden Age, The Axial Age and the times of Lao Tzu, the Buddha and Confucius. I focused mostly upon the wisdom and teachings of Lao Tzu, Chuang Tzu, Lieh Tzu and the Buddha and not at all upon those of Confucius.

Learning that many past and present Chinese people embrace Taoism, Confuciaism and Buddhism; prompts me to finally investigate and explore the teachings of Confucius. 1 So, I decide to read, study and learn about *The Analects* of Confucius and to consider writing a rendition with commentaries relating to psychotherapy practice.

I hadn't been interested in Confucius out of an uninformed projection that his teachings involved; 1) an authoritarian patriarchy and social hierarchy between 'superior' man and common people; 2) misogynistically ignoring women and 'the feminine' and 3) strictly adhering to rigid rules, prescriptions and fixed rituals of moral conduct and behavior.

This impression is fueled by a legendary account of an alleged meeting between Confucius and Lao Tzu to discuss the imperial archives wherein the former is portrayed as immature and the latter experienced as a dragon. There are numerous tales in *The Chuang Tzu* text that playfully counter the Confucian virtues of benvolence, righteousness and ritual propriety; poke fun at Confucius; attribute Taoist qualities to him, put Taoist words his mouth and make him up to be a convert to Taoism.

After a cursory reading of one translation of *The Analects*; I become aware of how much I basically agree with, value and have been living Confucian virtues such as filial piety, benevolence, righteouness, respect, loyalty, sincerity, reciprocity and a love of learning. I can see how these virtues contribute to establishing and sustaining social order and harmony and personal freedom, intimacy, peacefulness and happiness.

My love of reality, truth and language found validation in Confucius's 'rectification of names and social roles', whereby words accurately define the realities to which they refer, roles accurately embody the realities for which they are intended and there is a trustworthy congruence between our words and our actions, i.e., when we 'walk our talk'.

Human multi-dimensionality and multi-tasking abilities aside; I want a physician, therapist and spiritual teacher to just only be a physician, therapist and spiritual teacher and one who is a specalist trained, knowledgeable, practiced and competent specifically in the respective realities of our human body; our human being, living and relating and our human Soul, Spirit and enlightenment. When my car requires good and right repairing, what matters is that the mechanic is an expert and not an enlightened human being.

I recall that, once very much earlier in my life, I have the unsolicited realization that real and true 'freedom' is the result of conforming to, complying with and 'playing by' the rules rather than resisting and rebelling against them and harboring the illusion of being 'free'. But in that initial reading of *The Analects*, I am still bothered by the frequent use of words such as 'ought', 'should', 'must', 'always' and 'never'; the patriarchal, gender, hierarchical and class issues and what appears to be a kind of reductionistic and simplistic overemphasis on the importance of ritual.

Given this, I wonder how can *The Analects* ever be applied to the practicing of psychotherapy and how can I ever write psychotherapeutic commentaries of it. After reading, studying, reflecting upon and absorbing several more translations of *The Analects*, consulting a few bi-lingual translations and discovering the etymological meanings of some of the principal original Chinese terms; I decide to begin writing.

Very quickly, after somewhat laboriously rendering particular Book sayings, I am surprised and pleased by how easily and consistently psychotherapeutic commentaries of them just naturally 'come to mind' without my having to 'think' about making them. So, most all of the psychotherapy commentaries that you are reading happened in just this way with only a few later minor revisions and additions.

I hope that you find this rendition of *The Analects* and the commentaries of some value, meaning, use and benefit for you and for your life and relationships and, if you are a counselor or psychotherapist, for your clients and the conduct of your practice as well.

I also hope that this book; 1) will assist in correcting any negative preconceptions, misconceptions or misunderstandings that you may have about Confucius and/or Confucianism and 2) will contribute to a more educated, realistic, learned and compassionate including, accepting, understanding and appreciating of its ethical and moral socio-political philosophy and Way of being, living and relating.

Writing this book is a positive and heartwarming experience that completely changes any of my own negative preconceptions about Confucius and Confucianism. I appreciate having a sense of the human being and personhood of Confucius in ways that I hadn't had in regard to Lao Tzu, Chuang Tzu, Lieh Tzu and the Buddha.

I also appreciate how the three Spiritual traditions of Taoism, Confucianism and Buddhism are naturally, culturally and essentially a tripartite complementary unity in Chinese culture, among the Chinese people and within our own consciousness and life.[1]

Please simply enjoy reading the book and reflecting upon its teachings and their meaning; knowing how much I happily enjoyed and dutifully recorded its spontaneous unfolding and how much I humbly offer it to you and kindly share it with you.

Raymond Bart Vespe
Scotts Valley, California
Spring Equinox 2025

水

TAO TE CHING QUOTES

There are too many commonalities between Taoism and Confucianism in Lao Tzu's *Tao Te Ching* to quote. The following quotations refer; 1) to ego-invested and ego-attached benevolent 'be-gooders' and righteous 'do-righters'; 2) to 'filiality' as a formal obligatory and heartless obedience; 3) to 'virtue' as ego-motivated quasi-'virtuous' appearances and 4) to 'learning' and 'knowing' in the usual sense of their meaning of acquiring conceptual 'knowledge' and not in the Confucian sense of learning as self-cultivation, self-improvement and self-refinement.

When Dao is forgotten, 'benevolence' and 'righteousness' appear ... When the relationships between father and son, elder and younger brother and husband and wife are disordered, there are 'filial' children. (TTC 18).

Cease being 'benevolent' and 'righteous' and human beings will naturally be filial and return to being loving. (TTC 19).

Human beings of lowest 'virtue' never stray from being 'virtuous' and, therefore, don't have true virtue ... Human beings of lowest 'benevolence' and 'righteousness' act from ulterior motives and, when no one responds, resort to force. When Dao is lost, there is 'virtue'. When 'virtue' is lost, there is 'benevolence'. When 'benevolence' is lost, there is 'righteousness'. When 'righteousness' is lost, there is 'ritual propriety'. When there is 'ritual propriety', there is a loss of real loyalty, true fidelity and genuine trust and the beginning of disaster. (TTC 38).

When the least developed students hear about Dao, they laugh out loud. (TTC 41).

In the pursuit of 'learning', more is 'known'. In the pursuit of Dao, less is 'done'. (TTC 48).

Human beings who truly know may not 'speak' and those who 'speak' may not truly know. (TTC 56).

Even if human beings are not 'good', they aren't abandoned. (TTC 62).

Not to truly know and to 'think' that one truly knows is a sickness to be sick of. (TTC 71).

水

Chuang Tzu Quotes

Some portrayals of Confucius in Chuang Tzu's *The Chuang Tzu* have him preaching his conventional morality and others playfully jest with Confucius, often portraying him as professing and speaking Taoist ideas, beliefs and values and/or being a convert to Taoism. The following quotations illustrate more contra-Confucian notions:

When the Way and words depend upon small words and showy deeds, we have the rights and wrongs of Confucianism. (**Chapter 2**).

A madman wanders by Confucius's gate shouting, 'Phoenix, phoenix, how your virtue has failed ... forget about teaching human beings virtue!'. (**Chapter 4**).

Confucius certainly hasn't reached the stage of a Perfect Man, has he? ... He's after the illusion of fame and reputation. (**Chapter 5**).

Men like me wander within the realm. Beyond and within the realm can never meet ... The petty man of Heaven is a gentleman among men. The gentleman among men is the petty man of Heaven ... You and I – we are dreaming and haven't awakened yet ... Yen Hui says 'I'm improving'. Confucius asks, 'What do you mean?'. Yen Hui answers, 'I've forgotten benevolence and righteousness ... rites and music'. (**Chapter 6**).

There is no more unity to Virtue ... the crime lies in meddling with men's minds ... now come the Confucianists ... so lacking in shame ... benevolence and righteousness are their fetters and manacles. (**Chapter 11**).

Lao Tzu asks Confucius, 'Do benevolence and righteousness belong to the inborn nature of human beings?' Confucius answers, 'Yes, what else could they be?' ... Lao Tzu adds, 'Why are these banners of benevolence and righteousness so courageously raised ? ... you'll bring confusion to the nature of human being'. (**Chapter 13**).

Regarding Confucius's teaching in other states, a Master says to one of his disciples, 'Your Master hoping to bring the practices of former dynasties to these states is like pushing a boat over land – a great deal of work, no success and certainly dangerous ... rituals change with the times'. In a visit, Lao Tzu says to Confucius, 'Benevolence and righteousness are the dwellings of former kings; you can stay in them for a night but not for any longer ... *The Six Classics* are the worn-out paths of former kings and not the ones who walked the paths'. (**Chapter 14**).

A time came when Virtue declined ... there was compliance but no unity ... purity was defiled and simplicity shattered. The Way was separated for the sake of goodness. True Virtue was endangered for the sake of conduct ... inborn nature was abandoned ... 'culture' came next and destroyed the substantial (The Way) ... people became confused and disordered. (**Chapter 16**).

What the ancient Five legendary Emperors passed on, the Three Kings of the former dynasties fought over, the benevolent grieve about and the responsible labor over ... Confucius passed himself off as learned because he talked about it and them. (**Chapter 17**).

Confucius is beseiged and his life endangered when traveling to an adjoining state and a sympathetic person offers some reasons, 'The straight-trunked tree is felled first and the well of sweet water dries up first. Now you – you display your wisdom to astonish the ignorant, work at good conduct to distinguish yourself from the disreputable and travel around bright and shining as though holding the sun and moon. That's why you can't escape'. (Chapter 20).

Confucius says to a Master, 'I've been driven out of my home State Lu twice and in my travels to neighboring states; people chopped down a tree on top of me, wiped away my footprints, made trouble for me and beseiged me. I've met many calamities. My associates, followers and friends drift farther apart and one after the other leave. How come?' The Master mentions an example of someone who relinquished profit-obtained jade in favor of a Heaven-brought baby and says, 'The friendship of a gentleman is insipid as water and leads to affection and the sweetness of a petty man leads to revulsion. Those with no reason to join together will part for no reason'. Confucius reportedly abandons his studies and gives away his books and his disciples stop bowing to him but their affection for him is greater than ever before. (Chapter 20).

Confucius says to Lao Tzu, 'Your virtue is the very complement of Heaven and Earth and yet even you must use perfect teachings in order to cultivate your mind'. 'Not so!', replies Lao Tzu. 'The sound of water is its natural talent, not something done deliberately. The Perfect Man has the same relationship with virtue. Without cultivating it, he has it to such an extent that no one can draw away from him. It's as natural as the height of Heaven and the depth of earth and the brightness of the sun and moon. What is there to be cultivated?'. (Chapter 21).

Chuang Tzu visits the Ruler of the State of Lu who says that there are a large number of Confucians in the state but few who follow Chuang Tzu. Chuang Tzu says that there are only a few Confucians but many who dress in Confucian apparel and says, 'A gentleman can embrace doctrines without the apparel and may wear the apparel without understanding the doctrines. Why not issue an order proclaiming that anyone who wears Confucian apparel without practicing the doctrine will be sentenced to death?'. The order is issued and in five days only one old man in the state is wearing Confucian apparel. **(Chapter 21)**.

Confucius asks Lao Tzu to discourse on the Perfect Way which he does specifically and at length and concludes by saying, ' Your Way – the 'Way of the gentleman' that you teach is superficial, is it not?. But that which sustains the ten thousand things without fail, is this not the real and true Way?'. **(Chapter 22)**.

Confucius is speaking with a disciple about 'the men of old' and 'the men of today' and says, 'Among gentlemen there were those like Confucians who became 'teachers' and, as a result, people began using 'rights' and 'wrongs' to contend with each other. And it's much worse today'. **(Chapter 22)**.

Confucius is meeting with the ruler of a neighboring state who asks him to speak about the wisdom of the ancients. In the process, Confucius says, 'The unity of the Way is something that virtue can never master ... To apply names in the manner of Confucians is to invite trouble'. **(Chapter 24)**.

Confucius is visiting another state. A crowd is gathered around a sage and one of Confucius's disciples asks if the sage should be called over. Confucius objects, saying 'He knows that I'm out to make a name for myself and will assume that I'm trying to get the ruler to give me a position and will take me for a self-seeking flatterer'. **(Chapter 25)**.

The Confucians rob graves in accord with *The Odes* and ritual. The big Confucian says, 'The East grows light. How is the matter going?'. The little Confucians answer, 'We haven't got the graveclothes off yet but there's a pearl in his mouth'. (Chapter 26).

Lao Tzu summons Confucius and says to him, 'Get rid of your proud bearing and that knowing look on your face and you can become a gentleman ... You can't bear to observe the sufferings of one age and you make trouble for the next ones that come ... Don't you have the sense to understand the situation?. You take pride in practicing charity and making people happy – the shame of it will follow you for all of your days ... What good are these actions of yours? They end in nothing but boasts!'. (Chapter 26).

An old fisherman comments on Confucius, saying, 'As far as benevolence goes, he is benevolent but I fear that he won't escape harm. To weary the mind, wear out the body and put Truth in danger is being separated from the Great Way by a vast distance!'. (Chapter 31).

A stranger comments to Confucius saying, 'Now you scrutinize the realm of benevolence and righteousness ... yet you barely manage to escape harm. If you were diligent in improving yourself, held fast to the Truth and would let others handle external matters; you could avoid entanglements. But now, without improving yourself, you make demands upon others – that's not the way to go about things, is it?'. Confucius asks the stranger what he means by 'the Truth' who answers, 'Rites are created by the common men of the world. Truth is that which is received from Heaven ... There is no greater misfortune than for a man to lack benevolence and yet you alone dare to invite such misfortune!'. (Chapter 31).

The Ruler of the State of Lu asks a minister, 'If I made Confucius my supporting pillar, would it improve the well-being of the state?'. The minister warns, 'Be careful – that way is very dangerous!. Confucius will decorate things with feathers and paint, conduct affairs with flowery phrases and mistake side issues for crucial ones. He'll disregard his inborn nature in order to be a model for the people without realizing that he's acting in bad faith. He takes everything to heart and submits all to the judgment of Spirit. How can he be put in charge of the people? ... One who encourages the people to turn their backs on reality and to study hypocrisy is hardly fit to be a model for them'. (Chapter 32).

水

TITLE CHINESE CHARACTERS

CONFUCIUS

孔 　 夫 　 子

KONG
FAMILY NAME

FU
BIG MAN
DISTINGUISHED
MASTER
GREAT TEACHER

ZI
PHILOSOPHER
HUSBAND/FATHER

THE ANALECTS

論 　 語

LUN
DISCUSS

YU
SPEECH

YAN - WORDS + LUN - ARRANGE　　YAN - WORDS + WU - I/ME

言 + 侖 　 言 + 吾

CONFUCIUS
KONG FU ZI

CONFUCIUS

Confucius reportedly is born in 551 BCE in Qu Fu, the capital of the Chinese State of Lu, shortly after the family flees from the Chinese State of Song during the Spring and Autumn Period (770-475 BCE) of the Eastern Chou Dynasty (770-221 BCE). He is named Kong Qiu by his mother Yan Zeng Zai and his honorific name is Zhong Ni, the second son born near Mt. Ni.

The Kong family reportedly is descended from a lower nobility rank and military background, but loses their Song ancestral hereditary titles, status and privileges in Lu. Because of their humble economic circumstances, Confucius is considered to belong to the Shi class of common gentlepersons and public servants between the aristocracy and the common people. 6 He comes to be named Kong Zi, Master Kong and Kong Fu Zi, Great Master Kong, which is Latinized to 'Confucius' by Jesuit missionaries in the late 16th-early 17th Centuries CE.

His father, Kong He, dies when Confucius is three years old and he is raised and educated by his mother in relative poverty. Confucius reportedly has an early love of learning and a respect for moral values. At age 19, he marries Lady Qi Guan and their first child, a son Kong Li, is born when Confucius is 20 years old. Two daughters are born later, one of whom dies and the other of whom, named Kong Jiao, survives. Confucius later outlives all of his children.

In his 20s, Confucius reportedly works as a bookkeeper in a granary and as an animal caretaker. His mother dies when Confucius is 23 years old and he ritually observes the traditional three year mourning period. He reportedly studies music at 28 years of age and holds a minor administrative position in a small local town. At 30 years of age; in spite of a hierarchically

1

stratified society of scholars, farmers, artisans and merchants; Confucius opens a school to educate persons of any social class or neighboring state whose only qualification is a sincere interest in, and commitment to, learning and a tuition of dried meat.

Learning, for Confucius, is both the 'lesser' learning of ritual, music, arithmetic, calligraphy, archery and charioteering and the 'greater learning' of *The Five Classics* and *The Four Books*, discussing them and composing essays and poetry. Greater learning doesn't involve learning abstract knowledge but is self-development and self-improvement prompted by life's unfolding and through the cultivation and refinement of the moral virtues of cultured gentlepersons.

When 35, Confucius is exiled to a neighboring state after supporting a defeated rebel ruler, is absorbed in studying peace music and is rejected for court membership. He receives death threats and returns to Lu when 36 years of age.

Throughout his lifetime, Confucius reportedly often declines official positions but does hold several relatively minor administrative positions in the State of Lu; namely, Police Commisioner, Minister of Works, Minister of the Interior, Minister of Crime and Minister of Justice/Law. However, he maintains a steadfast and heartfelt commitment to being an independent teacher of the common people as well as being an educator and trainer of the sons of gentlemen/Jun Zi in virtues proper to members of the ruling and aristocratic class.

Confucius believes that good and right moral conduct leads to developing good and wise human beings, political order and social harmony. He adheres to the earlier dynastic legacy of what is good and right in antiquity, e.g., the root moral virtues of ancestor veneration, filial piety and ritual propriety and the core virtues of benevolence, righteousness, respect, sincerity, learning, wisdom, loyalty and trustworthiness.

Confucius believes that good rulership and right governance, like that of legendary Ancient Sage-Rulers, should be conducted in terms of the essential needs and best interests of human beings and by the moral virtues of kindness and fairness rather than by the strict orders and harsh punishments of Legalism. The good ruler is self-cultivated and self-disciplined, exemplifies and models ethical principles and moral virtue/de, is non-coercive and non-punitive and respectfully and dutifully cares for the welfare and well-being of the people and the order and harmony of society.

Confucius advocates for; 1) the precursor of a virtue-based ruling meritocracy based upon ability rather than nobility and 2) the influence of the moral virtue, integrity, energy and power/ de of rulers creating social order and harmony that naturally radiates from family, to the community, to the society, to the state, to the world and, ultimately, to all of humanity.

There is an ethically good, morally right, socially proper Way of human being and living and social harmony is fostered by rectified and clearly defined identities, roles and duties.

Gentlepersons cultivate, develop, embody and enact the moral power of virtues such as filial piety, benevolence, righteousness, propriety, learning, sincerity and reciprocity and are living a Way of Goodness, Rightness and Properness.

Confucius reportedly has twenty or so close disciples, the most favorite one being Yan Hui. And *The Analects* are books of the sayings of Confucius and dialogues with disciples and others that are recorded, collected and compiled by his first and second generation disciples and later generation followers, some of whom are masters in their own right, occupy official positions and develop branches of Confucianism.

Confucius longs for a governmental political office that would allow him to keep alive, transmit and put into practice the Way, ethical principles and moral rituals and the Goodness of the legendary Ancient Sage-Rulers; Shun, Yao and Yu and the Duke of Zhou and King Wu of the three previous Xia, Shang/ Yin and Western Zhou Dynasties. However, again, because of his social status, he is not allowed to assume higher official government positions only reserved for the nobility and aristocrats of elite society.

During the decentralization of states, the disruption and disintegration of the feudal system and the ensuing political turmoil and social unrest of the Spring and Autumn Period (770-475 BCE) prior to the bloody internecene battles of regional feudal lords for hegemony of the Warring States Period (475-221 BCE); Confucius meets with various government officials of the Lu State in an attempt to promote the moral values and ethical practices of the Ancient Sage-Rulers as ways of creating order, harmony and peace in the country. However, his advocating of reforms, such as restraining governing power and razing fortified city walls, is unfavorably received, results in creating a falling out with the ruler and making enemies of, and being politically persecuted by, officials within the Lu State.

After failed attempts to uproot ruling families and to restore ignored ceremonial rites; in 497 BCE at 54 years of age; Confucius resigns from administrative positions, risks losing followers, goes into self-exile and leaves the State of Lu to become an itinerate teacher. He reportedly travels to neighboring states with his three closest disciples; Yan Hui, Zigong and Zilu, in hopes of finding rulers who are receptive to and understand his teachings and who would possibly offer him an official position in their government.

During 497-484 BCE, Confucius travels for fourteen years to the neighboring States of Qi, Wei, Song, Chen, Cai, Zheng, Chu et al advising rulers and officials on matters of governance and politics and counseling rustics and recluses on matters of human character and moral conduct. In the process, Confucius experiences repeated rejections, undergoes numerous hardships and reportedly avoids ambushes and escapes an assassination attempt.[4]

Confucius returns to Lu in 484 BCE at 68 years of age to devote himself full-time to teaching. In the ensuing years, he reportedly gains a following of some three-thousand students and seventy some disciples. He and/or some disciples write or edit *The 5 Confucian Classics* and *The 4 Books*. Confucius suffers the deaths and losses of his wife, his only son and his closest disciple.

At 73 years of age in 479 BCE, Confucius reportedly has a dream of a coffin sitting atop an altar surrounded by a large number of people paying obeisance. He considers the dream to be a premonition of his impending death, writes the following expression and dies seven days later.

'The great mountain must crumble.
The strong beam must break.
The wise man must wither away like a plant'.

Confucius, is considered to be a 'commoner' and, as such, could not hold any major political office or governmental position. He attains no particular rank or status as a publicly important figure and devotes his entire life to teaching. Confucius reportedly doesn't regard himself as a Divine Sage or even as a truly Good human being but as a life-long learner who; 1) is committed to the moral cultivating, self-improving and refining of character that is every human being's capacity and potential and who; 2) loves investigating and transmitting the best of the ethical, moral, Good and Right Way of the legendary Ancient Sage-Rulers.

Confucius is not the human being whom he is often portrayed as being, either positively or negatively, and is generally misinterpreted, poorly understood and underappreciated in his own lifetime. He struggles for most of his life attempting to find and convince rulers and governmental officials of the necessity, value and corrective cultural and social benefits of; 1) restoring and adopting the Way of Heaven and the natural harmony of Heaven, Earth and Humanity as a standard and of; 2) the benevolent and righteous ways, customs, rituals and practices of legendary Ancient Sage-Rulers as a model for being and living, social harmony and political order.

Confucius never succeeds in reforming the current state of affairs of his time by finding good, wise and courageous rulers and officials to implement his transmitted teachings. However, he certainly is not a complete failure and, in later centuries, his seemingly lofty ideals and noble aspirations achieve the acknowledgement that he and they deserve not just in China but throughout Asia and the rest of the world.

It appears that Confucius's high standards and self-expectations of moral virtues and conduct and his humility and modesty prevent him from objectively acknowledging and evaluating his actual accomplishments and the benefits that he gifts to the students and disciples of his time and that later are bequethed to the people and country of China.

Confucius says, 'Do I possess wisdom? Far from it!'. (9-8). 'In practicing the ritual duties of gentlepersons in life, I'm not there yet'. (7-33). 'I can't claim to be a Divine Sage or even a gentleperson'. (7-34). 'No one understands me'. (14-35). 'Things are declining for me'. (7-5). 'I'd rather not speak'. (17-19). 'I want to settle among the barbarians'. (9-14).

Confucius, as a human being, philosopher, educator and politician is finally regarded;

1) as the founding 'father', earliest teacher and elder statesperson of Chinese society who inspires, leads and guides the lives, culture, government and society of the Chinese people and nation for 2,500 years,

2) as embodying and realizing the highest potential Goodness attainable by a human being;

3) as being a proponent of virtue ethics, moral self-cultivation, self-improvement and self-refinement; social harmony and ethical governing by morally virtuous leaders and

4) as being the singlemost personally, socially, ethically, morally, culturally, educationally and governmentally influential

human being in China's 5,000 year history, heritage and Way of human being, living and relating.

Confucius has the longest lineage of recorded pedigreed descendents in human history, now numbering an estimated three million in eighty-three continuous generations and that include both women and men who have enjoyed or are currently enjoying dignity, respect and honor; social status and official positions and family and economic benefits.

Confucius styles himself as a 'transmitter' rather than an originator or innovator of the ethical principles and moral virtues of the ancient tradition that he espoused. Learning is imitating the Way of Ancient Divine Kings and Emperors, the Sons of Heaven, and Divine Sage-Rulers, i.e., 'Sageliness within and Kingliness without'. Learning is the self-cultivating of individual character, ethical values, moral virtues and self-improvement that leads to personal integrity and social, poltical and national order, harmony, peace, prosperity and happiness.

Over the years, 'Confucian-ism'; as a humanistic and virtue-based ethical philosophy, political ideology and moral way of being;

1) has become institutionalized as Confucianism and later transformed into Neo-Confucianism by early disciples and later generation followers of Confucius, e.g., Meng Zi/Mencius (372-289 BCE), Xun Xi (c.300-c.230 BCE) and Han Yu (768-824 CE), Cia Ao (772-841 CE) and Zhu Xi (1130-1200 CE) and

2) has been syncretically integrated with Chinese Taoism and Buddhism and synthesized with certain aspects of various Western religions.

The peoples of Asian countries such as Japan, South Korea and Vietnam are strongly inspired and influenced by the ideology, philosophy and teachings of Confucius and pay tribute and homage to him by holding annual memorial ceremonies and celebrations in his honor.

The original Spirit and human Soul of Confucius acknowledges and appreciates the essentially good inner nature, ethical character, moral virtues, right conduct, social harmony, political order, wisdom, radiant beauty and love of humanity and human beings.

Confucius values, cherishes and teaches an ideal, positive and optimistic conviction that ethical and moral human beings are the foundation, heart, potential and hope of and for a harmonious family and community; a well-ordered government, society and world and the proper Way of an integral and reciprocal relationship of Goodness and Rightness between human beings and between human beings and Heaven and Earth. 5

'Beauty is everywhere but not everyone sees it.'

水

CONFUCIANISM

CONFUCIANISM

As with Taoism and Buddhism, there is some question as to whether Confucianism is a religion (L. re-ligio - rebind, reverence) or a philosophy (Gk. philos - dear, love, friendly + sophia - wisdom) or a Way (OE. wegan - to move) of life (OHG leben - to live); since there is no deity to venerate (L. veneratis - love), revere (L. revereri - fear) or worship (ME. worshipe - respect).

1) religion is defined as 'the service and worship of God and the supernatural'; 2) philosophy is defined as 'a pursuit of wisdom' and 3) philosophy of life is defined as 'an overall vision of or attitude toward life and the purpose of life'.

The question arises from the artificial dualistic separation of the sacred (L. sacrare - holy) = devoted to the worship of a deity and the profane (L. profanus - before temple) = unconcerned with religion or religious purposes and the secular (LL. saecularis - coming once in an age) = temporal, worldly and not overtly or specifically religious. In general, 'religion' (L. re-ligio - rebind, tie together, reverence, religion) unifies, integrates, bonds and heals this separation.

'Religious'/Dao Jiao Taoism; early Theravada and later Buddhism, e.g., Pure Land Buddhism; and Xia, Shang and early Zhou Dynasty pre-Confucianism have some form;

1)   of a venerated providential Ultimate Reality, 'Higher or Heavenly Power', anthropomorphic deity or of nature deities, gods and goddesses;

2)   of spiritual doctrines, ethical principles, moral teachings, ritual practices, sacred observances, sacrificial offerings and prescribed devotional duties;

3)   of holy shrines, temples, sanctuaries, hermitages, monasteries and places of veneration and practice.

4) of an ancestral lineage of authenticated spiritual masters, clergy and teachers;

5) of devoted, humble, supplicant, prayerful and dutiful disciples, believers, devotees, followers and adherents;

6) of a spiritual, metaphysical, cosmological, mythological, theological and/or ontological ideology and a defined and/or codified ethical belief system;

7) of traditional sacred scriptures, sutras, canons, classics, texts and books of teachings;

8) of meditative postures, movements, recitations, chanting, mantras, mudras, yantras and mandalas;

9) of personal, interpersonal, social, transpersonal and spiritual purposes, objectives and goals and

10) of a sectarian division, hierarchical organizational structure and successional ancestral lineage.

In the Xia Dynasty (c. 2100 -1600 BCE) 'religion' is believed to have been some form of folk belief, animism, shamanism, divination and the worship of polytheistic heavenly, cosmic, Nature and mythological 'gods' and 'goddesses' and the ancestors who could communicate with them. However, to date there is little or no archaeological evidence or formal records of its culture and 'religion'.

In the Shang Dynasty (c. 1600-1045 BCE) 'religion' is shamanic, oracular and divinatory and is both polytheistic and monothistic with a belief in;

1) a Heaven realm/Tian (sky, heaven, firmament, celestial vault, overhead, Nature and the great whole);

2) an anthropomorphized Supreme Being, Lord Above and Highest Deity/Shang (high, highest, primordial, first, superior, up, above) Di (God, Deity, Supreme Being, sovereign, emperor and ruler) and Tian Di (Heaven and Earth) who is

both transcendent and immanent and omnipotently responsible for the nature, control, course and destiny of humanity;

3) a pantheon of gods and goddesses such as the mythological
    Creatrix/Mazu and Creator/Pangu of humanity, The Great
    Emperor/Tai Di and The Yellow Emperor/Huang Di, The
    Jade Emperor/Yu Di and The Queen Mother of the West/
    Xi Wang Mu and various polytheistic nature, sky, sun, moon,
    star, earth, river, fire, rain, etc. goddesses/mothers and gods/
    fathers of whom the sky god/Tian and goddesses/Niwa and
    Douma are the most powerful and

4) a Heaven yang and Hell yin realm, yang gods and spir-
    its/shen, yin demons and ghosts/gui and a Heavenly yang
    human Soul/hun and an Earthly yin human Soul/po.

The first recorded history of the introduction of Christianity
into China reportedly is that of a heretical form of Nestorian
Christianity in 635 CE which lasts until all 'foreign' religion is
banned by imperial decree in 907 CE. 8 Eastern Christianity
is a major religious influence during the Mongol empire (c.
13th-14th Century CE). John of Montecorvino (1247-1328
CE) reportedly is an Italian Franciscan missionary who is one
of the first to visit China and to found Catholic missions in the
14th Century CE and Franciscan friars from Europe begin missionary work in China.

Russian Orthodox Christanity reportedly is practiced in parts
of China during the 14th-16th Centuries CE, Roman Catholic
priests are missionaries in China during the 16th Century and portions of *The Holy Bible* are translated into the Chinese language.

In the 16th Century CE, Francis Xavier (1506-1552 CE),
Michele Ruggieri (1543-1607 CE) and Matteo Ricci (1552-
1610 CE) are Spanish and Italian Jesuit missionaries who bring
orthodox Christianity to China and are considered to be the
founding 'fathers' of establishing Christian missions in China.

As history unfolds; Xaviar dies during arrival in China,

Ruggieri leaves China early and the majority of missionary work is left up to Ricci. Ricci reportedly is less concerned with converting the Chinese people to Christianity and more interested in;

1) learning about the Chinese culture, learning the Chinese language and studying the 'civil religion' and virtue-ethics philosophy of Confucianism;

2) validating and verifying the Chinese belief in Shang Di/ Lord of Heaven as an absolute, immutable, infinite, eternal, omnipresent, omniscient, omnipotent, holy, loving, gracious and faithful Christian-like God (Ricci authored *The True Meaning of the Lord of Heaven*) and

3) integrating certain beliefs of Chinese religion and Confucianism, e.g., ancestor worship and traditional sacrificial ceremonies and rituals, with Christian beliefs and practices.

The French Jesuit Francois Noel (1651-1729 CE) reportedly arrives in China in 1687 and professes that Christianity is the ancient religion of China. Robert Morrison (1782-1834 CE) is the first Protestant missionary arriving in China in 1823 CE, is considered to be the 'father' of Protestantism in China, is followed by Protestant missionaries throughout the 19th Century CE and reportedly is the first to make a complete translation of *The Holy Bible* into the Chinese language. James Hudson Taylor (1832-1905 CE) arrives in China in 1854, establishes numerous Baptist missions throughout China and is regarded as the greatest missionary to China. Sinologist James Legge (1815-1897 CE) is historically instrumental in the cross-cultural East-West integration by being the first to translate all of the foundational classic Chinese texts into the English language.

More recently, there is scholarly integral religious work being done demonstrating that the embedded meanings of some ancient Chinese language characters and writings identify a Christian-like monotheistic God/Shang Di, parallel religious ideologies and corresponding events that are described in

The Holy Bible, e.g., the creation of Heaven, Earth and human beings described in the Book of Genesis, Eve and Adam and the Garden of Eden, the Great Flood and Noah's Ark, sacrifice, the Crucifiction and Resurrection of Jesus Christ and other events mentioned in Old and New Testament gospels.

It is more pragmatic and useful to disregard the dualistic 'either-or' problematic question of whether Confucianism is a religion or a philosophy and to adopt a non-dualistic 'both and' solvent answer of harmonious integration. Confucianism, like Taoism and Buddhism is, at once, a Way of being and living, a philosophy of life and a religion in the sense of having all of the above constituents and characteristics and spiritual-humane ideologies, ethical-moral principles, ritual-observational practices and personal-transpersonal purposes.

Suffice to say, in all three spiritual traditions, the profane and the secular are sacred and they each can be regarded as a 'religion' that ties and binds them together and unites their spiritual traditions, teachings, practices and practitioners.

Tao/Dao is our inborn Human nature, Dharma is our innate Buddha nature and the gentleperson is our intrinsic Moral nature; 1) the harmonious integration of Ultimate Heavenly, Divine and Spiritual Reality and the intimate earthly, human and material actuality of the ten-thousand things, dharmas and phenomena of human consciousness and experience and 2) the laws, rules, methods and energies creating, governing, regulating, sustaining and evolving the multiverse, our planet, our social world and our human being, living, conduct and relationships.

Human being and human living are sacred and hallowed. The ordinary is infinitely in all ways extraordinary and the everyday is eternally as always forever. And, like Lao Tzu and the Buddha; Confucius is venerated, revered, honored and respected; not because of being a divinity or demi-god but for being a real, true, highly evolved and exceptionally outstanding human being who has unquestionably, immeasurably and compassionately encouraged, benefited, improved and advanced our personal identity, social civility, governmental morality and cultural humanity.

Confucianism is essentially and preferably known as Ruism or Ru Classicism, a system of thought, behavior and government in ancient China. The Ru are Confucian educated and refined scholars, intellectuals and *literati*. Ru Jia is the educational school of Ruism and Ru Jiao is the religious doctrine of Ruism. 7

Confucianism; 1) originates with Confucius (551-479 BCE); a teacher, philosopher and politician during the Spring and Autumn Period (770-475 BCE) who transmits the cultural traditions, social values and governmental practices of the earlier Xia Dynasty (c. 2100-1600 BCE), Shang/Yin Dynasty (c. 1600-1045 BCE) and Western Zhou Dynasty (1045-771 BCE) and 2) is organized and developed by his first, second and subsequent generation disciples, Zeng Zi (505-435 BCE), grandson Zisi (481- 402 BCE), Meng Zi/Mencius (372-289 BCE) and Xun Xi (310-238 BCE). Through the ensuing years, Confuciansm undergoes numerous transformations, e.g., into the Neo-Confucianism of Zhu Xi (1130-1200 CE) and others but retains its fundamental and essential core ideology of;

1) The Way of Heaven and the harmonious co-existing of Heaven, Earth and Human Being.

2) Heaven endows and regulates the moral nature of human life and of the social world.

3) The Ancient Sage-Kings of early dynasties as examples and models of Good governing.

4) Governing by ethical principles and moral virtues for the Good and welfare of people.

5) Early governing by The Mandate of Heaven and later by meritocratic ability, not nobility.

6) Good and Right governing is a macrocosm of the microcosm of Good and Right families.

7) It is the moral virtue/de of a ruler, as an agent of Heaven that creates social harmony.

8) Moral and ethical leaders govern and 'rule' by virtue and the power of their presence.

9) Ancestor veneration, filial piety and reverence and respect for all elder human beings.

10) The importance of ritual, ceremony and sacrifice that honor ancestors and one's family.

11) Morality is filial piety, benevolence, righteousness, propriety, knowledge and sincerity.

12) Moral virtues of modesty, humility, respect, honesty, trustworthiness, loyalty and fidelity.

13) Filial piety is the root virtue and cultivating being a gentleperson is a central objective.

14) Being a gentleperson is the ultimate beginning and ending of the human life journey.

15) Cultivating, practicing and refining one's character, moral virtues and ethical conduct.

16) Cultivating and practicing moral virtues and ethical conduct creates social harmony.

17) De is the natural moral virtue, integrity, energy and efficacious power of the Way/Dao.

18) Moral cultivation radiates from the person to the family, society, nation and the world.

19) Harmonious human life is self-cultivation in a morally ruled and socially ordered world.

20) Reciprocity and mutual responsibility in relationships and living by the 'GoldenRule'.

21) The Golden/Silver Rule of 'Not doing to others what you don't want them to do to you'.

22) Fulfilling one's obligations, commitments, agreements, duties and responsibilities.

23) Human beings are inherently good, teachable, improvable, refinable and perfectable.

24) Much can be learned from ancient historical cultures and ethical and moral ancestors.

25) Studying, reading, memorizing and reciting traditional teachings at a very early age.

26) True learning is self-studying, self-cultivating, self-improvement and self-refinement.

27) Being friendly, courteous, civil, obedient, compliant and deferent with one's fellows.

28) Openly following the 'spirit' of Confucianism and not rigidly adhering to its 'letter'.

29) Speaking, acting and relating virtuously and truthfully in an appropriate timely manner.

30) Not desiring, pursuing and gaining name, fame and wealth at the expense of morality.

31) Being a loving caring human being living the Way/Dao and virtues for their own sake.

32) Being as good a human being as you can be and doing the best that you can do as such.

33) Being devoted and dedicated to assisting and benefiting all fellow human beings.

Confucius and/or his disciples either wrote, compiled or edited some of the principal foundational classics and books of the Confucian vision and ideology and of Confucianism which are:

The 5 Classics:

1) *The Classic of Changes* – divination, yin-yang interactions, organismic and dynamic unity.

— one of the oldest of Chinese texts (c. 10th-8th Centuries BCE).

2) *The Classic of Odes* – anthology of the oldest poems, songs, hymns from 1000-600 BCE.

— convey inspiring, uplifting and elevating human feelings.

3) *The Classic of Documents* – compilation of historical speeches founding humane ruling.

— ancient rulers Yao, Shun and Yu of Xia and Shang Dynasties.

4) *The Classic of Rites* – ceremonies of the Zhou/Early Han Dynasties and Warring States.

— social classes of scholars, farmers, artisans and merchants.

5) *The Spring and Autumn Annals* - chronicles of Eastern Zhou Dynasty (770-221 BCE).

— reanimating perspectives of Confucius's Lu State. [9]

The 4 Books:

1) *The Doctrine of the Mean* – the virtues of moderation and practicing the Middle Way.

2) *The Great Learning* – guidance for the self-cultivation of learning and virtuous conduct.

3) *The Analects* – compilation of the sayings of Confucius and dialogues with his disciples.

4) *The Mencius* – conversations of Meng Zi . Good governing by rulers following the Way. [9]

The 5 Constants and other Virtues of Confucian ethical and moral character, virtue, integrity, energy and power/de and conduct are the following:

1) REN - benevolence, humaneness

2) YI - righteousness, justice

3) LI - properness, rituals

4) ZHI - knowledge, wisdom

5) XIN - sincerity, faith, trust

1) XIAO - filial piety

2) GONG - respect

3) CHENG - uprightness, honesty

4) ZHONG - loyalty, fidelity

5) JIE - self-restraint of desires

6) RANG - modesty, humility

7) SHU - kindness, forgiveness

8) WEN - gentleness

9) YONG - courage, bravery 11/12/13

The 5 Relationships that contribute to personal, social and political order and harmony are hierarchical and each involve and require reciprocal and obligatory respect, deference, responsibilities and duties. They are those:

1) Between ruler and subject.

2) Between father and son (father-daughter, mother-daughter, mother-son?).

3) Between husband and wife (or wives?).

4) Between older and younger brothers (brothers-sisters, sisters-sisters?).

5) Between older and younger friends (of the same or opposite male-female gender?). [10]

Confucius observes that the Eastern Zhou Dynasty's rulers during the Spring and Autumn Period and approaching the Warring States Period are deviating from the Way; are degenerating and lack the ethical principles, moral virtues and ritual practices that he believes contribute to governmental order, social harmony, the welfare of the people and individual peacefulness, prosperity and happiness.

Confucius observes moral hypocrisy, ritual improprieties, lust, greed, sloth and corruption on the part of rulers; their concern with externals and superficial appearances and disputes over succession. Individual states are decentralized into separate states fighting for hegemony and the heads of wealthy families are usurping the power of rulers and becoming *de facto* rulers of principality states.

Confucius's socio-political ideology and teachings of the self-cultivation of unfaltering good ethical virtues and unerring right moral conduct as leading to social and governmental order and harmony are not appreciated, understood or implemented during his lifetime and, following his death, Confucianism goes in and out favor during subsequent dynasties following the Eastern Zhou Dynasty.

In the Qin Dynasty (221-206 BCE), Legalism is prominent and Confucianism is suppressed, its books are burned and reportedly its scholars are buried alive. Confucianism becomes the State religion and the dominant cultural, social and political ideology in the Han Dynasty (202 BCE- 220 CE) and Confucius is recognized as a great sage by its rulers. *The 5 Confucian Classics* and *The 4 Confucian Books* are required reading in school curricula at all levels and are the basis for imperial civil service examinations.

Confucianism is eclipsed by Buddhism and Taoism in the Sui (581-618 CE) and Tang (618-907 CE) Dynasties and fully and officially revived in the Song Dynasty (960-1279 CE) as Neo-Confucianism and becomes the core philosophy of the scholarly class emphasizing the importance of education, learning and moral self-cultivation and development as the basis for harmonious social, governmental and political order.

Official Confucianism ends in 1905 CE when the examination system is abolished and Confucianism as a State religion ends in 1912 CE, along with the end of the imperial monarchical epoch and the establishment of the Republic of China. During the Cultural Revolution (1966-1976 CE), attempts are made to erase China's ancestral and cultural past, as during the Qin Dynasty (221-207 BCE). Once again, books are burned, scholars are murdered, cultural relics are destroyed and sacred sites are razed.

A slow but progressive revival of Confucianism begins after 1976 CE, mostly among China's scholars and intellectuals. Since the 2,000s CE, there is continued increasing interest in, recognition of and acceptance of Confucianism and it spreads to schools, institutes, non-governmental and social organizations and churches. Confucianism also spreads throughout Asian countries; most notably Japan, South Korea and Vietnam. Approximately four million human beings in China and six million human beings world-wide identify as Confucian believers, adherents, followers and practitioners.

Overall, Confucianism is a prominent world-wide humanistic virtue-ethics philosophy and is seen as being the foundation and integral part of Chinese civil-ization and as having fundamentally, positively and centrally influenced, contributed to and shaped the historical development of social mores and norms, cultural rituals and practices, governmental and political policies, the national legacy and identity of the Chinese country and the daily lives and relationships of its people for 2,500 years.

Some principal interpretive objections to, and criticisms of, Confucianism that reportedly have accounted for its relative lack of greater popularity and influence are:

1) its predominantly authoritarian, dominating, controlling and oppressing patriarchical, hierarchical and unequal social structure of prestigious male superiority that misogynistically relegates and subjugates women to an inferior, restricted and limited social position;

2) the centrality of ethical principles, moral rules, traditional customs and prescribed rituals that, while instituted to create social and governmental order, goodness, correctness and harmony, are rather ideal rigid standards that are difficult to model, transmit and adhere and live up to; 13

3) the reality that it is considered to be a non-theistic virtue-ethics belief system, moral philosophy, political ideology and way of life rather than a religion in the traditional sense and

4) that it has not, in fact, led to as great as possible modern cultural advancement, economic progress and actualization of its full potential due to some of its beliefs, customs and practices that may create, constitute and pose limitations upon and resistances to such growth and development, e.g., ancestor worship, being focused on the remote past, obligatory and deferential relationships, 'self as community' and not encouraging, supporting, promoting, facilitating and reinforcing greater individualism.

However, Confucianism is currently experiencing a renaissance and is still very much alive; 1) in the vast and magnificently beautiful geographical landscape of the mountains, lands, valleys and waters of China; 2) in the State preserved and protected treasured relics dating as far back as the Shang and Zhou Dynasties and 3) in the collective historical consciousness and culturally united hearts of all social classes of Chinese people; especially those who, in spite of, or because of, modernization; long for the stable grounding and deeper centering of traditional historical roots and cultural branches.

There are nearly five-hundred Confucian institutes world wide. Numerous commemorative statues of Confucius, Confucian temples, statuary and iconography exist throughout the homeland of China and still outnumber its cellphone towers, shopping malls, highway roadsigns and advertising billboards.

水

THE ANALECTS
LUN YU
TEXT

THE ANALECTS
LUN YU
TEXT

The Analects (Gk. ana-/up, back, again + - legein/gather) are Lun/discuss + Yu/speak - the collected sayings, speeches, conversations, discussions and question and answer dialogues of Confucius (551-479 BCE) on matters of moral virtue and conduct, ethical politics and governmental and social order and harmony during the Spring and Autumn Period (770-475 BCE) of The Eastern Zhou Dynasty (770-221 BCE) that are recorded and compiled by his first, second and later generation disciples beginning in the Warring States Period (475-221 BCE) and throughout the Han Dynasty (206 BCE-220 CE).

The Analects is a work of the life teachings of Confucius and the single most important book in Chinese history. Also, no other book in world history has made the greatest influence on the largest number of human beings over the longest period of time. *The Analects* survived book-burning (213 BCE) in the tyrannically ruled anti-Confucian Qin Dynasty (221-206 BCE); the ups and downs and ins and outs of historical dynasties and has profoundly influenced and shaped Chinese culture, society and families; government, politics and education and the ways of being and living of Chinese people for two-thousand five-hundred years.

There exists a Xi Ping stone carving of some *Analect* sayings dating c. 175-180 BCE. The oldest partial extant bamboo strip copy of the *Lun Yu* reportedly is discovered in the Chinese Haihunhou tomb excavation in 2011. The dating of this partial copy reportedly is seventeen years before two other partial bamboo strip copies, the 55 BCE Ding Zhou and the 50 BCE Pyong Yang, respectively found in 1973 in Chinese and in 2003 in North Korean tombs.[16]

Three existing versions of the *Lun Yu* are: 1) the *Gu Lun* of 21 Books, only two of which are reportedly found in a wall of Confucius's home and the remainder are lost in the Han Dynasty (206 BCE-220 CE), 2) the *Qi Lun* of 22 Books and 3) the *Lu Lun* of 20 Books. The latter two are edited and synthesized by He Yan (170-249 CE) into an eclectic version of 20 Books that is considered to be the received text of *The Analects* that is used for most translations.

The Analects consist of 20 Books. Books 1-10 are considered to be the earliest and Books 3-9 the oldest. Books 11-18 are later ones and Books 19 and 20 are the latest additions. Books 14 and 17 are considered to be the addition of an anti-Confucian scholar. The 20 Books don't follow any particular continuous sequential order and their contents are found, at times repetitiously, throughout *The Analects* . The Books are originally untitled and, after the invention of paper in 105 CE, titles are usually just the opening words of each book. Most translators simply number the twenty Books 1-20.

The first Western translation of *The Analects* is the Latin version *Confucius Sinarum Philosophus* by Ludovici Magni in 1687. Other early translations are made by 18th Century Jesuit scholars Prosperi Intercetta, Christiani Herdtrich, Frabcusco Rougemont and Phillipi Couplet. Popular early English translations are made James Legge in 1861, William Soothill in 1910, Lionel Giles in 1910 and Arthur Waley in 1938.

Over the years, numerous commentaries of *The Analects* have been made and serve to keep the virtue ethics of Confucianism alive, relevant and continually transforming. The commentaries of Zhu Xi (1130-1200 CE) are the most popular and have been the standard since the 12th Century. Liu Baonan's (1791-1855 CE)

Collected Commentaries of The Analects /Lun Yu Zeng Yi is the first and most authoritative commentary collection and which reportedly took this Qing Dynasty (1644-1912 CE) politician and Confucian scholar twenty-seven years to complete.

水

THIS RENDITION

THIS RENDITION

Several bi-lingual and other translations of *The Analects* are consulted, considered, reflected upon and integrated in the process of creating this rendition. The etymological roots of many key terms are investigated since they provide additional and often deeper meanings than customary definitions typically made by translators. This rendition involves some literal translation, some interpretation, some synonymizing and some paraphrasing.

For ease of reading and understanding by English speaking readers, the Chinese names of people and places are eliminated and generalized with nouns, pronouns and, in the case of people, titles or role-relationships. I hope that in doing so, I'm not squeezing the last bit of juice out of the fruits of Confucius's teachings or removing the last bits of flesh from their already skeletal remains. I don't feel that this modification takes away from the original and essential meaning of ideas, concepts, speeches, question-answer interchanges or dialogues.

Most all of the Confucian 'never', 'always', 'must', 'should', 'ought' and 'need to' directives to human beings are changed to less imperative ones of 'does', 'do', 'can', 'may', 'might' and 'will'. References to 'one', 'someone', 'persons' and 'people' are usually changed to 'human beings'.

Since in *The Analects* rulers, officials, disciples, individuals etc. are predominantly males; in the interest of gender equality, gender-free plural designations are used and 'they', 'them' and 'their' are substituted for 'he', 'him' and 'his', e.g.,

'The sage is a very wise man' is changed to 'Sages are very wise human beings'.

'A man does whatever he wants' is changed to 'Persons do whatever they want',

'A reward wasn't given to him' is changed to 'Rewards weren't given to them',

'A common man obeys his ruler' is changed to 'Common people obey their ruler',

'The gentleman embodies Good' is changed to 'Gentlepersons embody Good'.

To bring the material to a current and more active sense, past tenses are usually changed to the present tense and some nouns are changed to their gerund form of -ing, e.g.,

'Disciples respected masters' is changed to 'Disciples respect (or are respecting) masters'.

'In the Shang and Western Zhou Dynasties, the gentleman respected his prince' is changed to

'In previous dynasties, gentlepersons respect (or are respecting) their ruler'.

Again, in the interest of unburdened and economical readability, sentences are freed of Chinese names, are parsed into the present tense and are condensed, e.g.,

'Ziyou was a disciple of the Master who served as a steward in the town of Wucheng in Lu State and asked the Master ...' is changed to 'A disciple of Confucius who serves as an official asks Confucius ...'.

'The Master said ...' that usually introduces each saying is changed to 'Confucius says ...'

For the simplicity, economy and consistency of writing and reading:

Ren is translated as 'Good' and 'Goodness'.

Yi is translated as 'Right' and 'Rightness'.

Li is translated as 'Proper' and 'Properness'.

Junzi is translated as 'Gentlepersons'.

Dao and 'the Way' are used interchangeably and De is usually defined as the 'moral virtue, integrity, energy and power of Dao'.

For the locations and cast of characters in *The Analects*, the following generic designations are:

'Ancient Sage-Rulers' for the legendary rulers Yao, Shun and Yu the Great.

'Previous three Dynasties' for Xia, Shang/Yin and Western Zhou Dynasties.

'The State' for the Empire, Kingdom, nation, country, land and state.

'Rulers' for Sons of Heaven, Emperors, Kings, Lords, Dukes, Princes and Sovereigns.

'Officials' for stewards, retainers, counselors, ministers and scholar-officials.

'People' retain designations as common, lower, inferior, small and petty persons.

'Gentlepersons' for gentleman and gentlemen.

水

THE COMMENTARIES

Over many years there have been numerous commentaries on *The Analects* from different historical, spiritual, religious, philosophical, personal, social, organizational, governmental and political perspectives. Such commentaries contribute greatly to understanding the original sayings and appreciating their broad, useful and helpful applications.

This commentary is made from the interpretative standpoint and perspective; 1) of the theory and practice of Western psychology and psychotherapy and 2) of a psychology teacher and educator and practicing counselor and psychotherapist.

The specific foundation of this perspective is the phenomenological philosophical attitude and approach that; 1) suspends any preconceptions and presuppositions about the phenomena (in this case, the human being of clients and psychotherapists) that are being considered, investigated, explored, understood and 2) that simply lets them be 'just as they are' and just as they are presencing themselves in their 'givenness' to human consciousness.

This state of freedom from preconceptions and presuppositions is a consciousness and conscious awareness that is awake, clear and empty and open to the actual reality, essential qualities and true nature of any phenomenon just as it presences itself and enables an accurate and comprehensive description of it.

The psychotherapy model used for the psychotherapeutic commentaries of this rendition of *The Analects* is that of individual one-with-one outpatient private psychotherapy in office settings. However, the client-psychotherapist relationship applies to psychotherapy conducted in inpatient psychiatric hospitals and institutions and outpatient treatment centers and clinics.

And more generally, virtuous psychotherapy, at its root and heart, characterizes and can practically, usefully and beneficially apply to any and all essentially good, right and proper humane relationships between human beings.

For the psychotherapeutic commentaries:

1) Psychotherapists are referred to as virtuous psychotherapists per Confucian ethics.[2]

2) Text references to rulers refer to psychotherapists and their virtues and conduct.

3) Text references to rituals refer to psychotherapy techniques, methods, processes and procedures.

4) Text references to persons/people refer to students, trainees, interns and clients.

The principal ethical-moral value-concepts of *The Analects* are correlated with the corresponding attitudes, approaches and conduct of virtuous psychotherapists and the psychotherapy relationship process with clients as follows:

1) REN – the virtue of goodness —

The being of the psychotherapist is impartial, unprejudiced unbiased and non-judgmental.

The being of the psychotherapist is humble, respectful, caring, kind, gentle and patient.

2) YI – the virtue of rightness —

The being of the psychotherapist is interested, engaged, involved, connected and attentive.

The being of the psychotherapist is aware, understanding, empathic and compassionate.

3) LI – the virtue of properness —

The conduct, interactions and interventions of the psychotherpist are ethical and moral.

The techniques, methods and processes of psychotherapy are appropriate and beneficial.

4) Xin – the virtue of integrity —

The being of the psychotherapist is authentic, genuine, sincere, honest and truthful.

The being of the psychotherapist is dedicated, committed, faithful, loyal and trustworthy.

5) Shu – the virtue of reciprocity —

The relating of the psychotherapist is equal, mutual, reciprocal, cooperative and collaborative.

The relating of the psychotherapist follows the Golden Rule of corresponding 'doing to'.

5) Zhi – the virtue of wisdom —

The being of the psychotherapist is insightful and knowledgeable in psychological theory.

The being of the psychotherapist is wise, skillful, competent and proficient in therapy practice.

6) Yong – the virtue of courage —

The actions of the psychotherapist involve assertiveness, directness and straightforwardness.

The actions of the psychotherapist involve vulnerability, self-confidence and risk-taking.

In the same way that the ethical integrity and moral virtue/de of Confucianist sage-rulers result in political order, social harmony and the peacefulness, happiness and prosperity of human beings; so does the ethical integrity and moral virtue of virtuous psychotherapists result in meaningful, effective and beneficial psychotherapy and the health and well-being of clients.

The Confucian focus upon governing virtuously, cultivating moral virtues and improving oneself and refining and perfecting one's moral nature have a parallel application to the intentions, goals and objectives of virtuous psychotherapy, i.e., self-regulating, self-acculturating, self-developing, self-actualizing and self-evolving.

The Taoist 'Dao'; the Way of Ultimate Reality, Nature, the Multiverse, all beings and all things is parallel to the Confucian 'Dao'; the Way of Heaven, human morality, the ordered human social world, good and right human beings and a good and right world. The Taoist 'De'; the inborn nature, individualization, integrity, virtuosity, energy and power of Dao is parallel to the Confucian 'De'; the inner character, individual ethics, moral virtue, energy and power of the Way.

The most essential factor in the conduct and progress of efficient and effective and meaningful and beneficial psychotherapy and client progress is the quality, level, degree, extent and depth of the emotional, intellectual, psychological, social, moral, ethical and spiritual being and development of virtuous psychotherapists and their humaneness, availability, accessibility and approachability.

To be a credible, valued, respected, worthwhile, trustworthy, effective, meaningful and beneficial virtuous psychotherapist involves;

1) rigorous education, training, supervision and practice in learning, knowing and applying psychological theories and in mastering and utilizing psychotherapeutic techniques, methods, procedures and processes wisely, cautiously, relevantly, appropriately, flexibly, skillfully, usefully and effectively; 3

2) conducting the psychotherapy relationship process with devotion, dedication, commitment, intention, resolve, diligence, effort, straightforwardness, competence, proficiency, responsibility, dependability, reliability and accountability;

3) being as fully present as possible, paying as close attention as possible, having the best interest of clients at heart and doing the best psychotherapy work that can be done in the shortest amount of time;

4) embodying, personifying and manifesting the moral virtues of humaneness, goodness, rightness, properness, respect, equality, empathy, compassion, honesty, truthfulness, humility, sincerity, mutuality, reciprocity, kindness, loyalty, faithfulness, trustworthiness, learning, wisdom, courage et al and most of all, the virtuous moral integrity and efficacious power/de of Dao/the Way;

5) being economical and non-reactive in verbalizing, exploring, reflecting, giving feedback, clarifying, explaining, questioning, interpreting, summarizing, suggesting, interacting, intervening, probing, responding, confronting and challenging, etc.;

6) a career-long valuing of, commitment to and cultivating of learning, self-awakening, self-reflecting, self-investigating, self-exploring, self-understanding, self-accepting, self-developing, self-transforming, self-improving, self-actualizing, self-refining, etc. and

7) inspiring, supporting, encouraging, facilitating, stimulating, activating, potentiating, reinforcing, validating, fostering, promoting, inducing, evoking and nourishing client experiencing and developing of:

   a. self-awareness, insight, understanding, realization, acceptance and appreciation;

   b. self-interest, care, study, examination, education, learning, exploration and discovery;

   c. self- growth, development, cultivation, improvement, progression and refinement;

   d. self-support, reliance, confidence, empowerment, expression, assertion and actualization;

   e. self- control, regulation, integration, unification, harmony, change and transformation;

f. self-solidity, stability, security and solitude, silence, simplicity, sufficiency and serenity,

g. self-relatedness, strength, balance, flexibility, responsiveness, adaptability and resilience;

h. self-satisfaction, fulfillment and freedom, peacefulness, intimacy and happiness and

i. enthusiasm, motivation, a therapeutic alliance, compliance, cooperation and collaboration.

The virtuous one-with-one psychotherapy relationship is first and foremost a real, true, good, right, proper, mutual, reciprocal and humane relationship between two interrelated, interconnected and interacting worthy, dignified and equal human beings.

Etymologically, in the English language, the word 'psychotherapy' is derived from;

1) the Greek, 'psyche' - breath, mind, life, Soul and Spirit and

2) the Greek, 'therapeuein' - attend and treat.

Psychotherapy is attending and treating the human mind, life, Soul and Spirit.

Etymologically, in the Chinese language, 'psychotherapy' is derived from;

1) 'psyche' - a) XIN LING = XIN - heart, mind, core, center, intentions, affections, motives + LING - Soul, Spirit, spiritual enegy and force, supernatural, deity, divine, flexible, nimble, efficacious transcendent power (YOU - rain + LING - large falling drops + WU - Spirit and rain-invoking dancing witches and wizards), b) LING HUN = LING + HUN - Soul, Spirit, Mind, evanescence (GUI - spirits of the deceased + YUN - clouds) and c) HUN PO = HUN + PO - Soul, Psyche (GUI + BAI - pure, white) and

2) 'therapy' LIAO FA = Liao - treat, heal, cure (NI - sickness, illness, disease + LIAO - sacrifices to heaven) + FA - rule, law, art, model, pattern, method, means, way and Buddhist teachings (SHUI - water + QU - to go).

Psychotherapy is the art, way, means and methods of treating, healing and curing the illnesses, sicknesses and dis-eases of the human heart, mind, Psyche, Soul and Spirit.

Virtuous psychotherapy is a sacred reality, spiritual activity, soulful relationship and efficacious art wherein and whereby the Heart, Mind, Psyche, Soul and Spirit of human beings are attended to, treated, understood, healed and cured.

For virtuous psychotherapists, there is no difference between human being; moral self-cultivation, self-improvement and self-refinement; psychotherapy practice and being, living and sharing a human and humane life of; 1) Good Earth-grounded ethical principles, 2) Right Heart-centered moral conduct and Proper Heaven-elevated social behavior.

It is my heartfelt hope that these commentaries on this rendition of *The Analects* of Confucius contribute meaningfully, constructively, creatively, practically and beneficially to your personal growth and life, your professional development and work and your spiritual evolution, light and love throughout the most blessed gift and most cherished treasure of your most sacred, precious, evanescent and ephemeral human being, living and relating.

水

THE VIRTUES

The following terms are principal Confucian virtues of human beings that ground, center and sustain individual, family, societal, political, governmental unity, order and harmony.

1. JEN/REN - the individual supreme virtue and forms of Heaven, humaneness, goodness, human-heartedness, respect, kindness, tolerance, caring, benevolence, empathy, compassion, altruism, charity, generosity, courage, resolve, diligence, moderation, humility, modesty, selflessness, trustworthiness, gratitude, forgiveness, freedom from insecurity, worry and unhappiness and a natural deep inner love for fellow human beings that prompts ethically good and morally correct and just deeds.

These moral virtues/de are the individual internalization of Dao/the Way and are cultivated for their own sake and not for the purpose of acquiring reward, merit, expiation or salvation.

$$ 仁 = 亻 + 二 $$

JEN/REN - humaneness = JEN/REN - human being, humankind + ERH/ER- two, another, above.(The two horizontal lines often symbolize earth-heaven and yin-yang bipolar unities).

The highest co-existing, connecting and communing of human beings with each other.

2. I/YI - the virtues of righteousness, uprightness, correctness, obligation, duty, accord with moral principles, integrity, honesty, right and fitting conduct, meaningfulness, honor, impartiality, fairness, justice, selflessness and sacrifice.

The correct and appropriate outer actions from an inner morally virtuous and benevolent heart.

義 = 羊 + 我 = 戈 + 手

I/Yı - right conduct = YANG/YANG - good, sheep + Wo/Wo - I, we + Ko/GE - lance + SHOU/SHOU - hand.

Following ethical and moral codes of conduct that are good and right in human beings.

3. Lı/Lı - the virtues of propriety, social etiquette, public decorum, normative and proper conduct, reverence, respect, courtesy, politeness, good manners and form, ritual, rites, ceremony, worship, offering, observing and adhering to prescribed behavioral protocols, e.g., nodding, hand-clasping, bowing, yielding, deferring, etc.. The correct and appropriate external forms of observing, following and expressing inner ethical principles and moral virtue/de, e.g., in dress, demeanor, behavior and activities; mourning and burial ceremonies, sacrificial rituals and song, music and dance.

Ritual harmony with the laws and order of Heaven. The natural state of the human heart and 'the always so'.

禮 = 礻 + 豊

Lı/Lı - ritual, manners = SHIH/SHI - proclaim, show, reveal, signs from Heaven + Lı/Lı - sacrificial vessel.

Manifesting of Heaven-bestowed proper and appropriate social decorum, ritual behaviors and sacrificial offerings.

4. HSIAO/XIAO - the supreme virtue of filial piety; respecting, honoring, obeying, serving, caring for and having reverence for and being devoted to ancestors, parents and elders and observing the five cardinal relationships between parent-child, ruler-subject, husband-wife, older-younger brothers and older-younger friends.

The ethical-moral-familial-social foundation of all cardinal and other virtues.

孝 = 老 + 子

HsIAO/XIAO - filial piety = LAO/LAO - old + TZU/ZI - child.

Respectful, reverential, devotional, dutiful, obedient caring for parents and elders.

5. SHU/SHU - the virtues of reciprocity, mutuality, equality, correspondence, consideration, mercy and forgiveness in relationships and adhering to the maxim of not doing to fellow human beings what you do not want them to do to you, i.e., the 'Golden Rule'.

恕 = 心 + 如 = 女 + 口

SHU/SHU - reciprocity, forgiveness = HsIN/XIN -heart + JU/RU - as, like, same as, as good as, go to + NU/NU - woman + K'OU/ KOU - mouth.

Going to same-hearted relationships and speaking the virtues of mutuality and reciprocity with womanly skill, as good as it gets. Acting in harmonious accord with fellow human beings.

6. CHUNG/ZHONG -the virtues of loyalty, fidelity, devotion, dedication and faithfulness.

忠 = 心 + 中

CHUNG/ZHONG - loyal = HsIN/XIN - heart, mind, moral nature + CHUNG/ZHONG - center, middle.

Moral qualities of human beings that reside in and issue from the center of one's heart.

7. CH'ENG/CHENG AND HSIN/XIN - the virtues of sincerity, integrity, being true to oneself, authenticity, genuineness, uprightness, straightness, honesty, belief, faith, trust, fidelity, faithfulness, trustworthiness and standing by one's word.

誠 = 言 + 成　　信 = 亻 + 言

CH'ENG/CHENG- sincerity = YEN/YAN - words, speech + CH'ENG/CHENG - to become, to complete, to perfect and HSIN/XIN - sincerity = JEN/REN - human being + YEN/YAN- words, speech.

Human beings speaking their words perfectly and completely and standing by their words.

8. HSUEH/XUE AND CHIH/ZHI - the virtues of studying, observing, reflecting, learning, knowledge, understanding, insight and wisdom.

學 = 臼 + 子　　知 = 矢 + 口

HSUEH/XUE - study, learn, practice = TZU/ZI - child, son, philosopher + HSIAO/XIAO - study, learn and CHIH/ZHI - know, knowledge, wisdom = SHIH/SHI - arrow + K'OU/KOU - mouth.

Both hands of the master acting from above the disciple. Learning that contributes to self-awareness, self-understanding, self-developing, self-improving and self-refining. Learning as ethical/moral cultivating, developing, refining and practicing of the cardinal virtues of goodness, rightness, properness and learning and the virtue of speaking wisdom like arrows.

9. CHUN TZU/JUN ZI - a ruler's son, prince; the ultimate human being of complete moral virtue; the cultured, refined, noble, honorable, exemplary and ideal gentleman, mister, sir and not the HSIAO JEN/XIAO REN - small, little and petty human being

who doesn't live the cardinal virtues of goodness, rightness, properness and other human virtues.

Superior, well-educated, cultivated, developed and refined in character, ethical virtue, moral conduct and social responsibility. Cultivating, personifying, living and enacting the virtues of benevolence, righteousness and propriety and respect, humility, sincerity, wisdom, courage et al.

君 = 彐 + ノ + 口 + 子

CHUN TZU/ JUN ZI - gentleperson = CHI/JI - boar's head + P'IEH/ PIE - left downstroke indicating action and motion + K'OU/KOU - mouth, opening + TZU/ZI - son, philosopher.

Human beings who are cultivating, embodying, living, enacting and transmitting the above virtues and who are modeling, inspiring, encouraging, supporting, potentiating and assisting fellow human beings in realizing and actualizing the above virtues by being, living, doing and sharing that which is real, true, good, right, appropriate, fitting, harmonious and beneficial. [14]

10. TAO/DAO - road, lead, say, teach, The Way. TE/DE - virtue, goodness, energy, conduct.

道 = 辶 + 首

CHO/CHUO - run fast and stop, halt
SHOU/SHOU - chief, head
Traveling on the principal Way.

德 = 彳 + 直 + 心

JEN/REN - human being + CHEN/ZHEN - real, true + CH'IH/CHI - step taken, in action + HSIN/XIN - heart
True-hearted human being in action.

In Confucianism, Tao/Dao and te/de have the meaning of cultural reality and the ethical Way of humanity and its moral character and power that are cultivated by good and wise gentlepersons. Tao/Dao and te/de don't have Taoism's meaning of Ultimate Reality and the Universal Way of Nature and its individualization, integrity, energy, force, power and efficacy in all beings and things.

水

THE ANALECTS
BOOK THEMES

BOOK ONE

The characteristics, qualities and behavior of true gentlepersons, human beings and the nature and characteristics of Goodness, e.g., dutiful respect for parents and superiors; moderation, modesty, deference, courteousness, cordialty, loyalty and harmony in relationships. Obedience to what is right and diligence in work, adhering to ritual and pursuing the development of the moral power/de of the Way.

BOOK TWO

The characteristics, qualities and behavior of gentlepersons, e.g., reverence, respect, filial piety and obedience to parents; being authentic, straight, unbiased, trustworthy, courageous and having good thoughts; dignity, attentiveness and encouragement toward fellow human beings and ruling and governing by the moral power/de of the Way and ritual and not by coercion and punishments. Political order through moral self-cultivation.

BOOK THREE

The qualities, attitudes and behavior of gentlepersons, e.g., non-competetive; appropriate for social station and proper for ancestral sacrificial and mourning rituals; being reverential and right with Heaven and ancient culture and appreciating the Goodness and beauty of ritual songs and peace dances. Critique of ritual impropriety.

BOOK FOUR

Filial piety, relationships with parents; the value, beauty and effects of not departing from Goodness; hearing, caring for and complying with the Way; setting one's heart upon, adhering to and doing what is right and consideration of and loyalty to fellow human beings.

BOOK FIVE

The desirable course and qualities of moral self-cultivation for human beings, rulers, officials and disciples, e.g., Goodness, uprightness, courtesy, good faith, steadfastness, reciprocity, justice, loyalty, generosity, diligence, reverence and cherishing.

BOOK SIX

The qualifications, qualities and conduct of rulers, officials and disciples. The love of learning and commitment to Goodness and following and delighting in the Way. Wisdom, security and happiness. The characteristics of gentlepersons. The moral power/de of the 'Middle Way'.

BOOK SEVEN

The transmission rather than the innovation of teachings and learning. The qualities of good students and learners. Appropriate ways of mourning behavior and legitimate means of attaining wealth. Commitment to teaching students and diligence in investigating the past. The immunity and invulnerability of the Heaven-bestowed power/de of the Way. The love of knowledge and the availability of Goodness. Qualities of impartiality, courtesy, deference, calmness, at-easeness, friendliness and politeness.

BOOK EIGHT

The moral power/de of the Way. The value of ritual and generosity. A Master's illness and the qualities of his friend and those of a gentleperson. The way of being of truly good and not so good human beings. The way to learn. The greatness of legendary Ancient Sage-Rulers. The moral power/de of a king and dynasty.

BOOK NINE

Adherence to ancient rituals and culture. Divine sagehood versus practical accomplishments. Signs of respect for mourners and ceremonialists and blind and younger human beings. The challenges of rigorous instruction. The vicissitudes of Confucius's life and sayings.

BOOK TEN

Further vicissitudes of Confucius's life, characteristics, behavior and sayings. The ritual requirements of dress, habits and conduct of gentlepersons.

BOOK ELEVEN

Confucius's sayings regarding ritual and music, the behavior of various disciples, mourning the death of a favorite disciple, serving ghosts and spirits, the difficulty in ascertaining true gentlepersonness, responses to hearing maxims, the service of ministers and wishes made by disciples.

BOOK TWELVE

About the favorite disciple of Confucius. Inquiries by disciples and rulers about Goodness, being a gentleperson, illumination, government, accumulating moral power/de, public business, the art of ruling, being influential, being a good ruler and having friends.

BOOK THIRTEEN

More disciples asking Confucius about governing and Goodness. The need to use knowledge practically and to educate the overpopulated. The need for the right human beings doing the right things in order to insure good government that ends cruelty and slaughter. Phrases that could save or ruin a country. A ruler and official asking Confucius about governing. The differences between gentlepersons and common people.

BOOK FOURTEEN

Various sayings of Confucius purportedly attributed to disciples about good human beings, the prevailing of the Way in the world, the accumulation of moral power/de, the qualities of gentlepersons, being loving and loyal, the perfect human being, the behaviors of a master and rulers, how to serve a ruler, the inner qualities and inner power of de and two examples of a disciple and a young boy uncommitted to self-improvement.

BOOK FIFTEEN

A ruler asks Confucius about gathering military troops and Confucius says that he has never studied warfare. Confucius's speaking about moral power/de, inactive ruling, getting along with people, uprightness and straightforwardness, truly wise human beings not wasting people or words, how to become Good, the making of a state, continuing self-examination, the qualities and conduct of gentlepersons and the characteristics and behavior of human beings.

BOOK SIXTEEN

The dilemmas, circumstances and considerations of the family of a powerful state contemplating attacking a smaller state. The nature and effects of the Way prevailing in the world. Three kinds of beneficial and harmful friends and pleasure. Three mistakes made when serving gentlepersons. Three things that gentlepersons guard against and three things that they fear. Nine cares that gentlepersons have. An interaction between Confucius and his son. A very sexist account of the wives of rulers.

BOOK SEVENTEEN

Sayings of Confucius on good and wise ruling, assisting an official, Goodness, usefulness to an official, six sayings and six degenerations, the ignorance of ritual and music, not serving a corrupt ruler, three faults of former common people, regretting having to speak, the length of mourning, people who idle away their lives instead of developing themselves, courage and the Right, the dislikes of gentlepersons and prejudicial statements about women, poor human beings and elders.

BOOK EIGHTEEN

Some criticisms of Confucius. The tales and behavior of rulers, a madman, two farmers, a recluse, six subjects whose services to the state are lost and a chief musician and band members leaving the state. A ruler's comments on the behavior of a gentleperson and a record of a state's eight officials who are four sets of twins.

BOOK NINETEEN

Disciple's comments about the good qualities of officials, about those who believe in the Way but without conviction and about social relationships and mourning. Numerous sayings from a master other than Confucius about the cultivation of gentlepersons; their love of learning, self-improvement and service and their appearance, demeanor, behavior and moral import and the master's responses to criticisms about his disciples. Another master's comments on not-yet-good, difficult and mourning persons and filial piety. A disciple comments upon the dwelling and faults of gentlepersons, where Confucius receives his learning, modesty about his own development and about Confucius's inability to be disparaged and equalled.

BOOK TWENTY

The Heavenly power of ancient legendary Sage-Rulers and their honoring of Good human beings and their taking responsibiity for all wrongs. A ruler who governs with reformations and the hearts of the subjects for whom he cares and is their joy. What a human being must do to be fit to govern the country. Gentlepersons are so because of understanding the will of Heaven, the rites and words and can, therefore, be gentlepersons who take their stand with human beings and understand them.

水

THE ANALECTS
BOOK QUOTATIONS

BOOK ONE

'To learn and at the right time repeat what has been learned is a pleasure'.

'Clever talk and a pretentious manner are seldom found in Goodness'.

'In acting on behalf of fellow human beings, have I been loyal to their interests?. In communion with friends, have I been true to my word?'.

'Good human beings do not grieve that fellow human beings do not recognize their worth. They only grieve if they do not recognize the worth of fellow human beings'.

BOOK TWO

'A human being who reanimates the old gains knowledge of the new and is fit to be a teacher'.

'True gentlepersons don't preach what they practice until they've practiced what they preach'.

'Human beings who learn but don't think are lost. Those who think but don't learn are endangered'.

'Knowledge is recognizing that and when you know something and that and when you don't know something'.

BOOK THREE

'What can human beings do with ritual and music if they're not Good human beings?'.

'Gentlepersons don't generally compete...but even when competeing, they still are gentlepersons'.

'Human beings in the wrong with Heaven have no means of forgiveness'.

'What is over and done with, taken its course and belongs to the past; do not discuss, criticize or censure'.

BOOK FOUR

'Human beings who are free to choose and don't prefer Goodness can't be called wise'.

'Good human beings are content with Goodness. Merely wise human beings pursue it because it pays to do so'.

'Without Goodness, human beings can't endure adversity or enjoy prosperity for long'.

'Human beings whose heart is in the slightest degree set upon Goodness dislike no one'.

BOOK FIVE

'I have yet to see a human being who is truly steadfast and not at the mercy of desires'.

'What I don't want fellow human beings to do to me, I don't do to them'.

'You may find someone who is as loyal and true to their word as I am, but not as fond of learning'.

'In vain have I looked for a single human being who has seen their own faults and taken responsibility for them'.

BOOK SIX

'A gentleperson helps the needy and doesn't make the wealthy richer'.

'Who expects to leave a house except by the door?. How is it that no one follows the Way?'.

'Human beings' very life is honesty and without it they would be fortunate to escape with their lives'.

'To prefer the Way is better than to only know it. To delight in the Way is better than to merely prefer it'.

BOOK SEVEN

'Set your heart upon the Way, support yourself by its power/de, rely upon Goodness and enjoy the arts'.

'I instruct and enlighten only those human beings who burst with eagerness and bubble with excitement'.

'When walking with three human beings, I can always learn something. Good qualities, I can imitate for myself and bad ones, I can correct in myself'.

'True gentlepersons are calm and relaxed. Small persons are irritable and uncomfortable'.

BOOK EIGHT

'Gentlepersons following the Way are free from violence and arrogance and act in good faith and properly'.

'Common human beings can be made to follow the Way but can't be made to understand it'.

'True gentlepersons can equally and confidently be entrusted with an orphaned child and a whole state'.

'Learn as if you are following someone whom you cannot catch up with and is someone whom you are afraid of losing'.

BOOK NINE

'Never take anything for granted or be overly positive, obstinate and egotistic'.

'Like this flowing stream, I could go on and on, never ceasing day or night'.

'I've never yet seen any human being whose desire to develop the moral power/de of the Way/is as strong as their love of female beauty'.

'Respect the young. How do you know that they won't be all who you are now?'.

BOOK TEN

'Gentlepersons dress appropriately, follow etiquette and observe customs'.

'Gentlepersons respectfully prostrate themselves, bow and clasp their hands together'.

'Gentlepersons ask about the animals as well as the people when a stable burns'.

'Gentlepersons leave at the first sign of an absence of Goodness and go to and settle where there is Goodness'.

BOOK ELEVEN

'Until you know how to serve human beings and the living, how can you know how to serve spirits and the deceased?'.

'Human beings who do not follow the Way of the Ancients, can't find their way into its Inner Sanctuary'.

'When one hears a maxim, it should immediately be put into practice'.

'It's upon ritual that the governance of a state depends'.

BOOK TWELVE

'Human beings who can submit themselves to ritual are Good human beings'.

'Gentlepersons look within, find no corruption and, thus, have no grief or fear'.

'Gentlepersons call attention to the good points in fellow human beings and not to their defects, faults, errors and failures'.

'Gentlepersons, by nature and culture gather friends around them and through these friends promote and expand Goodness'.

BOOK THIRTEEN

'When rulers are upright, all will go well even though they don't give orders'.

'Only if Good and Right human beings rule a country will there be no cruelty and slaughter'.

'If human beings don't put themselves Right, how can they put fellow human beings Right?'.

'Goodness is being courteous in private life, diligent in public life and loyal in relationships'.

BOOK FOURTEEN

'It's possible to be a gentleperson and lack Goodness but not to be a Good human being and not be a gentleperson'.

'Don't be too ready to speak of Goodness, lest the living of it proves to be beyond your power'.

'In olden days, human beings study and learn for self-improvement but nowadays they do so to impress fellow human beings'.

'Gentlepersons don't grieve that fellow human beings don't recognize their abilities. They grieve over their own inabilities'.

BOOK FIFTEEN

'Those human beings who understand the moral power/de of the Way/Tao are few'.

'Be loyal and true to your word and serious and careful about your actions and you'll get on well'.

'The demands that gentlepersons make are upon themselves and not upon fellow human beings'.

'To have faults and not amend them is to have another and greater fault'.

BOOK SIXTEEN

'Three kinds of friends are beneficial; the upright, the truthful and the learned'.

'Three kinds of pleasure are beneficial; ritual and music, focusing on the good points of human beings and having many wise friends'.

'Three things gentlepersons must guard against are lust when young, strife when middle-aged and avarice when old'.

'Three things gentlepersons fear are the will of Heaven, great human beings and the words of Divine Sages'.

BOOK SEVENTEEN

'Things are by nature near together and by practice far apart'.

'It's only the very wisest of human beings and the most stupid who can't change'.

'Goodpersons are courteous, broad-minded, of good faith, diligent and forgiving and, therefore, they are accepted, popular, trusted, successful and appreciated'.

'The six sayings are love of Goodness, love of wisdom, love of keeping promises, love of uprightness, love of action and love of courage'.

BOOK EIGHTEEN

'If the Way prevails under Heaven, we should not be trying to alter things'.

'Gentlepersons' service to their country consists in doing as much Good and Right as they can'.

'Good serving is having personal integrity; being highly resolved, unhumiliated and congruent in words and relationships; acting with prudence and being balanced when let go of'.

'Gentlepersons don't neglect kinsfolk, irritate retainers, dismiss loyals or expect one human being to be able to do everything'.

BOOK NINETEEN

'Go with those human beings with whom it is proper to go. Distance from those human beings from whom it is proper to distance'.

'Gentlepersons revere those human beings who excel but make room for everyone. They commend good human beings and have compassion for the unable'.

'True lovers of learning are conscious of what they lack and never forget what they have learned'.

'Gentlepersons study so that they can improve themselves in the Way'.

BOOK TWENTY

'Gentlepersons are bountiful without being extravagant, encouraging without arousing resentment, desirous without being covetous, proud but without being insolent and awe-inspiring without being fearsome'.

'Gentlepersons don't execute human beings without having first taught them, don't expect them to complete tasks without having warned them, don't delay giving orders to them and expect punctuality and don't give things to them grudgingly'.

'Human beings who don't understand the will of Heaven, the rites and words; can't be regarded as gentlepersons, take their own stand or understand fellow human beings'.

水

THE ANALECTS
BOOK ONE
STUDYING AND PRACTICING
XUE ER

學 而

VIRTUES AND CONDUCT

1. Text.

Confucius says, 'To learn, practice and pass on what has been learned is a pleasure. Like-hearted friends coming from far away to learn is a delight. To not resent it if one's learnings and teachings aren't recognized or understood is the mark of a virtuous gentleperson'.

Commentary.

Being a virtuous psychotherapist is a pleasurable experience and a delightful opportunity to unselfishly share and to humbly transmit one's knowledge to assist and benefit friendly clients seeking assistance and to be patient with their understanding and progress.

2. Text.

Confucius says, 'Human beings who are filial and deferential with parents usually don't resist or rebel against superiors and create disorder. Gentlepersons live respectfully at the solid roots of the family tree where the Goodness of the Way/Dao and human character grow and develop'.

Commentary.

Virtuous psychotherapists have sufficiently dealt with and/ or resolved parental issues in their family, don't have authority problems with superiors, don't feel or act superior to clients, don't engage in acting-out power struggles with them and respectfully conduct the psychotherapy relationship in ways that embody, reflect and support the Goodness of Dao and the human character of clients.

3. Text.

Confucius says, 'Clever talking and pretentiousness aren't found in the virtue of Goodness'.

Commentary.

Virtuous psychotherapists aren't pretentious and don't make clever observations, analyses, reflections, interpretations and explanations of, to and with clients. They're down-to-earth, realistic, concrete, clear, straightforward and understandable when communicating with clients.

4. Text.

Confucius says, 'Acting daily on behalf of fellow human beings; I ask myself whether or not I'm respectful, sincere, loyal and trustworthy; I'm doing the best that I can and I'm continually practicing and passing on the learning handed down to me'.

Commentary.

Virtuous psychotherapists act of behalf of clients; are sincere, respectful of, faithful to and trusted by them; do their best in conducting psychotherapy; remember and use their past learning and training experience and serve as good examples and role-models for clients.

5. Text.

Confucius says, 'Large states are well-governed when rulers

attend to business with respect and care, keep their word and promises, limit expenditures, treat people fairly and don't waste their time and effort performing unimportant duties and untimely projects'.

Commentary.

Virtuous psychotherapists enjoy a well-managed and successful professional practice by staying focused on the business of psychotherapy; keeping any contracts, agreements and promises made with clients; having fair requirements and charging reasonable fees and engaging clients in activities that are appropriate, relevant, significant, opportune and meaningful for them.

6. Text.

Confucius says, 'The duties of disciples are being filial at home and obedient away from home, being modest and respectful in demeanor, being trustworthy in speaking and keeping promises, having kind feelings for everyone and associating with good friends and, if energy and time remain; learning, cultivating and practicing the cultural arts'.

Commentary.

Some responsibilities of virtuous psychotherapists are to behave morally, respectfully and appropriately with clients, to keep any agreements and promises made with clients, to have no unkind countertransference feelings toward clients and to affirm the Goodness in clients and to have close friendships and to engage in creative artistic and cultural activities in addition to conducting their psychotherapy practice.

7. Text.

Confucius says, 'Human beings who honor parents unselfishly, serve rulers dutifully, treat superiors deferentially and relate to friends faithfully are learned human beings, even if they're unknowledgeable about certain matters'.

Commentary.

Virtuous psychotherapists are learned practitioners who honor, serve and treat clients unselfishly, responsibly, respectfully and faithfully in spite of not knowing certain psychological theories and psychotherapy techniques.

8. Text.

Confucius says, 'Gentlepersons are serious, dedicated, reliable and respected and loyal, faithful, trustworthy and do their best; associate with fellow human beings who share their same standard of Goodness and acknowledge and correct their faults, mistakes and errors'.

Commentary.

Virtuous psychotherapists are respected and trusted by clients and develop a successful psychotherapy practice by being loyal and faithful to clients and acting responsibly and reliably with them. They do their best and acknowledge and correct any errors in conducting psychotherapy and don't usually associate with professional colleagues who don't share their same ethical values and moral virtues.

9. Text.

Confucius says, 'When funeral rites are correctly performed at the time of the death of parents and properly continued in sacrificial ceremonies after it, the moral virtue/de of human beings reaches excellence'.

Commentary.

When virtuous psychotherapists appropriately honor and remember the deaths of clients and/or their family members, close relatives and friends and also acknowledge and recall the termination of a psychotherapy relationship; their moral virtue/de reaches its summit.

10. Text.

Confucius says, 'When visiting another state, its governmental policies and procedures need to be known. Information isn't acquired by usual direct questioning but by it being offered when respectful, courteous, modest and deferential'.

Commentary.

When interviewing and making inquiries of clients, virtuous psychotherapists are respectful, kind, mild-mannered and receptive rather than distant and formal through objectifying and alienating questioning. Clients naturally disclose and offer essential, relevant, pertinent and useful information.

11. Text.

Confucius says, 'When parents are alive, see the intentions of offspring. After they die, see the actions of offspring. They're filial daughters and sons if, after three years of mourning, the household continues unchanged'.

Commentary.

Whether or not the intentions and objectives of virtuous psychotherapists and clients are successfully realized and fully sustained often can only be known following the termination of psychotherapy through follow-up contacts or meetings.

12. Text.

Confucius says, 'In practicing rituals, harmony and the beauty of the Way of ancient Sage-Rulers are the best results. But in both small and great matters when harmony and beauty aren't supported by ritual, things don't go right'.

Commentary.

Effective minor and major interactions and interventions of virtuous psychotherapists are harmonious, beautiful and Dao-like when they are attuned to, integrated with and implemented by appropriate techniques and methods.

13. Text.

Confucius says, 'Being trusted is when promises accord with what's Right and are kept. Being respected is when ritual accords with what's Good and is consistent. Trust and respect continue when joining with friends who are faithful and dutiful to family'.

Commentary.

Virtuous psychotherapists are trusted and respected by keeping their word, being consistent and according with what is Right and Good in the conduct of psychotherapy. Clients are also usually trusting and respectful who have a history of being caring of and loyal to their parents, relatives and friends.

14. Text.

Confucius says, 'Gentlepersons who eat moderately, don't require comfort at home, are diligent in work, cautious in speech and associate with human beings of the Way to correct themselves are lovers of learning'.

Commentary.

Virtuous psychotherapists who are modest in habits, indifferent to comforts, diligent in psychotherapy work, considerate in speech and derive the self-correcting benefits of associating with Wayfaring colleagues are committed to learning, growing and improving personally, interpersonally and professionally.

15. Text.

A disciple asks, 'Being poor without subservience and being wealthy without arrogance. What else is there?'. Confucius replies, 'Not bad but better still is being poor and still happy in the Way and being wealthy and still loving ritual'. The disciple continues, 'Is this what the saying; 'Jade, stone, bone and horn are cut, chiselled, filed and polished' means?'. Confucius adds, 'You understand the steps of moral cultivation and refinement!'.

Commentary.

Virtuous psychotherapists, regardless of financial status, are happy living the constant reality of the Way/Dao and loving employing the consistent methods in and of the practice of psychotherapy. They're aware of and value psychotherapy practice as vitally contributing to cultivating and refining their personal growth, professional development and spiritual evolution.

16. Text.

Confucius says, 'Gentlepersons don't worry about fellow human beings not recognizing or understanding them. They worry about not recognizing or understanding fellow human beings'.

Commentary.

Virtuous psychotherapists are concerned more with not recognizing, acknowledging, appreciating and understanding clients and professional colleagues than with themselves not being recognized, acknowledged, appreciated and understood by them.

水

THE ANALECTS
BOOK TWO
THE PRACTICE OF GOVERNMENT

WEI ZENG

為 政

FILIAL RELATIONSHIPS AND LEARNING

1. Text.

Confucius says, 'Gentlepersons of moral virtue/de resemble the pole-star that remains in its place and centers other stars'.

Commentary.

Virtuous psychotherapists conduct psychotherapy by de; the virtue, integrity, energy, power and efficacy of Dao. Clients respect them and are often referral sources for new clients. When virtuous psychotherapists simply occupy their place, and by their presence alone, clients often fill silences and spaces between verbalizations and interactions with true, relevant and meaningful self-disclosures.

2. Text.

Confucius says, 'One phrase summarizes the poems and songs of *The Book of Odes*. 'Don't deviate from the path".

Commentary.

Virtuous psychotherapists don't deviate from the path of

Goodness and Rightness and the Way/Dao in their professional psychotherapy practice with clients and in their personal private lives with family and friends.

3. Text.

Confucius says, 'Human beings governed and controlled by strict rules and harsh punishments won't have a sense of shame, correct themselves or obey rulers. But when governed and guided by the moral virtue/de of Dao and ritual propriety, they'll have self-respect, regulate themselves and accept rulers'.

Commentary.

Psychotherapy won't be possible or effective and clients won't respect psychotherapists or themselves and will terminate psychotherapy when it's conducted by strict rules, rigid techniques and punitive consequences. Clients will respect themselves and will naturally continue engaging in psychotherapy when virtuous psychotherapists conduct psychotherapy by de; the moral virtue, integrity, energy, power and efficacy of Dao and with flexible techniques, methods and procedures that are appropriately suited to uniquely individual clients and their particularly specific issues.

4. Text.

Confucius says, 'I set my heart on learning at fifteen, ground myself in ritual at thirty, find my place at forty, understand Heaven's will at fifty, attune to truth at sixty and at seventy follow my heart without overstepping the line of what's Good, Right and Proper'.

Commentary.

Throughout the years of their professional career; virtuous psychotherapists continue to grow, mature and evolve in learning about human beings, psychotherapy and themselves; in establishing themselves in practice, in truly understanding and really treating clients and in conforming to and complying with the ethical standards of good, right and proper practice.

5. Text.

An official asks about treating parents. Confucius answers, 'Comply with them. While they're living, be obedient and serve them in compliance with ritual. When they die, be respectful and bury them in compliance with ritual and later on make sacrificial offerings to them in compliance with ritual'.

Commentary.

Virtuous psychotherapists comply with the ethical standards of psychotherapy practice, respect and serve clients, work within their uniquely individual frames of reference and remember and honor them after termination of the psychotherapy relationship.

6. Text.

Another official asks about treating parents. Confucius replies, 'Behave so that they only worry about your health'.

Commentary.

Virtuous psychotherapists don't conduct themselves in the psychotherapy relationship in ways that create clients' transference feelings of anxiety or worry about them except for the natural and normal human feelings of mutual care about health and well-being that they both have for each other.

7. Text.

A disciple asks about treating parents. Confucius answers, 'Nowadays, filial children insure that parents are sufficiently fed but it's reverence for them that makes this different from caring for animals'.

Commentary.

Virtuous psychotherapists regard, care about and treat clients with the dignity and respect that they as human beings deserve.

8. Text.

Another disciple asks about treating parents. Confucius replies, 'Be reverent. Filial piety doesn't just involve doing hard work for parents or serving them food and wine first'.

Commentary.

In addition to conducting psychotherapy in routinely professional personal and interpersonal ways, virtuous psychotherapists are aware and experience that the psychotherapy relationship process also involves higher and deeper realities, values and interactions of a reverential, transpersonal and spiritual nature.

9. Text.

Confucius says, 'I speak with this disciple for days without any disagreement from him as if he's unintelligent. But closely observing his actions, I see that he learns and practices what I teach him and certainly can't be regarded as unintelligent'.

Commentary.

When virtuous psychotherapists observe that clients are living the progress made in psychotherapy in their ongoing relationships, they can be regarded as internalizing the gains made in psychotherapy and intelligently being and successfully applying them in their everyday lives outside of psychotherapy.

10. Text.

Confucius says, 'See the aims of human beings and the means by which they're pursued and accomplished and see what brings them comfort, fulfillment and happiness and their true character and worth can't be hidden'.

Commentary.

By observing attitudes held, motives involved, means used and goals accomplished by clients and what brings them ease, satisfaction and fulfillment; virtuous psychotherapists can learn about their nature and character.

11. Text.

Confucius says, 'Human beings who remember, reactivate and use previous knowledge to acquire, learn and understand new knowledge; qualify as teachers'.

Commentary.

The teaching function, ability and success of virtuous psychotherapists involve being able to apply past psychotherapy work and former client experience to better understand new and current clients.

12. Text.

Confucius says, 'Gentlepersons aren't implements'.

Commentary.

Virtuous psychotherapists are not simply technical specialists or functionally instrumental utensils in psychotherapy relationships and work. They are, first and foremost, valuable and reliable human beings who are competent and proficient in using the moral virtue, integrity, energy, power and efficacy of Dao for the benefit and welfare of other human beings called clients.

13. Text.

A disciple asks about gentlepersons. Confucius replies, 'They practice what they preach before preaching about what they practice'.

Commentary.

Virtuous psychotherapists are most effective in psychotherapy relationships when they speak from what they really know and truly understand directly and concretely from their own lived-experience of psychotherapy practice.

14. Text.

Confucius says, 'Good gentlepersons are broad-minded, impartial and affiliate with individuals. Small human beings are narrow-minded, biased and associate in cliques'.

Commentary.

Virtuous psychotherapists are non-dualistic, open, impartial and unprejudiced; view questions, problems, issues and conflicts from both sides and multiple perspectives and usually prefer communing in intimate individual relationships rather than participating in partisan groups and movements.

15. Text.

Confucius says, 'Human beings who learn but don't think are lost and who think but don't learn are endangered'.

Commentary.

Virtuous psychotherapists meditate and thoughtfully reflect upon what they learn and aren't lost in their understanding of themselves, clients and the conduct of psychotherapy. They find informative, helpful and useful insights about, for example, safe interpretations, safe interactions and safe interventions that they ordinarily wouldn't have if they only simply think about themselves, clients and psychotherapy without learning anything.

16. Text.

Confucius says, 'Human beings who only work with one strange strand destroy the whole fabric'.

Commentary

Virtuous psychotherapists don't work only with strange phenomena and isolated client experiences, don't know only single and separate theories and don't use only routine and inflexible techniques and, therefore, don't negate the aliveness, uniqueness and wholeness of the psychotherapy relationship, process and experience.

17. Text.

Confucius says to a disciple, 'I'll teach you what knowldge is. Knowledge is knowing that you know something when you know it and knowing that you don't know something when you don't know it'.

Commentary.

Virtuous psychotherapists are knowledgeable in recognizing that which they truly know and truly don't know with regard to psychological theories, psychopathological conditions, psychotherapy techniques and their own experiences and those of clients.

18. Text.

A disciple is studying to gain an official position. Confucius advises, 'When studying, learn much, ignore what's doubtful and speak carefully about the rest and you won't be blamed. When observing, see much, avoid what's dangerous and act cautiously with the rest and you won't be sorry. Human beings who aren't blamed for what they say and don't regret what they do are successful and an official position follows naturally'.

Commentary.

Virtuous psychotherapists attentively study, listen to, observe and see clients closely; speak and relate to them carefully and cautiously and ignore what's doubtful and avoid what's risky. As a result, they aren't blamed for or regretful of reflections, interpretations, interactions and interventions and the psychotherapy relationship process unfolds naturally and successfully.

19. Text.

A ruler asks, 'How can I gain the people's support?'. Confucius answers, 'Elevate the straight above the crooked, don't elevate the crooked above the straight and they'll be supportive'.

Commentary.

Virtuous psychotherapists obtain the trust and support of clients by uprightly and straightforwardly promoting and elevating what is ethically and morally superior, correct and appropriate rather than what is ethically and morally inferior, incorrect and inappropriate.

20. Text.

A ruling family head asks, 'How can I induce people to be respectful, loyal and supportive?'. Confucius replies, 'Relate to them with dignity, filiality and kindness; promote the capable and teach the incapable and they'll be encouraged to be virtuous'.

Commentary.

Virtuous psychotherapists encourage respect, trustworthiness and support in and from clients by validating their dignity, respecting their worth, relating to them filially and kindly, reinforcing them in realizing and actualizing their potentials and abilities and assisting them in overcoming their limitations.

21. Text.

Confucius is asked why he isn't in government. Confucius answers, 'Being filial with parents and elders and friendly with fellow human beings are public services that are participating in, contributing to and influencing good government. There are many ways of serving human beings besides being in government'.

Commentary.

Virtuous psychotherapists participate in, and contribute to, the general welfare and well-being of their social community by conducting a viable and visible psychotherapy practice for children, adolescents, adults, couples, families and groups.

22. Text.

Confucius says, 'Human beings whose word can't be trusted have difficulty being useful. How can wagons and carriages be used without linchpins for their yoke- and collar-bars?'.

Commentary.

Virtuous psychotherapists are effective in assisting and facilitating clients to develop, grow and move forward in their lives by being essentially trustworthy and crucially useful connecting links in the psychotherapy process.

23. Text.

A disciple asks whether ten generations hence can be known. Confucius answers, 'The ways that ritual is conducted in previous dynasties and sequentially modified and transmitted are known and patterns are seen that enable predicting future trends'.

Commentary.

Virtuous psychotherapists are able to intuit and predict some aspects of the future life of clients by observing and understanding patterns and trends in their past and present ways of being, living and relating.

24. Text.

Confucius says, 'Just as sacrificing to ancestral spirits who aren't one's own is presumptuous, seeing what is Good and not doing it is uncourageous'.

Commentary.

Virtuous psychotherapists aren't typically devoted to psychotherapists with whom they haven't had an actual educational, training or therapy experience. They conduct their own psychotherapy practice courageously by doing what is ethically sound and morally correct.

水

THE ANALECTS
BOOK THREE
8 LINES OF 8 DANCERS

BA YI

八 佾

RITUAL AND PROPRIETY

1. Text.

A family accepts an offering proper only for a ruler. Confucius says, 'If this family can be excused for having eight rows of eight dancers performing in their courtyard, anyone and anything can be excused'.

Commentary.

Virtuous psychotherapists are able to accept and work with pretentious clients who make ostentatious displays and to assist them in conforming to and complying with appropriate social mores, expectations, actions and behavior.

2. Text.

Three ruling families misuse a sacrificial ode reserved for the ruler. Confucius says, 'Words such as 'Attending are the Great Lords, majestic is the Son of Heaven'. How can these families use this for their own sacrifices?'.

Commentary.

Virtuous psychotherapists use psychotherapy techniques, methods and procedures that are appropriate for, and applicable to, unique clients, specific issues and realistic abilities.

3. Text.

Confucius says, 'When human beings lack the virtue of Goodness, what can ritual and music do for them?'.

Commentary.

Virtuous psychotherapists suit psychotherapy techniques, methods and processes to the characterological constitutions, traits, predispositions, inclinations and behaviors of unique clients.

4. Text.

A disciple asks about ritual. Confucius replies, 'A great question!. Be sparing rather than lavish. Funeral rites are regulated by genuine grief rather than formal details'.

Commentary.

Virtuous psychotherapists are conservative and economical when using psychotherapy techniques, methods and procedures and appropriately suit them to the realities of client situations and circumstances and their emotional states and feelings.

5. Text.

Confucius says, 'Barbarians have rulers but they can't compare with a Chinese State even without one'.

Commentary.

Virtuous psychotherapists observe that the practices of some other colleagues who are employing less refined treatment methods don't compare with their own ones or even with the functioning of leaderless therapy groups.

6. Text.

The head of a family is planning to make a sacrificial offering to a sacred mountain which only rulers are entitled to perform. Confucius asks a disciple in the employ of the family, 'Can't you prevent this?'. The disciple replies, 'No. I can't'. Confucius adds, 'Well, the spirit of the sacred mountain isn't as ignorant of such violations of sacrificial ritual as this person'.

Commentary.

Virtuous psychotherapists only use psychotherapy techniques, methods and procedures that are appropriate to their degree of training, skill, proficiency and competence. Clients are often painfully aware if and when psychotherapists don't do so.

7. Text.

Confucius says, 'Gentlepersons don't generally compete with others but, if in contests like archery, they still bow and defer to others at the field and drink together at the celebration. They always remain gentlepersons'.

Commentary.

Virtuous psychotherapists remain as respectful gentlepersons at the beginning and ending of psychotherapy meetings and even during disagreements, conflicts and power struggles with clients.

8. Text.

A disciple asks the meaning of the ode, 'Her sweet engaging smile. Lovely eyes so clearly detailed. Colored designs on a white background'. Confucius replies, 'The colors of a painting come after the plain background'. The disciple states, 'So ritual follows virtue'. Confucius says, 'You understand the meaning and are ready to study and learn *The Odes*'.

Commentary.

In their conscious awareness, virtuous psychotherapists have their clear field of empty and open consciousness as a background upon which to illuminate and to clearly perceive the vivid content, phenomena and experiences presented by clients.

9. Text.

Confucius says, 'I can speak about the rituals of earlier states but there's little documented evidence from later ones and only a few learned human beings in them to record events'.

Commentary.

Virtuous psychotherapists rely upon client self-reporting and don't have direct evidence about the characteristics and behavior of other human beings in their lives unless some documented evidence is provided or they are interviewed in the process of psychotherapy.

10. Text.

Confucius says, 'At the ancestral sacrifice, what follows after the opening libation to the spirits is mechanical and superficial and I don't wish to witness it'.

Commentary.

Virtuous psychotherapists are equally present for both the initiation and conclusion of psychotherapy techniques, methods and procedures while they are occurring and not usually after the psychotherapy meeting ends, especially when they meet with clients back-to-back.

11. Text.

Someone asks about the meaning of the ancestral sacrifice. Confucius says, 'I don't know. Anyone who can explain it can understand everything under Heaven (the world) as easily as this'. And Confucius points a finger at the palm of his hand.

Commentary.

Virtuous psychotherapists humbly don't pretend to abstractly and conceptually know the nature of some of the mysteries and deeper meanings of human nature, human being, human existence and the inner worlds of clients.

12. Text.

Confucius says, 'Memorial ceremonies and ancestral sacrifices are conducted as if the person or spirit is present. But also, if I'm not truly present, it's as if there's no ceremony or sacrifice at all'.

Commentary.

Unless a virtuous psychotherapist and a client are fully present in the reality and true spirit of a psychotherapy meeting, it's not really happening.

13. Text.

An official asks what's the meaning of the saying, 'Better to honor the spirit of the kitchen stove than the spirit of the sacrificial altar?'. Confucius answers, 'It's not true. If you're not right with Heaven there's no way of being nourished'.

Commentary.

Virtuous psychotherapists usually prioritize transpersonal and spiritual realities over personal and material ones.

14. Text.

Confucius says, 'This dynasty extends and refines the great cultures of the two preceding ones. How magnificent is our culture and my following it'.

Commentary.

Virtuous psychotherapists benefit from studying, learning about, following, extending and refining the psychotherapy theories and methods of great former master psychotherapists and the literature of their case studies.

15. Text.

Whenever Confucius enters an ancestral temple, he asks questions about everything. He's erroneously regarded as a villager's son who knows nothing about ritual and has to ask about everything. Confucius hears about this and says, 'Asking questions is the correct ritual'.

Commentary.

Virtuous psychotherapists may continually ask clients questions not because they aren't knowledgeable but because doing so is an integral part of the psychotherapy relationship process.

16. Text.

Confucius says, 'The saying, 'In archery, it's not hitting the bull's eye or piercing the target that matters' because human beings differ in physical skill and strength. This is the ancient Way'.

Commentary.

Virtuous psychotherapists conduct psychotherapy by the virtue of Goodness and Rightness rather than by the use of power and force.

17. Text.

A disciple wants to eliminate the ritual of presenting a sacrificial sheep to the ancestors at each new moon. Confucius says 'You care about saving the sheep but I care about saving the ritual'.

Commentary.

Virtuous psychotherapists continue to use effective techniques and successful methods and don't eliminate them from their psychotherapy repertoire.

18. Text.

Confucius says, 'Today, anyone serving a ruler according to the full requirements of ritual propriety is considered to be a subservient flatterer'.

Commentary.

Virtuous psychotherapists appropriately use effective psychotherapy techniques, methods and procedures because they work and not out of needs to impress clients, professional colleagues or themselves.

19. Text.

A ruler asks how to employ subjects and how subjects should serve rulers. Confucius answers, 'Rulers should accord with the requirements of ritual propriety and subjects should be dutiful and loyal to their cause'.

Commentary.

Virtuous psychotherapists best serve clients by effective psychotherapy techniques, methods and procedures and clients best serve psychotherapists by a strong and faithful commitment to psychotherapy.

20. Text.

Confucius says, 'Oh *The Ospreys* (a song of longing for and realizing a loving union between two human beings)! Pleasure uncarried to the point of immodesty. Sadness uncarried to the point of self-injury'.

Commentary.

Virtuous psychotherapists model not taking the pleasures and pains of psychotherapy performance to their unethical extremes of immodesty and self-harm.

21. Text.

A ruler asks a disciple about the holy ground of the gods and spirits of the earth. The disciple replies, 'The sovereigns of earlier dynasties plant pine, cypress and chestnut trees to cause the common people to be in awe'. Confucius hears this and says, 'What's run its course, is completed and belongs to the past isn't commented on, discussed or criticized'.

Commentary.

Virtuous psychotherapists discuss past histories, relationships, actions and events with clients but they don't criticize or censure clients for them.

22. Text.

Confucius says, 'An official is said to be frugal. Yet he has three residences and a staff that doesn't perform double duties. How can he be called frugal?. He's also said to have knowledge of ritual propriety, yet he violates the rules and protocols appropriate to his position. If he's considered to be an expert in ritual, then who isn't one?'.

Commentary.

Virtuous psychotherapists aren't hypocritical and don't claim to be anyone other than or more than who they authentically, genuinely and truly are with regard to their personal character and professional knowledge, skills, proficiencies and competencies.

23. Text.

Confucius says, 'The music of the ancients, as far as I know, begins in unison. Then musicians are given freedom to improvise but the music remains harmonious right up until the end'.

Commentary.

Virtuous psychotherapists do their best to be equally harmoniously attuned to clients when beginning meetings, when adhering to standard forms of techniques or when improvising methods to suit varied clients and when ending meetings.

24. Text.

A frontier guardian asks for an audience with Confucius saying that all gentlepersons arriving at the border gate give him one. The followers of Confucius arrange a meeting after which the border guard says, 'Don't be discouraged by any failures of your master. It's been a long time since the Way is in the world and Heaven intends to use him to awaken the people'.

Commentary.

Virtuous psychotherapists aren't usually discouraged about failures and regard the client-psychotherapist relationship and its course to be a synchronistic event. And they progressively understand that they have somethings to teach clients and also somethings to learn about themselves when certain clients are presented to them.

25. Text.

Confucius says, 'Peace music is perfectly beautiful and perfectly Good. War music is also perfectly beautiful but not perfectly Good'.

Commentary.

Virtuous psychotherapists see the embodied beauty of clients with both peaceful and war-like personalities, behaviors and relationships but still usually regard the peaceful clients as embodying and reflecting Goodness.

26. Text.

Confucius says, 'High offices filled by intolerant human beings, rituals performed without reverence and rites of mourning made without grief. I can't bear seeing them!'.

Commentary.

Virtuous psychotherapists have difficulty accepting some professional colleagues who are intolerant of psychotherapy client behavior, narrow-minded in knowing psychological theories, perfunctory in using psychotherapy techniques and personally relatively unfeeling or emotionally inappropriate.

水

THE ANALECTS
BOOK FOUR
LIVING IN BROTHERLINESS

LI REN

里 仁

GOODNESS AND GENTLEPERSONS

1. Text.

Confucius says, 'Goodness is a community of beauty. Human beings who are free to choose but don't prefer to dwell in Goodness, can't be considered wise'.

Commentary.

Virtuous psychotherapists freely and wisely choose to live a personal and professional life and conduct a psychotherapy practice of Goodness in a community of beauty.

2. Text.

Confucius says, 'Without the virtue of Goodness, human beings can't long endure adversity or long enjoy prosperity. Good human beings are at home in Goodness. Unwise human beings use Goodness for profit'.

Commentary.

Virtuous psychotherapists are at home and at ease in Goodness and enjoy the ups and endure the downs of psychotherapy practice and realize that its success is measured by Goodness and not by financial profit.

3/4. Texts.

Confucius says, 'Virtuous human beings know how to like and dislike fellow human beings. Human beings whose hearts are set on Goodness dislike no one'.

Commentary.

The hearts of virtuous psychotherapists are grounded and centered in Goodness and they accept and work with clients without feelings of liking or disliking them.

5. Text.

Confucius says, 'Wealth and high status are desired by many human beings but if attained at the loss of the Way, they should be relinquished. Poverty and low status are disliked by most human beings but if they can't be avoided without the loss of the Way, they should be accepted. Gentlepersons who forsake Goodness don't deserve the name. Even for necessities, gentlepersons don't abandon Goodness. They're never so confused or unbalanced to do so'.

Commentary.

Virtuous psychotherapists live their personal lives and conduct their professional practices in ways that sustain the Way of Goodness in spite of wealth and high status or poverty and low status. They're never so busy, stressed out, confused or unbalanced that they lose touch with Goodness.

6. Text.

Confucius says, 'I haven't met human beings who fully love Goodness or fully hate its lack. Human beings who really love Goodness don't prioritize anything else. Human beings who really hate a lack of Goodness do Good that prevents it. Has anyone ever done Good with all of their being for even a day?. But I've also not met anyone who lacks the strength to do so'.

Commentary.

Virtuous psychotherapists love Goodness and do their best to consciously, intentionally and courageously remain committed to, prioritize and nourish a personal life and professional psychotherapy practice devoted to Goodness in the presence of both Good and not Good realities.

7. Text.

Confucius says, 'Errors of human beings relate to their character, virtues and qualities. Awareness of their errors is a means to recognize character and the extent of Goodness'.

Commentary.

Virtuous psychotherapists are aware of their errors in conducting the psychotherapy relationship process and of the errors of clients engaged in it. They cultivate and model the characterological virtues and personal qualities that contribute to and constitute Goodness.

8. Text.

Confucius says, 'In the morning, hear and practice the Way. In the evening, die content'.

Commentary.

Virtuous psychotherapists are content at the end of their psychotherapy work day due to not losing touch with and to living the Way/Dao throughout the day from beginning to end.

9. Text.

Confucius says, 'Human beings whose hearts are committed to the Way but who are ashamed of wearing ragged clothes and eating common food aren't worth speaking with about it'.

Commentary.

On the contrary. Virtuous psychotherapists accept and work with clients in spite of their lack of commitment to the Way or their poor station in life.

10. Text.

Confucius says, 'In relating with fellow human beings and dealing with the world, gentlepersons don't have preconceived notions or strong likes and dislikes. They base everything on what is ethically and morally Good and Right'.

Commentary.

Virtuous psychotherapists suspend any preconceptions about clients, don't like or dislike them in general and relate to and affiliate with what is Good and Right in them.

11. Text.

Confucius says, 'Gentlepersons set their hearts upon the moral virtue/de of Dao and its effects and common people set their hearts upon physical possessions and benefits'.

Commentary.

Virtuous psychotherapists are grounded and centered in the moral virtue, integrity, energy, and power/de of both Dao and the ten-thousand things of being and living.

12. Text.

Confucius says, 'Human beings ruled by busyness, advantage and profit create ill-will, unhappiness and resentment'.

Commentary.

Virtuous psychotherapists avoid being so busy and greedy that the humanness and humaneness of the psychotherapy relationship is lost and clients become unfriendly, unhappy and resentful.

13. Text.

Confucius says, 'When rulers govern states by ritual propriety and deference, there's no difficulty. But when they don't, then what good is ritual?'.

Commentary.

Virtuous psychotherapists conduct psychotherapy meetings with clients according to clear, effective and beneficial techniques, methods and procedures and by yielding to the unique characteristics, abilities and requirements of clients.

14. Text.

Confucius says, 'Gentlepersons don't worry about not holding an office but only how they can be qualified for one. They don't worry about not being recognized but only how they can be worthy of being so'.

Commentary.

Virtuous psychotherapists are unconcerned about, and unoccupied with, attaining a famous professional status or reputation. They're too involved with assisting as many clients as possible in as many ways as possible, as beneficially as possible and for as long as necessary.

15. Text.

Confucius says to a disciple, 'My Way has a single thread running through it'. The disciple agrees and later is asked what the saying means by other disciples. 'The Master's Way is loyalty to our moral nature and reciprocity toward fellow human beings'.

Commentary.

Virtuous psychotherapists hold to one principle of exhibiting the virtues of respect for and loyalty to the unique moral nature of clients and empathy for and reciprocity with them.

16. Text.

Confucius says, 'Gentlepersons are concerned with what is morally Good and Right and small persons are concerned with what is economically advantageous and profitable'.

Commentary.

Virtuous psychotherapists are concerned with the ethics and morality of Good and Right psychotherapy practice with clients rather than its financial advantages and profitability.

17. Text.

Confucius says, 'When with Good human beings, see how you can equal them. When with not Good persons, look within and examine and correct your own self'.

Commentary.

Virtuous psychotherapists take good clients and relationships as opportunities for imitation, self-awareness and self-validation and take not so good clients and relationships as opportunities for introspection, self-correction and self-improvement.

18. Text.

Confucius says, 'In serving parents, if gently objecting to them and they fail to change, continue being respectful, deferent and obedient. Feel discouraged but not resentful'.

Commentary.

Even virtuous psychotherapists experience resistance, objections, disagreements, conflicts and power struggles in the psychotherapy relationship but they don't engage in overtly aggressive confrontations, don't harbor wishes to defeat clients, don't resent and lose respect for clients and don't lose sight of the real value, true meaning and essential purpose of psychotherapy.

19. Text.

Confucius says, 'While parents are alive, gentlepersons don't travel far away from them but if they do, they make their itinerary known to them'.

Commentary.

Virtuous psychotherapists usually reside close to where they practice psychotherapy and meet with clients and they make them aware of any of their travels and ways to remain available and accessible if and when necessary.

20. Text.

Confucius says, 'If daughters and sons continue a household in the same way for three years of mourning after their parents die, they're good filial human beings'.

Commentary.

Virtuous psychotherapists often remain in touch with clients after they terminate psychotherapy through communications or follow-up meetings to assess sustained progress.

21. Text.

Confucius says, 'It's good to know the age of parents but it'll be either a comfort if they're young or a concern if they're old'.

Commentary.

Virtuous psychotherapists aren't usually concerned about the ages of clients and their own age unless, in some way, it's a relevant psychotherapy issue or concern.

22. Text.

Confucius says, 'In olden days, human beings are careful with their words out of a fear of shamefully failing to keep them'.

Commentary.

Virtuous psychotherapists are true to their words in psychotherapy relationships with clients and are avoiding any shame or untrustworthiness that might result from not doing so.

23. Text.

Confucius says, 'Few are those human beings who err by caution and restraint in keeping to the essentials'.

Commentary.

Virtuous psychotherapists keep to the essential conduct of psychotherapy with caution and restraint, don't rigidly adopt a general position of either strictness or flexibility and are able to be either when necessarily or appropriately therapeutic.

24. Text.

Confucius says, 'Gentlepersons are slow with words and prompt with actions'.

Commentary.

Virtuous psychotherapists generally use words cautiously, thoughtfully and minimally but make interactions and interventions quickly and in a timely manner, especially in crisis and emergency situations.

25. Text.

Confucius says, 'Moral virtue/de doesn't exist in isolation and inevitably brings neighbors'.

Commentary.

The moral virtue, integrity, energy and power of/de of virtuous psychotherapists are magnetic, attractive and contagious and draw clients to them and to their psychotherapy practice.

26. Text.

Confucius says, 'In serving rulers, continued censuring leads to disgrace and in friendships leads to estrangement'.

Commentary.

Virtuous psychotherapists maintain continuing engaged, connected, involved and friendly psychotherapy relationships with clients and, of course; don't scold, berate or censure them and provoke derailing or terminating; although they may at times be required to object to or to be critical of their behavior in a psychotherapy meeting.

水

THE ANALECTS
BOOK FIVE
GONGYE CHANG

GONGYE CHANG

公 冶 長

SELF AND RELATIONSHIPS

1/2. Texts.

Confucius says, 'A wrongly imprisoned man and a man who is virtuous enough to hold office in a country ruled by the Way and to escape punishment in a country not ruled by the Way are both worthy of being married to family members'.

Commentary.

Virtuous psychotherapists don't accept or reject human beings as clients based upon their commendable or questionable histories or their positive or negative qualities.

3. Text.

Confucius says, 'This disciple truly is a gentleperson and learns this by emulating virtuous gentlepersons living in our state'.

Commentary.

Virtuous psychotherapists are virtuous human beings who are likely raised by, grow up with and identify with virtuous parents and human beings as models and examples.

4. Text.

A disciple asks, 'What do you think of me?'. Confucius says, 'You have specific capacities and abilities that can be used but lack Goodness. But nonetheless you have good capacities and abilities'.

Commentary.

Virtuous psychotherapists are often direct, honest, realistic and candid in giving feedback to clients interested in it and are accepting of their capacities and abilities as well as their limitations and shortcomings.

5. Text.

Someone said of a disciple, 'He's virtuous but a poor speaker'. Confucius says, 'Why does he need to be a good speaker?. Glib speakers end up being hated. I don't know if he's virtuous but why does he need to be a good speaker?'.

Commentary.

Virtuous psychotherapists value clients being virtuous human beings whether or not they are articulate speakers.

6. Text.

A disciple is encouraged to take office but acknowledges that he hasn't yet adequately cultivated and perfected himself in virtues. Confucius is pleased to learn this.

Commentary.

Virtuous psychotherapists appreciate when clients voluntarily and honestly acknowledge the realities of their limitations, shortcomings, inadequacies, etc., as well as their strengths, resources, assets, abilities, etc..

7. Text.

Confucius says to a disciple, 'If the Way isn't practiced in this country, I'll get on a raft and go out to sea and you'll accompany me'. The disciple is happy about the prospect. Confucius adds, 'You exceed me in courage and physical daring but are lacking in good judgment?'.

Commentary.

Virtuous psychotherapists may have difficulty finding students, trainees, interns, colleagues and clients who share their commitment to cultivating and practicing the Way/Dao and exercising good judgment, but they don't leave their psychotherapy practice because of it.

8. Text.

An official asks if three disciples are Good persons. Confucius answers, 'I don't know. In a city with a thousand families, in a state with a thousand chariots or in a court attending to a thousand guests; they'd each be responsible, trusted and successful but I don't know if they're Good persons'.

Commentary.

Virtuous psychotherapists experience that being responsible, competent and successful aren't necessarily criteria for ascertaining whether or not clients are Good human beings.

9. Text.

Confucius asks a disciple, 'Do you regard yourself or this other disciple as more superior?'. The disciple answers, 'I don't compare with him. He learns one part and understands ten and I only understand two'. Confucius adds, 'Neither one of us is his equal!'.

Commentary.

Virtuous psychotherapists are willing to realistically acknowledge when students, trainees, interns, colleagues and clients exceed them, for example, in intellectual gifts, cognitive skills and intuitive abilities.

10. Text.

Confucius says, 'This disciple sleeps during the day. Rotten wood can't be carved. Dried dung can't be plastered. What's the use of reprimanding him? In the past, I attentively listen to people and believe that they'll do what they say. Now I not only listen to them but I also watch to see what they actually do. This disciple teaches me to do this'.

Commentary.

Virtuous psychotherapists rarely consider a client as 'a lost cause' and are attentive to whether or not students, trainees, interns, colleagues and clients say what they do and do what they say, i.e., 'walk their talk'.

11. Text.

Confucius says, 'I've yet to meet human beings who are steadfast in integrity'. A disciple names one and Confucius comments, 'Him?. He's so full of desires. How can he be steadfast?'.

Commentary.

Virtuous psychotherapists are steadfast in integrity through generally being unmotivated, uninfluenced and undriven by their desires.

12. Text.

A disciple says, 'What I don't want others to do to me, I don't do to others' (The 'Silver Rule'). Confucius says, 'You haven't reached that stage of reciprocity yet'.

Commentary.

Virtuous psychotherapists abide by the reciprocal 'Golden Rule' of 'Do unto others as you would have them do unto you' in psychotherapy relationships with clients and treat them equally, honestly, fairly and reciprocally.

13. Text.

A disciple says, 'We hear about Confucius's views of culture and the arts but not about human nature and the Way of Heaven'.

Commentary.

Virtuous psychotherapists are open to natural, supernatural, preternatural and transpersonal realities and experiences of clients and are willing to work with them in psychotherapy if and when they are relevant, appropriate and useful.

14. Text.

A disciple hears some precepts, is unsuccessful in putting them into practice and is afraid that he won't do so before hearing yet another precept.

Commentary.

Virtuous psychotherapists are sensitive to pacing reflections, insights and interpretations so as to allow clients space to fully understand and assimilate them and to not be overwhelmed.

15. Text.

A disciple asks why another disciple is called cultured. Confucius answers, 'He's eager and quick to learn and loves learning so much that he's willing to learn from inferiors'.

Commentary.

Virtuous psychotherapists are committed to gaining knowledge about human psychology, psychopathology and psychotherapy and are open to learning from students, trainees, interns, colleagues, clients who may seem to 'know' less.

16. Text.

Confucius says, 'This official possesses four virtues of a gentleperson. He's humble in relating to others. He's respectful in serving superiors. He's generous in providing for people. He's fair in employing people'.

Commentary.

In their relationships with students, trainees, interns, colleagues and clients; virtuous psychotherapists exhibit four virtues of humility, respect, generosity and fairness.

17. Text.

Confucius says, 'This official exemplifies good relationships with fellow human beings. For as long as he knows them, he always remains respectful'.

Commentary.

Virtuous psychotherapists maintain respect for clients throughout the duration of both short-term and long-term psychotherapy relationships.

18. Text.

Confucius says, 'This official keeps ritual objects in his home that properly are only the privilege of rulers. How can he be considered virtuous and wise?'.

Commentary.

Virtuous psychotherapists usually and wisely only keep objects in their offices that are appropriate for use for psychotherapy techniques, methods and procedures and that won't create irrelevant distractions (but admittedly may become 'grist for the mill' of treatment).

19. Text.

An official is appointed to and deposed from office three times but isn't happy or disappointed. Each time he dutifully assists successors with the transition. Another official leaves the state, after an adulterous sovereign is assassinated, for two other states that he finds equally as corrupt. A disciple asks, 'What can be said about them?'. Confucius answers, 'One is loyal and the other principled, but I don't know if they can be called wise or Good'.

Commentary.

Virtuous psychotherapists are aware that some behaviors of clients that seem or are dutiful, loyal and ethical may not reflect that they are wise or Good moral human beings.

20. Text.

An official typically thinks three times before acting. Confucius comments, 'Twice is sufficient'.

Commentary.

Virtuous psychotherapists usually cautiously reflect, contemplate and think at least twice before speaking and interacting with clients and making psychotherapy interpretations and interventions.

21. Text.

Confucius says, 'An official is wise when the Way prevails in the state but foolish when it doesn't. His wisdom can be equaled but not his foolishness'.

Commentary.

Virtuous psychotherapists conduct psychotherapy with wisdom regardless of whether or not it's harmonious, effective and progressing well.

22. Text.

Confucius is traveling in another state with some disciples and says, 'Let's return home!. Let's go home!. The disciples there are careless and unruly. They're developing outward signs of cultural virtues but aren't being guided in using them'.

Commentary.

Virtuous psychotherapists are able to discern when clients outwardly appear to have changed but inwardly haven't really transformed and can benefit from psychotherapeutic guidance.

23. Text.

Confucius says, 'Two brothers don't hold onto the past wrongdoings of human beings and don't engender their feelings of ill-will and resentment'.

Commentary.

Virtuous psychotherapists model for clients the value of being aware of, working through and letting-go of their wrongdoings and those of fellow human beings and not engendering any concomitant feelings of ill-will and resentment.

24. Text.

Confucius says, 'How can we call this person straight, upright, honest and truthful? When asked for vinegar, he borrows some from neighbors and claims that it's his own when he gives it away'.

Commentary.

Virtuous psychotherapists assist clients in being straight, upright, honest and truthful with themselves, about their behavior and in relation to fellow human beings.

25. Text.

Confucius says, 'Clever speech, overdone politeness, false respect and feigning friendship are shameful'.

Commentary.

Virtuous psychotherapists assist clients in being their genuine, authentic, real and true selves; not being falsely respectful and polite and in becoming aware of and able to honestly express and communicate 'negative' or 'unfriendly' feelings such as frustration, anger, etc..

26. Text.

Confucius asks two disciples to share their heart's desires with him. One desires to share his carriages, rugs and clothes with friends and the other desires not to boast about his goodness or to impose upon others. They ask Confucius about his desires and he says, 'I desire to comfort the aged, trust friends and cherish the young'.

Commentary.

Virtuous psychotherapists typically comfort elders, trust friends and cherish children; model these virtues, values and behaviors for the clients with whom they meet in psychotherapy and also relate to them with the same comforting, trusting and cherishing.

27. Text.

Confucius says, 'It's hopeless!. I don't meet any human beings who see their own faults, look within and judge and correct themselves'.

Commentary.

Virtuous psychotherapists support and assist clients in becoming aware of their limitations, shortcomings, faults, mistakes, errors and failings; to look within themselves and to responsibly acknowledge, own and take steps to correct them and to improve themselves.

28. Text.

Confucius says, 'In any small village you'll find some persons who are as faithful and trustworthy as I am, but no one with such a love of learning'.

Commentary.

Virtuous psychotherapists have a love of learning and are professionally committed to encouraging, supporting, fostering and facilitating clients in learning about themselves and in becoming and being more self-aware, self-reflective, self-understanding, self-accepting, self-actualizing, self-developing, self-improving and self-refining.

水

THE ANALECTS
BOOK SIX
THERE IS YONG

YONG YE

雍 也

DISCIPLES AND QUESTIONS

1/2. Texts.

Confucius says, 'I consider these two disciples worthy of being a ruler. They're respectful, morally upright in conduct and simple in dealing with people but not with themselves or in conducting business'.

Commentary.

Virtuous psychotherapists value students, trainees, interns and clients who are committed to psychotherapy and working on themselves, respectful and morally upright in their conduct and uncomplicated in relating to fellow human beings.

3. Text.

A ruler asks Confucius which disciples have a love of learning. Confucius says, 'There's one who doesn't vent anger, blame others or repeat faults. But his life is short and he dies recently. I've not since met anyone else with a love of learning. Now there's no one'.

Commentary.

Virtuous psychotherapists sometimes discover that only a few clients are genuinely, sincerely, deeply and fully committed to a love of learning and self-improvement in spite of the apparent affirmative rhetoric and behavior of many.

4/5. Texts.

A disciple asks Confucius if the mother of another disciple can receive an allowance of grain. Confucius grants her an increasing amount of grain after her son's several requests for more and more. The son is later seen wearing furs and driving well-cared-for horses. Confucius says, 'Gentlepersons provide for the needy but don't make the rich richer'. Another disciple declines a large offering of grain after becoming an official and Confucius says, 'You could've given it to needy people'.

Commentary.

Virtuous psychotherapists generally value providing for genuinely needful clients rather than adding to the excesses of wealthy ones.

6. Text.

Confucius says, 'People hesitate to use a reddish-brown ox for sacrifices but the gods and spirits of the mountains and rivers wouldn't reject it'.

Commentary.

Virtuous psychotherapists realize that the accepting or rejecting judgments clients receive about their worth, significance, suitability and usefulness are subjective, relative and often unfortunately dependent upon their physical appearance alone.

7. Text.

Confucius says, 'This disciple keeps his heart focused upon the virtue of Goodness for three months at a time. Other disciples only can do so for a day or maybe a month'.

Commentary.

The clients of virtuous psychotherapists vary in their ability to intensively and extensively focus on cultivating virtues or to successfully engage in meditative practices like counting breaths, one-pointed concentration and focused visualization.

8. Text.

Confucius is asked whether three disciples are suitable to hold office. Confucius replies, 'They're intelligent, faithful and skilled and are all capable of holding office'.

Commentary.

Virtuous psychotherapists can confidently recommend clients as being suitable for various career positions who are knowledgeable, determined and capable.

9. Text.

A ruling family wants to make a disciple governor. He politely refuses the offer and says that if his excuse is rejected and he's still sought after, he'll move to a neighboring state.

Commentary.

Virtuous psychotherapists support and assist clients in making necessary, essential and crucial self-assertions that are honored and don't force them to make major unchosen and disruptive changes in their lives.

10. Text.

An ill disciple is visitied by Confucius who holds his hand through a window and laments, 'It's all over for him. Heaven so ordains it. How else can this person have this illness?. How else can such a person have such an illness?'.

Commentary.

Virtuous psychotherapists empathize with ill clients and grieve their demise as they naturally would a close relative, friend or colleague but don't necessarily attribute their condition to the will of a higher power.

11. Text.

Confucius says, 'How worthy is this disciple!. A handful of rice to eat, a cupful of water to drink and a middling place to live in. Other people would be depressed but it doesn't affect his happiness. Incomparable indeed!'.

Commentary.

Virtuous psychotherapists happily value simple and minimalist living without feeling deprived, insufficient, depressed or unhappy.

12. Text.

A disciple says to Confucius, 'Your Way is commendable but I don't have the strength for it'. Confucius replies, 'Human beings whose strength is really insufficient naturally give up somewhere along the way but you deliberately and arbitrarily stop ahead of time'.

Commentary.

Virtuous psychotherapists often support and assist clients in discovering and experiencing their real capacities, strengths, abilities and limitations through challenges made during the course of the psychotherapy relationship process. They respect client limits and limitations and encourage them to continue in the work of psychotherapy without just deliberately stopping at some arbitrary point.

13. Text.

Confucius says to a disciple, 'Cultivate and practice the virtues and conduct of the fifteen attributes of The Six Arts of gentlepersons and not those of petty persons.

> 1) Be accomplished in learning,
> 2) Be dignified in demeanor,
> 3) Be calm in readiness,
> 4) Be righteous in gains,
> 5) Be careful in words,
> 6) Be resolute in actions,

7) Be firm in convictions,

8) Be loyal in allegiances,

9) Be caring in justice,

10) Be tolerant in moderation,

11) Be generous in recommendations,

12) Be supportive in loyalty,

13) Be independent in thought,

14) Be courteous in self-restraint,

15) Be trustworthy in friendships'.

Commentary.

Virtuous psychotherapists cultivate, practice and model the character, virtues, qualities, relationships and actions of the arts of gentlepersons and inspire, encourage, support and assist clients in being and doing likewise.

14. Text.

Confucius asks an official if he finds good people where he lives. The official replies, 'There's a person who follows the Way without taking short-cuts and comes to see me only for conducting official business'.

Commentary.

Virtuous psychotherapists appreciate clients who exert the effort that it takes to remain committed to, focused on and engaged in psychotherapy without taking 'short-cuts', don't have social or financial relationships with clients and limit client relationships to conducting the 'official business' of psychotherapy.

15. Text.

Confucius says, 'This official doesn't boast. When his army is being defeated, he's the last one to flee. After everyone reaches safety, he modestly says, 'I'm not really courageous, it's just that my horse is slow''.

Commentary.

Virtuous psychotherapists usually straightforwardly acknowledge their courageousness and that of clients in psychotherapy and don't modestly rationalize, deny or hide its reality.

16. Text.

Confucius says, 'Nowadays, it's difficult to survive unless you've the beauty of certain aristocrats or the eloquence of certain priests'.

Commentary.

Virtuous psychotherapists accept, value and appreciate how language and speaking skills significantly and positively contribute to the psychotherapy work of assisting clients in understanding themselves and living their lives.

17. Text.

Confucius says, 'Who's able to exit a house without using a door?. Why is it then that no one uses the Way?'.

Commentary.

Some virtuous psychotherapists are puzzled by why more human beings don't choose to engage in psychotherapy or to follow a spiritual path as doorways through to a more improved, intimate, satisfying, fulfilling, peaceful and happier life.

18. Text.

Confucius says, 'When Nature supercedes culture, we have the crudeness of the rustic. When culture supercedes Nature, we have the narrowness of the pedantic. Only when Nature and culture are integrated and balanced do we have virtuous gentlepersons'.

Commentary.

Virtuous psychotherapists integrate and balance the co-existing and co-operating realities of Nature and culture in their consciousness, awareness, experience, lives and psychotherapy work with clients.

19. Text.

Confucius says, 'The very life of human beings is upright-ness and straightforwardness. Without them we can't escape with our life'.

Commentary.

Virtuous psychotherapists realize the crucial importance of integrity and honesty in living human life viably and vitally and are good examples and role-models for psychotherapy clients.

20. Text.

Confucius says, 'Loving the Way is better that just knowing about it and delighting in the Way is better than just loving it'.

Commentary.

Virtuous psychotherapists delight in knowing, choosing, following and loving Dao as a Way of being, living, relating and practicing psychotherapy.

21. Text.

Confucius says, 'For human beings above middling, we can speak of things higher yet. But to human beings below mid-dling, it's useless to do so'.

Commentary.

Virtuous psychotherapists typically don't evaluate and judge clients on a hierarchical scale of their stage of personal or spir-itual development and, when relevant, are open to discussing higher states of human consciousness, development and evolu-tion with them.

22. Text.

A disciple asks about wisdom and Goodness. Confucius answers, 'Human beings who respect and guide people to what is Good and Right and who revere and keep gods and spirits at the right distance are wise. Human beings who accomplish difficult things such as relinquishing a love of power, greed, success and wealth are Good'.

Commentary.

Virtuous psychotherapists are generally wise and Good human beings who are respectfully dedicated to guiding clients, have a reverent spiritual connection and who effectively and successfully accomplish psychotherapy objectives for their own sake and aren't enamored of ego-needs for power, wealth and status.

23. Text.

Confucius says, 'Wise human beings delight in water and Good human beings delight in mountains because the wise flow happily on and the Good stand securely in their lives'.

Commentary.

Virtuous psychotherapists are generally wise and Good human beings who integrate and balance activity and stillness in psychotherapy relationships with clients and who experience the happiness and security that such conduct affords.

24. Text.

Confucius says, 'One change can bring another state to the higher level of ours and another change can bring ours to the Way'.

Commentary.

Virtuous psychotherapists experience that there are levels of the progression of change and transformation in psychotherapy practice that become increasingly more elevated and can, ultimately, reach the highest level of Dao/the Way.

25. Text.

Confucius says, 'An improperly made or used horn-gourd drinking cup is not a horn-gourd drinking cup'.

Commentary.

Virtuous psychotherapists don't consider psychotherapy

techniques, methods and procedures as such unless they usefully serve their intended purposes and successfully achieve their intended objectives.

26. Text.

A disciple believes that Good persons would jump into a well to rescue another Good person even if falsely informed. Confucius replies, 'Why would they?. Gentlepersons can be deceived but not led astray'.

Commentary.

Virtuous psychotherapists are so fully identified with Goodness that they usually can't be deviated from the path of Dao/the Way.

27. Text.

Confucius says, 'Gentlepersons who are widely culturally learned and also use ritual for self-restraint are not likely to go wrong'.

Commentary.

Virtuous psychotherapists are well-versed in psychological theories and understand how to correctly, effectively and usefully use them; 1) in understanding and working with clients and 2) in informing their application in using psychotherapy techniques, methods and procedures.

28. Text.

A disciple is displeased when learning that Confucius visits a concubine. Confucius solemnly states, 'Whatever impropriety I've done, may Heaven reject me, may Heaven reject me!'.

Commentary.

If virtuous psychotherapists engage in any wrongdoing in the conduct of psychotherapy, they accountably acknowledge it, assume responsibility for it and may appeal to Heavenly Dao for retribution (as well as to the ethics committee of their professional organization!).

29. Text.

Confucius says, 'How balanced is the everpresent moral virtue and power/de of moderation and the Middle Way between extremes. But it's seldom found among and practiced by common people'.

Commentary.

Virtuous psychotherapists are by and large non-dualistic and experience the psychotherapeutic value and effectiveness of the middle way of moderation and balance between dualistic extremes in psychotherapy work with the experiences of clients.

30. Text.

A disciple asks whether rulers who benefit common people and save a whole state are Good persons. Confucius replies, 'It's not a matter of Good, since to do so, they'd have to be like the ancient legendary Divine Sage-Rulers. But if taking their stand is desired by people, Good persons help them to take it because they desire the same thing. Taking their own feelings as a guide for other persons is the Way of Goodness'.

Commentary.

Virtuous psychotherapists use their own feelings and experiences to empathize with clients and to assist them in realizing and actualizing similar objectives such as achieving personal independence, integrity, strength, courage and security, i.e., standing on their own feet, taking a stand, standing up to others, standing their ground, standing firm, etc.

水

THE ANALECTS
BOOK SEVEN
TRANSMISSION

SHU ER

述 而

CONFUCIUS AND SAYINGS

1/2/3. Texts.

Confucius says, 'I transmit what I learn and don't make up anything of my own. I love and am faithful to the ancient Ways ... I listen in silence, learn everything that's said and never tire of teaching what I learn. This is who I am. Not always cultivating moral virtue/de, deepening my learning, following what is Right or reforming wrongdoings concern me deeply'.

Commentary.

Virtuous psychotherapists learn, teach and use the psychological theories and psychotherapy techniques of preceding master psychologists and psychotherapists and listen well to clients but may have some concerns about neglecting further educational training for themselves and further therapeutic work on themselves.

4. Text.

The general manner of Confucius at home remains proper but is relaxed, cheerful and genial.

Commentary.

The general demeanor of virtuous psychotherapists 'at home' in their office is generally appropriate, relaxed, in good spirits, mild and friendly.

5. Text.

Confucius says, 'Things are declining for me. It's been a long time since I dream of the founding ruler of this state!'.

Commentary.

Virtuous psychotheraists may regret not thinking or dreaming about their significant master psychology teachers and psychotherapy trainers but don't usually interpret that reality as an indication of their personal or professional decline.

6. Text.

Confucius says, 'Set your heart upon the Way; accord with moral virtue/de, rely upon Goodness and enjoy cultivating the arts'.

Commentary.

Virtuous psychotherapists have their hearts grounded and centered in Dao/the Way; are supported by its virtue, integrity, energy and power/de and abide in its Goodness and enjoy actively cultivating and participating in various creative art-forms.

7. Text.

Confucius says, 'From the very poorest on upward, no human being comes to me who doesn't receive some instruction'.

Commentary.

Good virtuous psychotherapists are available and accessible to psychotherapeutically support and assist clients who are referred to and come to them, regardless of their social status.

8. Text.

Confucius says, 'I only teach and assist human beings who eagerly strive to learn and sincerely struggle to practice. I hold up one corner to show them but if they can't hold up the other three, I usually discontinue lessons'.

Commentary.

Virtuous psychotherapists appreciate clients who are inspired and enthusiastically motivated to engage and participate in psychotherapy and especially when they contribute to its progress through their amplified insights and transformed behavior.

9/10. Texts.

At a meal, when Confucius sits next to a person in mourning, he eats little and if he cries at a funeral, he doesn't sing for the rest of the day.

Commentary.

Virtuous psychotherapists respect clients who are grieving; are mild and moderate in their interactions and interventions with them and often remain empathically solemn throughout the remainder of their day.

11. Text.

Confucius says to his favorite disciple that he lives the maxim, 'Where wanted, go. When unwanted, stay'. Another disciple asks Confucius whom he would choose if he commands a whole army. Confucius replies ... 'Someone who approaches difficult situations cautiously and who plans crucial decisions strategically'.

Commentary.

Virtuous psychotherapists are considerate of, and responsive to, client needs and preferences and aren't intrusive or invasive in their interactions and interventions. They're cautious in dealing with difficult and crucial client and psychotherapy relationship issues and consciously employ carefully planned effective and beneficial treatment strategies.

12. Text.

Confucius says, 'If pursuing wealth is proper, I'd adopt any way to avoid poverty that doesn't entail wrongdoing. And if it does, I'll just continue doing what I love'.

Commentary.

Virtuous psychotherapists don't resort to unethical practices in order to have a lucrative psychotherapy practice and they continue conducting it based upon their love of just simply doing it.

13. Text.

Confucius pays careful attention to purification rituals preceding making sacrifices, conducting wars and treating illnesses.

Commentary.

Virtuous psychotherapists often begin psychotherapy meetings with some kind of ritual, e.g., closing eyes and being silent, attending to and lowering breathing, clearing thoughts and feelings, etc.. They also consider techniques, methods and procedures as ritually significant and meaningful in conducting psychotherapy and in treating clients and their issues.

14. Text.

After hearing peace music, Confucius doesn't eat meat for three months. He says, 'I haven't ever felt that music could reach such perfection and sublime beauty'.

Commentary.

Virtuous psychotherapists are mostly peaceful human beings who enjoy the perfection of splendid and sublimely beautiful music that inspires, celebrates, embodies and reflects peace and they may use such music in their psychotherapy work with clients.

15. Text.

Confucius is asked about who two brothers are. He says, 'They're Good human beings who live in ancient times, who seek and obtain Goodness and who have no regrets'.

Commentary.

Virtuous psychotherapists are so identified with and fulfilled by Goodness that they usually don't experience regrets in the conduct of psychotherapy practice.

16. Text.

Confucius says, 'With only simple food to eat, water to drink and a bent arm for a bedpillow, I still find happiness. To me, attaining rank and wealth by wrongdoing is like drifting clouds'.

Commentary.

Good gentle psychotherapists live simply and happily and won't and don't violate the ethics of psychotherapy practice in order to make money or to gain a professional reputation.

17. Text.

Confucius says, 'Allow me a few more years of cultivating Goodness and Righteousness until I'm fifty and perhaps I'll be able to avoid any great faults or mistakes'.

Commentary.

Virtuous psychotherapists use their whole professional psychotherapy career to learn how to progressively become freer and freer of faults, mistakes and errors.

18. Text.

Confucius uses correct language pronunciation when reciting texts and performing rituals.

Commentary.

Virtuous psychotherapists use language with clients that is respectful of, and appropriate for, the sacredness, uniqueness and meaningfulness of the psychotherapy relationship.

19. Text.

An official asks a disciple about Confucius but he doesn't reply. Confucius asks, 'Why didn't you say it's my character to be so committed and happy to be teaching that I forget hunger, worries, sorrows and aging?. That's who I am'.

Commentary.

Virtuous psychotherapists are so committed, by nature and profession, to assisting clients and doing psychotherapy work that they may, at times, forget to self-reflect on their current situation and to meet current needs.

20. Text.

Confucius says, 'I don't have innate knowledge. I simply love antiquity and diligently investigate it for knowledge'.

Commentary.

Virtuous psychotherapists are interested in; and earnestly explore, investigate and learn from; their own past life history and experiences and those of psychotherapy clients.

21. Text.

Confucius doesn't discuss supernatural omens, extreme physical feats, natural disasters or gods and spirits.

Commentary.

Virtuous psychotherapists tend to focus directly upon the concrete actualities of psychotherapy experience rather than upon abstractions, anomalies and supernatural realities unless doing so is relevant for specific psychotherapy work with particular clients.

22. Text.

Confucius says, 'When walking with three persons, I learn from them. I select good qualities to imitate for myself and bad ones to correct in myself'.

Commentary.

Virtuous psychotherapists continually learn about themselves from synchronistically meeting and empathically working with clients. They become aware of good qualities to foster and bad ones to correct in themselves.

23. Text.

Confucius says, 'Heaven begets de; the virtue, integrity, energy and power of the Way, within me. How can I fear ministers of war threatening to kill me?'.

Commentary.

Virtuous psychotherapists have internalized and assimilated the virtue, energy and power of Dao and are immune to fears of clients threatening or endangering them should that unlikely occasion ever occur in virtuous psychotherapy.

24. Text.

Confucius says, 'My disciples, I'm not concealing anything from you. I don't do anything that I don't share with you. This is me'.

Commentary.

Virtuous psychotherapists are open and self-disclosing with clients and collaborate with them in initial interviewing, diagnositic formulating, treatment planning, intervention strategizing and outcome evaluating; otherwise they wouldn't be the virtuous psychotherapists who they are.

25. Text.

Confucius teaches four things; cultural values, moral conduct, doing one's best and keeping promises.

Commentary.

Virtuous psychotherapists attend to the cultural values of clients, the ethical conduct of psychotherapy, doing their best and most beneficial work and responsibly and accountably keeping any psychotherapy contracts, agreements and promises made with clients.

26. Text.

Confucius says, 'I won't ever meet a Divine Sage but I'd be happy just finding a gentleperson of solid principles. Yet, I see nothing, emptiness and poverty pretending to be something, fullness and wealth. A gentleperson of constant and consistent principles isn't easy to find'.

Commentary.

Virtuous psychotherapists may not meet a realized spiritual master but they're able to meet clients who are principled gentlepersons in their psychotherapy practice amid the surrounding prevalence of personal pretense, social vacuity and cultural impoverishment.

27. Text.

Confucius uses a line and not a net when fishing and never shoots roosting birds when hunting.

Commentary.

Virtuous psychotherapists are fair with clients according to the ethical rules and guidelines of psychotherapy conduct and practice and don't use the power differential of their position and role to exploit or take advantage of clients.

28. Text.

Confucius says, 'There are human beings who act without knowledge but I'm not one of them. I see and hear much, take note of and remember it and select what's good to comply with and to follow. This is the lesser of the two kinds of innate and acquired knowledge'.

Commentary.

Virtuous psychotherapists value and make equal use of both innate and acquired knowledge. They gain knowledge about things indirectly through intelligence, reasoning and abstract concepts and gain knowledge of themselves and clients directly through intuition, insight and concrete experiences.

29. Text.

It's difficult to speak with some human beings about the Way. A boy comes to learn but two disciples have reservations about accepting him. Confucius says, 'In allowing him in, I'm not sanctioning anything that he may do while he's here. Why be so particular?. If anyone sincerely comes to learn in good faith, I'll accept them. It doesn't mean that I approve of what they did in the past or what they'll do after leaving us'.

Commentary.

Virtuous psychotherapists usually accept clients who have a high and enthusiastic interest in, and a sincere and genuine intention of, engaging and participating in psychotherapy. They are responsible to but not responsible for clients.

30. Text.

Confucius says, 'Is the virtue of Goodness that far away? When we really desire Goodness, it's right here at our side'.

Commentary.

Virtuous psychotherapists realize that Goodness is always present and being and living it is a direct function of the extent to which it is really and truly desired.

31. Text.

An official asks Confucius whether a certain ruler under-stands ritual propriety. Confucius answers, 'Yes'. After Confucius leaves, the official says to a disciple, 'A gentleperson is impartial, yet in his marriage this ruler is very partial ... if he knows the rites then anyone does'. When the disciple informs Confucius about this, Confucius sarcastically says, 'I'm so fortunate. When I make a mistake, everyone lets me know about it!'.

Commentary.

Virtuous psychotherapists are seldom incorrect in their assessments of students, trainees, interns, colleagues and clients but when they are, they inevitably hear about it.

32. Text.

Confucius doesn't join in when anyone sings a song that he likes but asks them to repeat it and then sings along with them.

Commentary.

Virtuous psychotherapists respectfully, courteously and patiently wait for clients to complete expressing themselves before joining with them in a dialogue.

33. Text.

Confucius says, 'Regarding cultural matters, I compare favorably with fellow human beings. But in practicing the virtues and duties of gentlepersons in life, I'm not there yet'.

Commentary.

Virtuous psychotherapists are well able to effectively and successfully manage difficult psychotherapy situations and client interactions and are humble about not yet reaching their full potentials as educators and healers.

34. Text.

Confucius says, 'I can't claim to be a Divine Sage or even a gentleperson of perfect virtue. I can claim making a steadfast effort to learn and cultivate and having a tireless patience to teach and practice'. A disciple comments, 'It's this that we disciples can't equal!'.

Commentary.

Virtuous psychotherapists don't pretend to be spiritual masters or perfectly good human beings but are deeply, earnestly and tirelessly committed to learning, cultivating, developing, refining and improving themselves personally and to teaching, practicing, assisting and healing clients professionally.

35. Text.

Confucius is ill and a disciple asks permission to ritually offer prayers for his recovery. Confucius asks if there are such prayers. The disciple answers that there is one that calls upon the sky-gods above and the earth-gods below. Confucius says, 'Well, if that's the case, then I've been offering prayers in my lifework for a long time'.

Commentary.

Virtuous psychotherapists take early and ongoing responsibility for themselves, their lives, their behavior and the conduct of their psychotherapy practice and typically don't require or depend upon rituals to expiate any faults, mistakes, errors, failures or wrongdoing.

36. Text.

Confucius says, 'Opulence leads to showiness and frugality leads to stinginess. But stinginess is more preferable than showiness'.

Commentary.

Virtuous psychotherapists aren't ostentatious and showy or parsimonious and stingy. They're both modest and generous in psychotherapy relationships with clients.

37. Text.

Confucius says, 'Gentlepersons are calm and at ease. Small persons are agitated and ill-at-ease'.

Commentary.

Virtuous psychotherapists are generally relaxed and comfortable personally and professionally and rarely become irritated and agitated by clients, even during intense confrontations, conflicts, power struggles and acting-out behavior.

38. Text.

Confucius's manner is friendly but not lax, commanding but not severe and polite but not rigid.

Commentary.

The demeanor of virtuous psychotherapists is generally friendly but firm, compelling but not dominating and refined but not inflexible.

水

THE ANALECTS
BOOK EIGHT
TAI BO

TAI BO

泰 伯

CONFUCIUS AND SAYINGS

1. Text.

Confucius says, 'A ruler's son exemplifies the highest moral virtue/de when he renounces the sovereignty of the empire three times without people learning of it or praising him for it'.

Commentary.

Virtuous psychotherapists gain the virtue, integrity, energy and power/de of Dao by relinquishing desires for wealth, name, reputation and fame and by declining opportunities to attain them and not being recognized or praised for doing so.

2. Text.

Confucius says, 'Respect and caution without ritual propriety are tiring and timid. Courage and uprightness without ritual propriety are unruly and rigid. When gentlepersons are dutiful toward family and remember friends, common people act humanely and loyally'.

Commentary.

Virtuous psychotherapists employ psychotherapy techniques and methods respectfully, cautiously, uprightly and courageously and clients don't experience them as boring, weak, harsh and rigid. When virtuous psychotherapsts are filial and friendly, clients act humanely and loyally.

3. Text.

An ill master summons disciples saying, 'Look at my feet, look at my hands ... I now feel that whatever befalls me, I'll make it through safely'.

Commentary

Virtuous psychotherapists certainly provide emotional support and assistance to clients during life-threatening health crises and discontinue healing interactions when clients feel that they have safely and sufficiently recovered.

4. Text.

A disciple visits an ill master who says, 'When birds are dying, sad are their songs. When human beings are dying, good are their words. Three important things that gentlepersons who follow the Way value above all else and for which they are trusted are: 1) serious actions free of enmity, 2) facial expressions free of insincerity and 3) spoken words free of impropriety.'

Commentary.

Virtuous psychotherapists who accord with and follow Dao and who are trustworthy are sincere, friendly and appropriate in their behavior, expressions and speaking when interacting with clients and making observations, reflections, interpretations and interventions in the psychotherapy relationship.

5. Text.

A Master says, 'Talented and capable but consulting with the less talented and capable, having and being full but seeming to lack and be empty and offended against but not resenting or retaliating. Once, long ago, I have a friend like this'.

Commentary.

Virtuous psychotherapists learn from students, clients, trainees, interns and colleagues who may be less talented, knowledgeable and skillful; don't react or retaliate if offended by or aggressed against by them and are unattached to being financially and materially prosperous.

6. Text.

A Master says, 'Human beings who can be entrusted with, and undeterred from, caring for both the welfare of an orphaned child and the sovereignty of a whole state even during times of an emergency or crisis are indeed gentlepersons'.

Commentary.

Virtuous psychotherapists can be confidently trusted to be caring, nurturing and trustworthy with clients and who are able to appropriately, effectively and successfully handle emergency and crisis situations.

7. Text.

A Master says, 'Gentlepersons need to be broad-shouldered and stout-hearted for their burden is heavy and their journey long. Goodness is a self-imposed burden carried until only death brings an end to their life-long journey'.

Commentary.

Virtuous psychotherapists are strong and courageous human beings who bear the heavy burden of Goodness for the entire length of their personal and professional life.

8. Text.

Confucius says, 'Human beings are first inspired by songs, then given a solid foundation through ritual and finally per-fected with music'.

Commentary.

Virtuous psychotherapists are well-versed in the ritual techniques and methods of psychotherapy and experience the psychotherapeutic and transformative value of bibliotherapy and music, dance and movement therapy for working with clients.

9. Text.

Confucius says, 'Common people can be made to follow the Way but may not be made to understand it or the reasons for following it'.

Commentary.

Virtuous psychotherapists are committed to understanding, according with and following Dao/the Way and to model its Way of being, living and relating for psychotherapy clients who, in their own time, come to understand it and their reasons for following it.

10. Text.

Confucius says, 'Human beings who are both courageous and resent poverty and human beings who are both virtuous and resent others will be insubordinate and rebellious'.

Commentary.

Virtuous psychotherapists understand that the etiology of, and motivation for, any insubordinate, rebellious and acting-out behavior on the part of psychotherapy clients has more to do with poverty, alienation and suffering rather than with any inborn characterological defects of their essential humanity.

11. Text.

Confucius says, 'When human beings have great talents and abilities are arrogant and mean-spirited, all of their gifts mean nothing'.

Commentary.

Virtuous psychotherapists value and model humility and kindness in themselves and for clients and see the destructive effects of arrogance and meanness on the talents and abilities of some clients.

12. Text.

Confucius says, 'A human being who studies for three years without any thought of reward is difficult to find.'

Commentary.

Virtuous psychotherapists are committed to study and learning for its own sake and value; for its use in improving themselves and psychotherapy practice and not for creating attractive resumes, as a means to the end of being hired by educational institutions or treatment centers, earning high salaries and being promoted or obtaining outstanding professional recognition.

13. Text.

Confucius says, 'Be of unwavering good faith, love learning and dwell in the Good and Right Way for life. Don't enter a dangerous state or remain in a disordered one. When the Way prevails in the state, show yourself and when it doesn't, conceal yourself. When the Way prevails in the state, be ashamed if poor and lowly and when it doesn't, be ashamed if wealthy and honored'.

Commentary.

Virtuous psychotherapists are of constant good faith, love learning and continually abide in Goodness and Rightness in their personal and professional life. They maintain psychotherapy practice as a safe place and a well-structured crucible, free of danger and disorder, where Dao prevails and they and clients can be open, honest and self-disclosing and not be ashamed of who they are, how they are being and what they are doing in the psychotherapy relationship process and in their lives.

14. Text.

Confucius says, 'Officials don't discuss policies and practices that aren't within the limits of their official position and duties'.

Commentary.

Human beings and psychotherapists who aren't virtuous psychotherapists or clients of virtuous psychotherapists; who aren't familiar with the philosophy, theories and practices of virtuous psychotherapy and who can't speak from their direct experience; usually don't discuss anything about it or how it is conducted.

15. Text.

Confucius says, 'When a music master conducts the climax of a performance of *The Ospreys* (a song of loving union between two human beings); what a splendid flood of sound fills my ears!'.

Commentary.

Virtuous psychotherapists are especially and deeply moved by music and musical performances of songs that are inspired by, involve and portray loving union between human beings. They also understand the power of such music and may often use it in their psychotherapy work with clients.

16. Text.

Confucius says, 'Impetuous but not upright, ingeneous but not honest, simple but not sincere; I can't understand such human beings'.

Commentary.

Virtuous psychotherapists typically don't personally or professionally choose to associate with deceitful, dishonest, insincere and untrustworthy human beings and clients.

17. Text.

Confucius says, 'Learn like you're following something that you can't catch up with and, if you do, learn like you caught up with something that you're afraid of losing'.

Commentary.

Virtuous psychotherapists often seek, experience, value and apply the learning gained by associating, studying and collaborating with teachers and collegial psychotherapists who are more advanced than they are.

18. Text.

Confucius says, 'How majestic are these two legendary ancient Sage-Rulers. All under Heaven (the whole world) is theirs. They receive it without seeking it and possess it without attaching to it'.

Commentary.

Virtuous psychotherapists don't seek and aren't attached to any name, status, reputation, fame or power that they obtain in or through psychotherapy practice.

19. Text.

Confucius says, 'Awesome is the legendary ancient Sage-Ruler who personifies the greatness of Heaven. So vast, all-encompassing and indescribable is his moral virtue/de and so sublime, brilliant and majestic are his cultural accomplishments'.

Commentary.

Virtuous psychotherapists embody, personify, manifest and transmit the vast, all-encompassing and ineffable moral virtue/de of Heavenly Dao and clients derive and share the benefits of their sublime, brilliant and majestic psychotherapy accomplishments.

20. Text.

A legendary ancient Sage-Ruler has five ministers and the whole empire is well governed. The ruler of a state boasts ten ministers ... yet only holds two-thirds of the state. The moral virtue and efficacious power/de of the ancient legendary Sage-Ruler is absolutely the greatest.

Commentary.

The moral virtue, integrity, energy and efficacious power/de of Dao of virtuous psychotherapists is sufficient to create and maintain the order, harmony and conduct of their psychotherapy practice.

21. Text.

Confucius says, 'I can't say anything against this legendary ancient Sage-Ruler. Simple in food and drink but displaying the utmost devotion in offerings to ancestors, deities and spirits. Everyday clothes are plain but ceremonial robes are magnificent. He lives in a humble abode and devotes all of his energy to opening irrigation channels and drainage ditches and controlling floods for the people. I find no fault with him'.

Commentary.

Virtuous psychotherapists tend to live simply, economically, humbly and contentedly and are faultlessly and humanely devoted and dedicated to supporting, assisting and benefiting the clients in their psychotherapy practice.

水

THE ANALECTS
BOOK NINE
THE MASTER SHUNNED

ZI HAN

子罕

QUALITIES OF CONFUCIUS

1. Text.

Confucius rarely speaks abstractly about Properness, Destiny and Goodness.

Commentary.

Virtuous psychotherapists typically don't generally abstractly discuss moral virtues and conduct and destiny unless they're specifically concretely relevant focuses and concerns of particular psychotherapy clients.

2. Text.

A villager sarcastically says that Confucius is a great man and widely learned but doesn't do anything to evidence this reputation. Confucius hears of this and humorously says to disciples, 'What should I take up?. Chariot driving, archery?. I think chariot driving!'.

Commentary.

Virtuous psychotherapists may experience that the practice of psychotherapy isn't understood by human beings who don't have first-hand experience with its inner nature, conduct, efficacy, value and benefit but they'd never take up another profession just because of it.

3. Text.

Confucius says, 'In ritual practices, I follow the current majority regarding the wearing of a non-traditional ceremonial cap but I still follow the traditional ritual practices regarding where and when to bow. Nowadays, the majority of people go contrary to many of the ancient ritual practices, but I don't'.

Commentary.

Virtuous psychotherapists typically conduct psychotherapy in traditional, conventional and orthodox ways using treatment approaches, skills, techniques and methods that have proven to be effective with a wide variety of clients and client issues for over a long period of time.

4. Text.

Confucius avoids four things: abstract theorizing, narrow-mindedness, inflexible obstinancy and egotistic self-centeredness.

Commentary.

Virtuous psychotherapists are experience-focused, open-minded, flexible and client-centered in their psychotherapy work with clients.

5. Text.

Confucius's life is endangered in a border town. He says, 'When the ruler dies, culture exists within me. If Heaven determines that culture should vanish, I won't still be here. And if Heaven doesn't determine to destroy culture, what do I have to fear about what these people can do to me?'.

Commentary.

Virtuous psychotherapists are internally and safely identified with Goodness and trust that the Heaven-bestowed Goodness within themselves and clients and the culture and society will prevail in spite of any seeming threats or actions to the contrary.

6. Text.

An official asks a disciple of Confucius, 'Is your Master a Divine Sage?. If so, why has he made so many mundane accomplishments?'. The disciple replies, 'Heaven intends him to be a sage and it's true that he has accomplished much'. Confucius hears about this and says, 'This official is right about me. When young I'm in humble circumstances and make many practical accomplishments in every-day matters. But gentlepersons don't need to make them'.

Commentary.

As virtuous psychotherapists develop themselves personally and professionally and evolve in their psychotherapy practice, some may have fewer needs to accomplish mundane things.

7. Text.

Confucius says, 'Not having to study and to be tested for or to occupy an official position, I've time to pursue learning and the arts'.

Commentary.

Virtuous psychotherapists temporarily take time to study for state licensing examinations and to attend continuing education programs to meet licensing requirements but still make time to pursue creative personal and professional interests.

8. Text.

Confucius says, 'Do I possess wisdom?. Far from it!. But if anyone sincerely comes and asks me a genuine question, I explore it thoroughly with them from beginning to end until we naturally reach a conclusion'.

Commentary.

Virtuous psychotherapists don't necessarily consider themselves to be wise human beings but they're receptive and willing to consider the genuine questions of sincere clients and to thoroughly dialogue with them until a satisfactory conclusive answer is reached.

9. Text.

Confucius laments, 'The phoenix doesn't arrive. The river offers no map. It's all over for me'.

Commentary.

Virtuous psychotherapists may but don't usually rely upon mythical creatures and natural phenomena to be magical signs and omens of their professional identity and destiny as virtuous psychotherapists, their ability to successfully work with clients or the current state and fate of their psychotherapy practice.

10. Text.

When Confucius sees persons who are in mourning, wearing ceremonial attire or are blind; he respectfully stands up or, if passing by them, respectfully quickens his pace according with prescribed ritual etiquette.

Commentary.

Virtuous psychotherapists show respect for clients coming to meet with them regardless of their physical condition or current circumstances.

11. Text.

A disciple sighs, 'The more that I look upward toward Goodness, the higher it goes. The more that I hone in on it, the harder it becomes. I look in front and it goes behind. Step by step, Confucius leads and guides me, expanding me with culture and focusing me with ritual. I can't stop even if I want to.

Just when I feel exhausted, some new resource arises. I long for Goodness but I'm not finding any way of reaching it'.

Commentary.

Virtuous psychotherapists have considerable experience with how Goodness eludes any conceptual objectifying or verbalizing of it and rely upon their own inner sense of its reality and the demonstration of its operation and positive effects in psychotherapy work with clients.

12. Text.

Confucius is very ill and a disciple obtains a retainer that he's not entitled to. Confucius says, 'The retainer is a pretense and deception. Pretending that I don't have a retainer, who am I deceiving, Heaven?. I'd rather die in the arms of you disciples than those of a retainer. Even if I'm not entitled to a state funeral and burial, it's not like I'm dying by the roadside'.

Commentary.

Virtuous psychotherapists may establish such intimate relationships with some clients that when they die, memorials are often held for them by current and former clients.

13. Text.

A disciple asks, 'If you have a beautiful jewel, would you wrap it up and keep in a box or sell it for the best price?'. Confucius replies, 'I'd sell it!. I'm still waiting for offers (for an official position)'.

Commentary.

Virtuous psychotherapists may consider and/or accept offers for more suitable and beneficial professional possibilities and circumstances in the field of psychotherapy rather than limit their opportunity and ability to assist clients solely by remaining with the status quo.

14. Text.

Confucius considers settling among barbarian tribes and is told that he might have difficulty tolerating their lack of refinement. Confucius says 'If a gentleperson settles among them, there wouldn't be any lack of refinement'.

Commentary.

Virtuous psychotherapists are flexibly able to connect, empathize and work with both so-considered 'cultured' and 'uncultured' clients in both refined and unrefined settings, contexts and circumstances and to bring their transforming virtues to them.

15. Text.

Confucius says, 'Only when I return home from traveling to neighboring states, am I able to edit and properly order music'.

Commentary.

Virtuous psychotherapists often contribute necessary and appropriate clarity, order and revisions to the professional literature of psychotherapy theory and practice through doing research studies, publishing journal papers and giving presentations.

16. Text.

Confucius says, 'I dutifully serve the ruler abroad and elders at home. I don't neglect mourning rites or get intoxicated. What else can I do?'.

Commentary.

Virtuous psychotherapists have no regrets about their professional psychotherapy conduct and career because they have complied with all of the ethical standards and professional requirements of good clinical practice.

17. Text.

Confucius is standing beside a stream and says, 'Can we flow on and on like this without stopping day or night!?'.

Commentary.

The good psychotherapy work of virtuous psychotherapists flows on and on, day and night.

18. Text.

Confucius says, 'I've yet to meet human beings who love moral virtue/de as much as female beauty'.

Commentary.

The desire and commitment of virtuous psychotherapists to increasing the moral virtue, integrity, energy and power/de of Dao often equals, or is identical with, their desire and interest in enhancing the beauty of clients and human beings.

19. Text.

Confucius says, 'Teaching human beings is like making a mound of dirt or leveling the ground. If they've only one shovelful left to add to the pile of dirt and stop, I stop teaching. If they've only lifted one shovelful to remove dirt from the earth but start working, I start teaching'.

Commentary.

Virtuous psychotherapists faithfully and diligently continue working with clients whether they add to or take away from their stage or progress in psychotherapy.

20. Text.

Confucius says, 'This one disciple can be counted on to attentively listen to what I say and to quickly put it into practice'.

Commentary.

Virtuous psychotherapists, in spite of a respectful attitude of equality for all psychotherapy clients, are nonetheless sometimes aware of some who are reliably more attentive, receptive and able to better implement insights and suggestions.

21. Text.

Confucius says, 'I see this disciple (who dies early) go forward but, alas, don't have the chance to see where his progress finally leads him. How sad!'.

Commentary.

Virtuous psychotherapists are aware of the progress that clients are making but most often they don't see how the progress is actualized after termination of psychotherapy, unless they schedule periodic follow-up check-in meetings at regular intervals.

22. Text.

Confucius says, 'There are plants that spring up but never flower and others that flower but never bear fruit' (re: the disciple who dies early).

Commentary.

Virtuous psychotherapists see and work with clients in accord with their own unique nature, character and personality; their length of time in psychotherapy and the extent to which they are able to effectively actualize their potential development.

23. Text.

Confucius says, 'Respect the young for they may one day equal all who we now are. If human beings are forty or fifty years of age and still remain unlearned, there's no need to respect them'.

Commentary.

On the contrary, virtuous psychotherapists are respectful of both youth, adults and elders who may or may not have yet learned or accomplished anything noteworthy at their age.

24. Text.

Confucius says, 'Moral sayings can move us but what matters is that they are correctly understood and change or reform us by being ritually carried out. For human beings who understand moral sayings but don't correctly understand, heed and carry them out, I can't do anything'.

Commentary.

Virtuous psychotherapists make the most progress in psychotherapy with clients who actualize insights that result in changes and that are put into practice in their lives and relationships.

25. Text.

Confucius says, 'Be trustworthy in what you say to fellow human beings and faithful in doing your best for them, refuse the friendship of those who aren't your equal, and admit your mistakes and correct them'.

Commentary.

Virtuous psychotherapists are trustworthy in what they say to clients and are faithful in doing their best for them. They don't usually associate with colleagues who don't share their virtue of Goodness and they acknowledge and correct mistakes and errors in psychotherapy conduct and relationships.

26. Text.

Confucius says, 'Armies may lose their commander-in-chief but you can't deprive common people of their purposes'.

Commentary.

Psychotherapy clients can often accept transfer referrals made by virtuous psychotherapists better than they can change the willful intentions and purposes of their egos.

27. Text.

Confucius says, 'Wearing shabby clothes yet standing unembarrassed next to those wearing furs applies to this disciple. The ode applies, 'Not covetous, not envious, how can he not be Good'?'. The disciple keeps repeating the ode over and over and Confucius finally says to him, 'C'mon, saying these words over and over isn't going to make you Good!'.

Commentary.

Virtuous psychotherapists are typically unconcerned with differences in dress between them and clients. Some clients of virtuous psychotherapists take their words too seriously and obsessively and compulsively repeat them as if they are sacred mantras and magical formulas rather than simply relevant observations and supportive feedback.

28. Text.

Confucius says, 'Only in Winter do we see that the pine and cypress trees are the last to lose their leaves'.

Commentary.

Virtuous psychotherapists realize that a relative context is needed to assess and appreciate the changes and progress of individual psychotherapy clients; the appropriate timing of reflections, feedback and interpretations and the realities of end-setting and termination.

29. Text.

Confucius says, 'Human beings who are Good, wise and courageous aren't worried, confused or fearful'.

Commentary.

Virtuous psychotherapists are, for the most part; Good, wise and courageous in that order and don't usually experience any worry, confusion or fear in psychotherapy meetings with clients.

30. Text.

Confucius says, 'Some human beings can be joined with in studying the Way but not in progressing along it. Some human beings can be joined with in progressing along the Way but not in establishing it. Some human beings can be joined with in establishing the Way but not in moral discerning'.

Commentary.

Virtuous psychotherapists usually have some colleagues who can be associated and collaborated with for focused psychotherapy study, shared psychotherapy progress, establishing psychotherapy practice and ethical psychotherapy conduct through study groups, peer supervisory consultation, co-counseling, individual psychotherapy and control psychoanalysis.

31. Text.

> 'Flowering branches of the cherry.
> How quickly they rebound
> after blossoms are plucked!
> It's not that I don't love you
> but your home is so far away'.

Confucius says, 'This person doesn't really love. If they really love, distance doesn't matter'.

Commentary.

Some clients of virtuous psychotherapists fail to make sufficient progress in their psychotherapy work, self-development and self-improvement because they don't want to, or are unable to, 'go the distance' to realize who they fully are, what they really desire and who and what they truly love, e.g., awakening, enlightenment, transformation, liberation, peace, intimacy, happiness, etc.. That the objective or goal appears too distant to achieve or reach or that the psychotherapy office or resource is too far away to get to aren't legitimate excuses for abandoning working to realize the full potentials of personal growth, interpersonal intimacy and transpersonal evolution.

水

THE ANALECTS
BOOK TEN
AMONG THE XIANG AND DANG

XIANG DANG

鄉 黨

CONFUCIUS AND RITUALS

1. Text.

At home in his native village, Confucius's manner is relaxed, simple and respectful and he speaks little. But in the ruler's ancestral temple or in court, he speaks confidently and at length, though always cautiously choosing his words.

Commentary.

Virtuous psychotherapists are usually at home in their office or place of conducting psychotherapy and are relaxed and respectful, typically listen more than they speak and when speaking, choose their words thoughtfully.

2. Text.

In court when interacting with lower officials, Confucius's attitude is gracious and friendly. With upper officials, it's respectful and formal. When the ruler is present, it's reverential and constrained.

Commentary.

Virtuous psychotherapists flexibly adapt their attitudes and conform their demeanors to appropriately suit and meet the conventional protocols of various different treatment settings and varied situations of, and relationships with, clients and colleagues.

3. Text.

When receiving guests, Confucius's appearance, stance and movements are solemn and courteous and when addressing colleagues, they're dignified and majestic ... he meets visitors enthusiastically and informs the ruler as soon as they've departed by saying, 'The guest isn't looking back'.

Commentary.

Again, good gentle psychotherapists flexibly and appropriately adapt their attitudes, posture and demeanors to suit the conventional protocols of differing treatment settings and professional role-relationships.

4. Text.

Entering the palace gate, Confucius respectfully and humbly draws himself in when nodding, clasping his hands and bowing. While he observes the protocols for entering, moving and standing; he often appears hesitant, shaky and to be holding his breath. When exiting, he appears relieved and recovers an air of dignity.

Commentary.

Virtuous psychotherapists are sometimes awkward and uncomfortable in formal and highly hierarchically structured professional situations that involve rigidly stratified power dynamics, protocols and behaviors.

5. Text.

When holding the jade tablet at ruler's investitures, Confucius hunches over as if bearing a great weight and recoils as if avoiding something dreadful. But when ritually giving out official presents, he's relaxed and friendly and during private audiences he's happy and animated.

Commentary.

Virtuous psychotherapists are sometimes awkward and uncomfortable executing responsibilities in formal and highly rigidly structured hierarchical social situations involving power dynamics and are usually more comfortable in one-with-one relationships, e.g., in an individual private practice psychotherapy office setting.

6/7/8/9/10/11/12/13/14/15. Texts.
(Condensed, Combined and Paraphrased).

Gentlepersons don't wear certain colored clothes. In hot weather, cool clothes are worn but covered in public. Certain clothes and skins are paired. All clothing is worn according to specific protocols of propriety for specific occasions, duties and purposes. Food, eating habits, seating arrangements and wine consumption are also highly regulated and ritualized according to protocols and rules of correct etiquette and conduct. Gentlepersons dress and act ritually at community festivals and prostrate themselves with messengers when sending messages to, or receiving messages from, people in another state.

Commentary.

Virtuous psychotherapists abide by certain clearly defined ethical standards, codes and treatment protocols that are highly regulated and monitored by the administration of their respective professional associations and organizations. Some ritual-like structures of psychotherapy practice are how meetings are scheduled, when client fees are paid, the length of meeting times, seating arrangements, how meetings are conducted and concluded, etc..

16/17/18/19/20/21/22/23/24/25/26/27. Texts.
(Condensed, Combined and Paraphrased).

Gentlepersons refuse gifts of unknown medication. If stables are burned down, they ask about the fate of animals as well as of people. Sacrificial offerings are made when receiving food and gifted live animals are reared. If ill, they receive visitors being dressed in specific ways and by assuming certain positions. When summoned to the palace, they leave immediately and when entering the ancestral temple, they ask about every detail of rituals. If deceased friends have no relatives, they assume responsibility for conducting funerals. They exhibit respect, proper solemn attitudes, demeanors and behaviors with people in mourning. They exhibit appropriate responses to gifts and events and assume specific positions when in bed, when alone and when mounting and riding in carriages. They know the correct reasons and time to leave the state.

Commentary.

Virtuous psychotherapists are committed to ethical principles, treatment protocols and role-relationships with clients that are regulated but also are generally those that constitute good normal relationships of and between Good normal human beings.

水

THE ANALECTS
BOOK ELEVEN
THOSE OF FORMER ERAS

XIAN JIN

先 近

CONFUCIUS AND DISCIPLES

1. Text.

Confucius says, 'My first disciples studying and learning rituals and music are rustics and later disciples are aristocrats. I prefer the rustics'.

Commentary.

Virtuous psychotherapists typically don't have social class preferences regarding clients. They can't begin their private psychotherapy practice until they are first sufficiently educated, trained, supervised and well-versed in schools and models of psychotherapy theories, techniques and methods and they are state licensed. The students, trainees, interns and clients of virtuous psychotherapists may change as they evolve from early to later on in their psychotherapy practice.

2. Text.

Confucius says, 'None of the disciples who travel with me to neighboring states are with me now'.

Commentary.

Most of the students, trainees and interns of virtuous psychotherapists don't usually continue relationships with them following graduation, employment and licensing.

3. Text.

Of several disciples Confucius says, 'They live by moral virtue/de, speak well, handle affairs ably and are culturally learned and refined'.

Commentary.

Virtuous psychotherapists work with students, trainees, interns and clients with many different interests, abilities, occupations and degrees of self-development from the personal and practical to the transpersonal and spiritual.

4. Text.

Confucius says, 'This disciple isn't of any help to me. He accepts everything I say'.

Commentary.

Virtuous psychotherapists experience that personal, social and professional new learning and growth occur through interpersonal relationships and dialogue and that differences of opinions, positions and perspectives often contribute to more learning and growth than unquestioned acceptance and agreement does.

5. Text.

Confucius says, 'This disciple is a very good filial son and no one argues with the good that his parents and brothers say about him'.

Commentary.

Virtuous psychotherapists value good family relationships characterized by filial respect, fidelity and harmony and work significantly with clients on exploring, understanding, working through and resolving any of their crucial family-related issues.

6. Text.

A disciple often and correctly recites a powerful ritual verse about a white jade tablet three times and Confucius sanctions the marriage of his elder brother's daughter to him.

Commentary.

Virtuous psychotherapists value clients who demonstrate the combination of reverent aesthetic sensibility and devoted dignified speaking.

7. Text.

An official asks Confucius which of his disciples has a love of learning. Confucius answers, 'There is only one but, unfortunately, he dies young and now there is no one'.

Commentary.

In spite of considering all clients as essentially equal, virtuous psychotherapists, for various reasons, may have some favorite ones.

8. Text.

A disciple dies and his father asks Confucius if he can use his carriage for a coffin enclosure. Confucius says, ... 'When my son dies, he has a coffin but no enclosure. I don't go on foot so that he can have one. Because of my rank it's not proper for me to do so'.

Commentary.

Virtuous psychotherapists observe the usual conventional protocols if and when choosing to attend the funerals of clients or their family members.

9/10. Texts.

When a favorite disciple dies, Confucius laments, 'Alas, Heaven has bereaved me, Heaven has bereaved me!' and wails without restraint. Some of his other disciples suggest that the wailing is excessive and Confucius says, 'Is it?. If any human being's death justifies abandoned wailing, it certainly is this disciple's!'.

Commentary.

Virtuous psychotherapists grieve the deaths of their clients with the same respect and emotional feelings as those for a loving parent, close teacher or good friend.

11. Text.

When the favorite disciple dies, other disciples want to give him a grand funeral but Confucius says that it'd be improper to do so. Nevertheless, they give him a grand burial and Confucius says, 'This disciple relates to me as a father. But I'm kept from relating to him as a son by burying him in the way that I feel is appropriate'.

Commentary.

Virtuous psychotherapists aren't typically involved with the surviving family members of deceased clients in making funeral arrangements but may do so for memorials.

12. Text.

A disciple asks about death and serving spirits. Confucius answers, 'Until you learn about living and how to serve human beings how can you know about death and how to serve spirits?'.

Commentary

Virtuous psychotherapists are usually skilled, competent and proficient in working with clients on issues relating to death and spirits, e.g., with near-death experiences, past life memories, parapychological phenomena, seances, communicating with the deceased, soul retrieval, etc..

13. Text.

The demeanor of one disciple attending Confucius is respectful restraint. That of a second one is impatient energy and that of a third one is relaxed geniality. Confucius is pleased with all three but suggests that the second disciple won't die a natural death.

Commentary.

Virtuous psychotherapists are pleased to work with a wide variety of clients and value the opportunity to experience and empathize with uniquely different ways of their human being and being human and to understand corresponding aspects of themselves.

14. Text.

Some residents are planning to rebuild a state treasury and a disciple suggests, 'How about restoring it along the old lines rather than completely restructuring it?'. Confucius comments, 'This disciple doesn't speak much, but when he does, he hits the mark'.

Commentary.

Virtuous psychotherapists typically listen to clients more than they speak; but when they do speak, they are accurately reflective, empathic and facilitative of client's awarenesses and insights.

15. Text.

Confucius says, 'This disciple's zither playing is inappropriate in my school' and the other disciples stop respecting the disciple. Confucius then adds, 'He hasn't the Goodness to enter the inner sanctuary but at least he has the courage to come as far as the guest-hall'.

Commentary.

The clients of virtuous psychotherapists range along a continuum of virtues from wisdom to courage to Goodness.

16. Text.

A disciple asks who of two other disciples is more worthy. Confucius says that one goes too far and the other doesn't go far enough. 'Going too far is the same as not going far enough'.

Commentary.

Virtuous psychotherapists hold to the 'middle way' between extremes of overdoing and underdoing with regard to psychotherapy interpretations, interactions and interventions.

17. Text.

A royal family is wealthier than a ruler and a tax-collector continues to give the family more tax revenues so as to increase their wealth. Confucius says, 'This tax-collector is no follower of mine. Disciples, beat the war drum, go after and publically expose him'.

Commentary.

Virtuous psychotherapists consistently treat clients equally and fairly regardless of their socio-economic status. They don't charge more wealthy clients higher fees to earn more income but they may have sliding-fee scales to benefit lower income clients. They don't conduct a Robin Hood (or Robbing Hood) type of psychotherapy practice.

18. Text.

Speaking of the faults of four disciples, Confucius says that one is slow, one is dull, one is formal and one is unruly.

Commentary.

Virtuous psychotherapists don't usually compare, evaluate and judge clients in terms of personality faults and work with clients of many different temperments, traits, characteristics, qualities, dispositions, behaviors, abilities and life-styles.

19. Text.

Confucius says, 'This disciple comes very close to perfect Goodness and still lives in poverty'. Of another disciple, Confucius says, 'He rejects his economic fate, takes to money-making and his business speculations hit the mark'.

Commentary.

Virtuous psychotherapists are encouraged by working with clients who are committed to decreasing desires and simpifying their lives as well as motivated to improving themselves and their circumstances.

20. Text.

A disciple asks about Good persons. Confucius says, 'Persons who follow the Way of the Ancients and not the ways of other persons can enter the inner sanctuary'.

Commentary.

Virtuous psychotherapists believe that the path to the 'inner sanctuary' of Goodness involves following the Way that previous Good and spiritually evolved human beings trail-blaze and live.

21. Text.

Confucius says of a disciple, 'His speech and demeanor seem sincere and proper but it's difficult to say whether he's really a gentleperson or simply appears to be like one'.

Commentary.

Virtuous psychotherapists are continually involved in accurately discerning whether clients are really being their true selves or are showing superficial masks, false facades and stereotypical personas.

22. Text.

Two disciples ask Confucius if a maxim should be put into practice as soon as it is heard. Confucius instructs one not to put a maxim into practice and the other to immediately put one into practice. Another disciple is confused by the apparent contradiction and asks Confucius for clarification who explains, 'One disciple is impulsive so I hold him back and the other is reticent so I urge him on'.

Commentary.

Virtuous psychotherapists skillfully and appropriately suggest different behaviors and apply different methods with different clients based upon their personality characteristics and the issues with which they're working, e.g., impulsiveness or compulsiveness.

23. Text.

Confucius and his disciples are escaping being trapped in a town and one disciple falls behind. After they regroup, Confucius says to the disciple, 'I thought that you died'. The disciple says, 'While you're alive, how dare I die?'.

Commentary.

Virtuous psychotherapists don't allow clients to overvalue and depend upon them so much that they'd be willing to die for them.

24. Text.

A disciple asks if two officials can be called great. Confucius answers, ' ... A great official serves a ruler without violating the Way or else resigns. I call these two 'stop-gap' or 'make-shift' officials'. The disciple asks, 'Does that mean that they'll do anything asked of them?'. Confucius adds, 'Yes, but not if they're asked to kill their father or ruler'.

Commentary.

Virtuous psychotherapists don't conduct their psychotherapy practice in any ways that violate sustaining and according with Dao/the Way.

25. Text.

One disciple appoints another disciple's son to be an official. Confucius thinks that it's a wrong decision and says, 'You're doing harm to another man's young son'. The disciple says,

'There are peasants to govern and the holy ground to maintain. Learning doesn't just consist of reading books'. Confucius says, 'Remarks like this make me dislike glib talkers!'.

Commentary.

Virtuous psychotherapists value book learning as well as practical learning and on-the-job training, speak truthfully and aren't glib conversationalists.

26. Text. (Edited, Condensed and Paraphrased).

Confucius asks each of four disciples what employment they would choose if their merits are recognized. The answers of two relate to having and ruling large kingdoms, overcoming great difficulties and benefiting the people. The answers of the other two relate; 1) to learning, participating in and conducting ceremonial rituals and 2) to communally enjoying Nature and poetry. Confucius favors the responses of the latter two disciples.

Commentary.

Virtuous psychotherapists typically enjoy Nature, human community and the creative arts and favor playing their meaningful and fulfilling role and part in unique, specialized and confidential individual psychotherapy meetings with a limited number of clients rather than being; 1) aggressive entrepreneurs networking for large private practices, 2) powerful administrators of large for-profit organizations or 3) under-regulated social media bloggers and influencers.

水

THE ANALECTS
BOOK TWELVE
YAN YUAN

YAN YUAN

顔 淵

CONFUCIUS AND DISCIPLES

1/2/3/4. Texts. (Condensed and Paraphrased).

Three disciples ask Confucius about gentlepersons of perfect virtue. Confucius answers,

'Gentlepersons:

1) restrain themselves and continually return to ritual,

2) have the source of Goodness within themselves,

3) look at, listen to, speak and do nothing contrary to ritual,

4) relate to people as guests at an important sacrifice,

5) don't do to others what they don't want done to them,

6) are cautious and careful in speaking about Goodness,

7) have no moral corruption within themselves and

8) thereby have nothing to regret, worry about or fear.'

Commentary.

Virtuous psychotherapists have Goodness within themselves, comply with all of the ethical regulations and practices of psychotherapy, treat clients as respected guests at the important event of a psychotherapy meeting, are thoughtful and cautious about what they say to clients, treat clients the same way that they themselves want to be treated, are not morally corrupt and are, therefore, free of regret, guilt, worry or fear in their psychotherapy practice.

5. Text.

A disciple laments not having brothers. Another disciple says, 'I've heard the saying, 'Death, life, wealth and rank are the decree and will of Heaven'. If a gentleperson attends to business and doesn't waste time, is respectful of and courteous with others and observes the rules of ritual propriety; then everyone is a brother. How can a true gentleperson lament not having brothers?'.

Commentary.

Virtuous psychotherapists are grateful for the bestowed opportunity of psychotherapy work, attend to the business of psychotherapy, don't waste meeting time, are courteous to clients, observe the ethical rules of treatment and sometimes have a sisterly and brotherly-like relationship with clients.

6. Text.

A disciple asks about discernment. Confucius answers, 'Words of defamation are as hurtful as bodily wounds. Human beings who aren't affected by unjustified complaints, slander and condemnation are discerning'.

Commentary.

Virtuous psychotherapists are moral and discerning human beings who are secure in themselves and unaffected by any unjustified criticism of, slander about or condemnation of them.

7. Text.

A disciple asks about governing. Confucius answers, 'Have sufficient food and weapons and the trust and confidence of common people'. The disciple asks which two of the three could be dispensed with. Confucius replies, 'Weapons and food. Death is the lot of all human beings but a state can't survive and the people can't stand without their trust in a ruler'.

Commentary.

Virtuous psychotherapists are trustworthy and inspire trust and confidence in clients through good relationships and meaningful and beneficial psychotherapy work with them.

8. Text.

An official says, 'Gentlepersons are so by virtue of their innate qualities. Culture can't create or refine them'... A disciple objects saying, 'Culture and inborn qualities are equally important. Skin a tiger or panther and their hairless hide looks the same as that of a dog or sheep'.

Commentary.

Virtuous psychotherapists are free of the dualistic issue of nature vs. nurture and integrally understand that the realities of human being are a complementary combination, interweaving and interplay of both innate and cultural factors, influences and determinants.

9. Text.

A ruler asks a disciple, 'It's a scarce year, revenues are insufficient and I can't meet the state's needs. What can I do?'. The disciple replies, 'Tithe the people' and the ruler counters, 'I'm already taxing them two-tenths and it's insufficient'. The disciple adds, 'When the people have plenty, how can a ruler not have enough and when the people don't have enough, how can a ruler have plenty?'.

Commentary.

Virtuous psychotherapists suffer the same economic downturns as clients and they may lose clients who can no longer afford fee-for-service psychotherapy.

10. Text.

A disciple asks about the meaning of 'increasing moral virtue/de' and 'being of two minds'. Confucius answers, 'They mean assuming loyalty and trustworthiness as guiding principles toward choosing and following what is Good and Right ... and simultaneously wanting something or someone to exist and not exist ...'.

Commentary.

Virtuous psychotherapists increase their moral virtue, integrity, energy and power/de by being loyal and trustworthy to clients; doing what is Good, Right and the best for clients in the conduct of psychotherapy and not having dualistic, antithetical, contradictory and ambivalent thoughts and feelings about things.

11. Text.

A ruler asks about government. Confucius answers, 'Rectification. Let a ruler, subject, father and son just and only be a ruler, subject, father and son.' The ruler adds, 'Very true!. When they each aren't being who they are, it creates so much insecurity that people don't know if they'll live to eat their next meal'.

Commentary.

Virtuous psychotherapists maintain clear, well-defined and solid interpersonal boundaries and role relationships between clients and themselves and thus insure the safety and security of the psychotherapy relationship and the viability of psychotherapy itself.

12. Text.

Confucius says, 'Deciding a lawsuit with only a few words!. This disciple is the one for doing that and never puts off a promise until the next day'.

Commentary.

Virtuous psychotherapists use their words pointedly, economically and effectively and make treatment decisions and interventions promptly.

13. Text.

Confucius says, 'I can try law suits as good as anyone but better yet is doing something to prevent them in the first place!'.

Commentary.

Virtuous psychotherapists adequately deal with current issues and conflicts in relationships with clients and practice early intervention and preventative maintenance in order to anticipate and forestall potential difficulties and crises in the lives of clients and in the conduct of psychotherapy.

14. Text.

A disciple asks about governing. Confucius replies, 'Carefully ponder policies and dutifully, carefully and untiringly do your best to carry them out when the time is right'.

Commentary.

Virtuous psychotherapists usually weigh possible psychotherapy interactions, interpretations and interventions within themselves before implementing them in a timely manner in the psychotherapy relationship process, i.e., when clients are ready and receptive.

15. Text.

Confucius says, 'Be broadly educated about cultural matters, focus them through the rules of ritual propriety and you won't go astray'.

Commentary.

Virtuous psychotherapists are educated about their own culture and also those of other human beings and are qualified to appropriately and effectively conduct cross-cultural psychotherapy with a wide variety of clients.

16. Text.

Confucius says, 'Gentlepersons cultivate and help perfect

the good qualities of people and not exploit their faults. Small persons do just the opposite'.

Commentary.

Virtuous psychotherapists focus upon facilitating the good qualities of clients rather than the psychopathological ones, although the latter may emerge in the negative transference projections and clinical issues of clients that need to be addressed and worked with.

17. Text.

An official asks about governing. Confucius answers, 'Governing is straightening things out. If you correctly lead people along a straight way in the right direction, who'll dare go by a crooked one and not do what's Right?'.

Commentary

Virtuous psychotherapists conduct psychotherapy by interacting with clients directly, straightforwardly, clearly and honestly and not by using dishonest, devious and manipulative strategies, tactics and interventions.

18. Text.

The same official then asks how to deal with robbers. Confucius advises, 'If you're free from your own excessive desiring and acquiring things by stealing from people, robbers won't steal from you even if you pay them'.

Commentary.

Virtuous psychotherapists don't desire to acquire, accumulate or amass clients, insights, successes or 'cures' in psychotherapy practice and thus don't lose them.

19. Text.

The same official asks about capital punishment saying, 'How would it be if I kill those who don't have the Way to save or help those who do?'. Confucius replies, 'Your position is to govern and not to kill. If you desire Good, the people'll be Good. The virtue of gentlepersons is like wind and that of small persons is like grass. When a wind blows through grass, it can't help but bend'.

Commentary.

The Goodness of virtuous psychotherapists is modeled by them and creates a compelling resonant and yielding responsive influence upon clients.

20. Text.

A disciple asks about what an accomplished official is like who is well-known and influential. Confucius says, 'Being well-known isn't necessarily being influential. Being influential, human beings are upright, straightforward and lovers of Goodness and Rightness. They examine the words of persons, observe their expressions and humbly consider them. They're accomplished regardless of being known or not and they're not just confidently pretending and appearing to be Good and do Right'.

Commentary.

Virtuous psychotherapists are truly influential for clients by carefully and skillfully listening to, observing and believing them and not because they may have a well-known professional reputation or a confident and authoritative personal demeanor (or wear a long white coat!).

21. Text.

A disciple strolling along with Confucius asks about accumulating moral virtue/de, correcting vices and resolving complications. Confucius answers, 'Good questions!. Serve first and consider rewards later; attack your inner vices and not those of others and don't allow anger to endanger your safety'.

Commentary.

Virtuous psychotherapists are usually deeply involved in the current work of psychotherapy rather than in its rewards. They usually engage in their own psychotherapy and participate in case conferences and peer supervision relationships in order to continue working on their own issues and countertransference feelings and insure that their psychotherapy practice is a safe, non-threatening, nourishing and humane holding environment and crucible for clients.

22. Text.

The same disciple asks about Goodness and wisdom. Confucius says, 'Love, care for and understand fellow human beings and by raising the straight above the crooked make the crooked upright and straight'. Later, the disciple asks another disciple about the meaning of Confucius's statements who says, 'What a wealth of instruction!. When two rulers hold the whole state, Good persons are chosen to be officials and are raised up and those who lack Goodness are distanced'.

Commentary.

Virtuous psychotherapists care for and understand clients and are effective in assisting them in elevating their Good over their not-Good qualities, traits and habits and thus increase their uprightness and straightness and decrease any crookedness.

23. Text.

A disciple asks about friendship. Confucius says, 'Advise human beings loyally and ably and guide them properly with Goodness. If that fails, withdraw. Don't be disgraced'.

Commentary.

Virtuous psychotherapists relate well to clients by faithfully educating them to the best of their ability and properly guiding them along the Way of Goodness.

24. Text.

A Confucian master who also is a disciple states, 'Gentlepersons by interest, education and culture gather good friends around them and through them support, promote and spread Goodness'.

Commentary.

The Goodness of virtuous psychotherapists attracts good clients and thus validates, fosters, reinforces and expands and extends Goodness.

水

THE ANALECTS
BOOK THIRTEEN
ZI LU

ZI LU

子 路

GOVERNING AND GENTLEPERSONS

1. Text.

A disciple asks about governing. Confucius says, 'Be an example, lead people and encourage people!'. The disciple asks for further instruction. Confucius says, 'Untiringly!'.

Commentary.

Virtuous psychotherapists inspire, encourage, support, assist and guide clients and are seemingly tireless in their psychotherapy work with them.

2. Text.

An official asks about governing. Confucius says, 'Be an example, excuse minor faults and promote those of superior ability'. The official then asks, 'How do you know who's of superior ability?'. Confucius says, 'Promote those you know are worthy and those human beings whom you trust recommend'.

Commentary.

Virtuous psychotherapists usually interview potential clients and meet several times before mutually deciding to work together and they accept client referrals from former clients and colleagues whom they know and trust.

3. Text.

A disciple asks Confucius what he would do first if governing a state. Confucius replies, 'Rectify names ... If language is incorrect, then what's said doesn't correspond with what's meant and what's done can't be accomplished. Rites and music won't flourish, rewards and punishments won't be properly given and people won't have anything stable to guide them. That's why gentlepersons use proper language to name things and speak about what is proper to carry out into action. They're correct, aren't careless in what they say and leave nothing to chance'.

Commentary.

Virtuous psychotherapists consciously and carefully choose the language and words that they use in asking questions and communicating information, observations, reflections, feedback, interpretations and suggestions. Their words directly and congruently relate to the conduct, objectives and effectiveness of psychotherapy activities and methods and enhance the security of clients and the stability of psychotherapy.

4. Text.

A disciple asks to learn about farming. Confucius says, 'You'd better ask farmers'. Confucius doesn't consider the disciple to have correct aspirations and says, 'When rulers love ritual, Rightness and trustworthiness; common people will be respectful, obedient and truthful and they'll flock to them. Why learn about doing farming yourself?'.

Commentary.

Virtuous psychotherapists have often responded to a calling to choose psychotherapy as a primary career vocation ('calling'); love their work and remain faithfully committed to and involved in it without dispersing, depleting and dissipating their energy moonlighting in second jobs and, as a result, attract a sizable clientele who are true to themselves, respectful, cooperative and collaborative.

5. Text.

Confucius says, 'If persons are able to recite all of *The Odes* by heart but can't carry out their duties in government or on missions, of what practical use are they to them?'.

Commentary.

Virtuous psychotherapists are usually very knowledgeable about psychological theories and psychotherapy methods but don't find such knowledge to be useful unless it can be put to practical, meaningful and beneficial use in treating clients in psychotherapy practice.

6. Text.

Confucius says, 'When rulers are upright and correct, people will be Good and do Right without being given orders. But if rulers aren't upright and correct, even though orders are given, people won't be Good and do Right'.

Commentary.

Virtuous psychotherapists are upright and straightforward, don't make demands upon and give orders to clients and clients naturally form cooperative and collaborative therapeutic alliances and psychotherapy proceeds well.

7. Text.

Confucius says, 'In their governing of two different states, two brothers are still brotherly'.

Commentary.

Virtuous psychotherapists maintain good friendly professional relationships with colleagues who may hold differing viewpoints of, and approaches to, psychotherapy practice and may even be co-therapists with them for some clients and/or their familiy members and partners.

8. Text.

Confucius says of a ruler, 'In spite of prospering, he sticks to simplicity and continues to live in the same residence. When the ruler is prospering, the residence is suitable; when he is prospering even more, it's adequate and when he becomes very wealthy, it's beautiful'.

Commentary.

Virtuous psychotherapists continue to value simplicity; even when they develop their psychotherapy practice and it progressively becomes more successful and financially remunerative.

9. Text.

A disciple takes Confucius to a neighboring state who observes, 'What a dense population!'. The disciple asks, 'When people multiply so much, what can be done for them?'. Confucius answers, 'Enrich them and teach them'.

Commentary.

Virtuous psychotherapists rarely have so many clients that they're unable to continue being instructive, helpful and beneficial to each and all of them.

10. Text.

Confucius says, 'If someone employs me in government for a year, I'll put things in order and in three years time, I'll complete real work'.

Commentary.

Virtuous psychotherapists do crisis intervention, brief/ short-term psychotherapy and appreciate the opportunity of doing longer-term psychotherapy that opens up the possibility of deeper and more complete work with clients.

11. Text.

Confucius says. 'If good rulers govern a country for a hundred years, it's possible to overcome violence, prevent cruelty and end slaughter'.

Commentary.

Virtuous psyhotherapists value being able to work with some clients in longer-term psychotherapy to assist them in working through deeper characterological psychological issues often related their early traumatic histories and more recent experiences of abandonment, neglect, rejection, abuse, violence, etc..

12. Text.

Confucius says, 'Even if a wise ruler appears, it'd still take a generation for the virtue of Goodness to prevail'.

Commentary.

The essential Goodness and efficacy of the psychotherapy work of virtuous psychotherapists are due to their wisdom and being and living the moral virtue, integrity, energy and power/ de of Dao that can improve the future of psychotherapy.

13. Text.

Confucius says, 'When officials are upright and correct in their conduct, they'll have no difficulty serving in any office. But if they aren't, how can they succeed in assisting other people in being upright and correct?'.

Commentary.

Virtuous psychotherapists are upright and correct in the

conduct of their psychotherapy practice and continue work-ing on their own personal growth, professional development and spiritual evolution and are better able to model for and to assist clients in their own growth, development and evolution as human beings.

14. Text.

A disciple returns from court and Confucius asks, 'Why are you so late?'. The disciple replies, 'Affairs of the state are discussed'. Confucius comments, 'They must be about private business. If real government business is going on, even though I don't hold office, I'd have heard about it'.

Commentary.

Sometimes the psychotherapy meetings of virtuous psycho-therapists go overtime due to the extensive issues and intensive feelings of clients.

15. Text.

A ruler asks Confucius, 'Is there one saying that can save a country?'. Confucius replies, 'No saying can ever do that but here's one that comes close; 'It's difficult to be a ruler and not easy to be an official'. Rulers who understand that come close to saving the country'. The ruler then asks if there is one saying that can ruin a country. Confucius adds, 'No phrase can ever do that but here's one that comes close; 'Rulers find pleasure in say-ing whatever they want and no one disagrees'. If what rulers say is Good, it's good to be unopposed but if what's said isn't Good and not opposed, the country's close to being ruined'.

Commentary.

Virtuous psychotherapists appreciate the difficulties of psychotherapy practice and they experience that even a single phrase can result in an 'aha' client insightful awakening or can completely derail a client relationship and come close to ending psychotherapy.

16. Text.

A ruler asks about governing. Confucius answers, 'Govern so that people who are near approve and those who are distant approach'.

Commentary.

Virtuous psychotherapists can measure the success of their psychotherapy practice by the number of clients who continue working with them and by the number of new client referrals that are made from past and current clients and previous and new referral sources.

17. Text.

An official asks about governing. Confucius says, 'Don't hurry matters and ignore minor considerations. Hurrying matters and minor considerations won't allow you to do anything thoroughly or to accomplish anything important'.

Commentary.

Virtuous psychotherapists allow psychotherapy to progress at its own pace without forcing or pushing the process and don't let attention to relatively minor issues interfere with the progress of addressing more important ones more thoroughly.

18. Text.

A ruler says to Confucius, 'In my state there's a person called 'Upright'. His father steals a sheep and he testifies against him'. Confucius says, 'In our state upright persons are quite different. A son and father cover for each other. This is also uprightness'.

Commentary.

Virtuous psychotherapists don't usually report crimes or ask that clients be arrested, except as mandated for very serious crimes or duty to warn offenses, e.g., homicide or threats of harm. If required to testify for clients, they don't deny a client's guilt for crimes committed, but do attempt to preserve their humanness as realistically as possible and to recommend consideration of mental health issues and psychological treatment needs and options in any sentencing determination.

19. Text.

A disciple asks about cultivating Goodness. Confucius says, 'In private life, be modest. In public life, be respectful. In relationships, be loyal. These virtues apply wherever you are, even among barbarians'.

Commentary.

Virtuous psychotherapists don't lose the Goodness of their virtues of modesty, respect and loyalty in whatever treatment setting they're working in or with whatever client population they're working with.

20. Text.

A disciple asks Confucius about the best gentlepersons. Confucius says, 'Persons who are upright in conduct in their home state and honor their ruler's orders in foreign lands'. The disciple asks, 'Who's next best?'. Confucius replies, 'Persons whom relatives commend for filial piety and the community considers respectful'. The disciple then asks, 'Who's next best?'. and Confucius says, 'Persons who stand by their word and complete actions they begin'. The disciple then asks about current government officials. Confucius says, 'Oh!. They're very small persons not worth considering'.

Commentary.

Virtuous psychotherapists are upright, loyal, respectful, true to their word, responsible and accountable and value and appreciate clients who share the same virtues.

21. Text.

Confucius says, 'If I can't find any persons who steer the middle course, I'll have to choose between cautious and impetuous persons. I'll settle for impetuous persons. At least, they get things done that cautious persons won't even try to do'.

Commentary.

Virtuous psychotherapists tend to appreciate clients who are moderate in their actions and often find that impulsive and assertive clients are easier to slow down than compulsive and unassertive clients are to speed up.

22. Text.

Confucius says, 'There's a saying, 'People who aren't steadfast can't be shaman-healers'. Well said!. If their moral virtue and power/de aren't stabilized, there's no point in consulting one. You don't have to be a shaman-healer to divine that!'.

Commentary.

Virtuous psychotherapists are morally upright and steadfast and their Goodness comes from the virtue, integrity, energy and power/de of Dao and enables them to not just deal with psychological-level issues with clients but to also activate and potentiate deeper healing and spiritual growth.

23. Text.

Confucius says, 'True gentlepersons are harmonizing but not necessarily agreeing. Common persons are agreeing but not necessarily harmonizing'.

Commentary.

Virtuous psychotherapists are generally harmonizing with clients but, at times, not necesarily agreeing with them. They maintain their integrity by not agreeing just for the sake of agreement and the false appearance of harmony.

24. Text.

A disciple asks, 'What can said about persons who are liked or disliked by the whole community'?. Confucius says, 'I don't know about them. But the best is that Good people like them and not Good people dislike them'.

Commentary.

Virtuous psychotherapists don't really like or dislike the clients with whom they work, even those who are either liked or disliked by members of their family and community.

25. Text.

Confucius says, 'Gentlepersons are easy to serve but difficult to please. They expect only what servers can do and aren't pleased by anything other than the Way. Common people are difficult to serve but easy to please. They're pleased by things other than the Way but expect servers to do anything and everything'.

Commentary.

Virtuous psychotherapists don't expect clients to do anything that they're not capable of doing with respect to psychotherapy techniques, methods and procedures and are pleased when some clients are able to share the Way of Dao.

26. Text.

Confucius says, 'Gentlepersons are dignified and not arrogant. Common persons are arrogant and not dignified'.

Commentary.

Vituous psychotherapists are dignified and not superior, proud or arrogant in psychotherapy relationships with clients.

27. Text.

Confucius says, 'Human beings who are straightforward, determined, diligent and modest are close to Goodness'.

Commentary.

Virtuous psychotherapists are close to Goodness when they're resolute, decisive, straightforward and modest in psychotherapy relationships with clients.

28. Text.

A disciple asks what gentlepersons are like. Confucius answers, 'They're earnest, congenial and harmonious with siblings and friends'.

Commentary

Virtuous psychotherapists are serious about conducting psychotherapy, are friendly (but not 'friends') and develop harmonious relationships with psychotherapy clients.

29/30. Texts.

Confucius says, 'Rulers who follow the Way see to it that people are educated and trained in moral virtues/de for seven years before considering them for participating in wars. Not doing so before sending them to war is betraying, endangering, abandoning and sacrificing them'.

Commentary.

Virtuous psychotherapists assist some clients in developing the moral power/de of Dao, but not usually for the purpose of humanely preparing them to participate in wars.

水

THE ANALECTS
BOOK FOURTEEN
XIAN ASKED XIAN WEN

XIAN WEN

憲 問

HUMAN BEINGS AND CONDUCT

1. Text.

A disciple asks about shameful conduct. Confucius says, 'Whether or not a state is ruled according to the Way, just being concerned with receiving rewards is shameful'. The disciple then asks, 'Can persons who are free of coveting, competing, boasting and resenting be called Good?'. Confucius says, 'Such persons do what's difficult but I don't know if they're Good'.

Commentary.

Virtuous psychotherapists find psychotherapy work with clients sufficiently rewarding just for and as what it is. They are relatively free of ego-attachment to coveting, competing, being rewarded and praised, boasting and resentment.

2. Text.

Confucius says, 'Gentlepersons who think only of the comforts of home aren't worthy of the name'.

Commentary.

Virtuous psychotherapists generally feel at home in their professional work setting which, however, at times may not be completely comfortable.

3. Text.

Confucius says, 'When the Way prevails in the state, speak and act righteously and when it doesn't, be righteous in action but cautious in speech'.

Commentary.

Virtuous psychotherapists are usually confident in speaking and acting cautiously and righteously regardless of the nature of circumstances and situations.

4. Text.

Confucius says, 'Human beings who have moral virtue/de are eloquent but those who are eloquent may not necessarily possess moral virtue. Good human beings are courageous but those who are courageous may not necessarily possess Goodness'.

Commentary.

Virtuous psychotherapists possess the Goodness, moral virtue, integrity, energy and power/de of Dao and are usually eloquent and courageous human beings.

5. Text.

A disciple comments to Confucius, 'A skillful archer and a strong warrior both don't die a natural death but two other persons devote themselves to agriculture and end up possessing the state'. Later Confucius says to another disciple, 'This disciple is a gentleperson and correctly understands moral virtue's integrity and power!'.

Commentary.

Virtuous psychotherapists tend to appreciate those clients who support and provide for the basic and essential needs of human beings rather those who possess war-like mentalities and abilities.

6. Text.

Confucius says, 'Some gentlepersons may lack Goodness but common persons don't usually possess Goodness'.

Commentary.

Virtuous psychotherapists don't lack Goodness and are gentlepersons.

7. Text.

Confucius says, 'When human beings are loving of and loyal to fellow human beings, how can they not encourage them to be Good and instruct them to do Right ?'.

Commentary.

Virtuous psychotherapists lovingly and loyally support and encourage clients to be Good and do Right and to make the effort that it often takes to engage in and to sustain deep psychotherapy work.

8. Text.

Confucius says, 'When government mandates are prepared; they are drafted, checked, discussed, edited, revised and polished by several officials before being issued'.

Commentary.

Any written professional documents reports, letters, etc. are thoroughly reviewed, discussed, revised and finalized by virtuous psychotherapists before being used or sent (now probably not 'mailed').

9. Text.

Confucius is asked about an official and says, 'He's a kind and generous person'. He's next asked about a second official and disparagingly exclaims, 'That person!. That person!'. He's then asked about a third official and commendably says, 'He's good, very capable and isn't even resented by a person whom he penalized'.

Commentary.

Virtuous psychotherapists are kind, generous, skilled and effective and capably do what needs to be accomplished in psychotherapy work and aren't resented by clients.

10. Text.

Confucius says, 'Being poor and not resentful is more difficult than being wealthy and not arrogant'.

Commentary.

In spite of having a thriving psychotherapy practice, possibly accruing considerable financial wealth and enjoying an admirable professional reputation; virtuous psychotherapists aren't arrogant. And if their practice isn't thriving, they aren't resentful.

11. Text.

Confucius says that a certain official is more fit to be the auditor of a noble family rather than a state minister'.

Commentary.

Virtuous psychotherapists are generally satisfied with, and fulfilled by, their individual psychotherapy practice and don't usually aspire to more restrictive administrative positions in academic institutions or treatment facilities.

12. Text.

A disciple asks Confucius about complete human beings. Confucius answers, 'They're wise, free of desire, courageous, skillful and cultivate ritual and music. Also, they pursue gain only if Right, risk their lives in danger, stand by what they say and keep promises that they make. These are complete human beings.'

Commentary.

Virtuous psychotherapists are knowledgeable; not greedy for clients; conduct psychotherapy meetings resourcefully and skillfully; are cultivated in the art and methods of psychotherapy, make correct and often courageous interventions and dependably stand by their words and reliably keep promises that they make with clients.

13. Text.

Confucius asks a disciple about his master who reportedly doesn't speak, laugh or accept things. The disciple says, 'People are exaggerating. The master only speaks when it's timely and appropriate, only laughs when genuinely delighted and only accepts things when it's right to do so.' Confucius replies, 'Is that so?. Is that really so?'.

Commentary.

The expressions, actions and interactions of virtuous psychotherapists in the psychotherapy relationship with clients are genuine, correct, timely, appropriate and reciprocal.

14. Text.

Confucius says, 'An official requests a ruler to grant a fief to his brother. It's said that no pressure is applied, but I don't believe it'.

Commentary.

Virtuous psychotherapists don't make deals with or put pressure on psychotherapy clients.

15. Text.

Confucius says, 'One ruler is upright and not crafty and another ruler is crafty and not upright.'

Commentary.

Virtuous psychotherapists are upright, aren't clever in making interpretations and aren't crafty in making interventions with psychotherapy clients.

16. Text.

A disciple asks, 'When this ruler assassinates his brother, one official dies attempting to save him and another does nothing. Did the latter official fall short of Goodness?'. Confucius says, 'Due to the latter official's support, this ruler's able to convene the rulers of many other states multiple times without resorting to force or warfare. This is his Goodness!'.

Commentary.

Virtuous psychotherapists experience that sometimes the seemingly incorrect actions of clients result in benefits and that the seemingly correct ones may not.

17. Text.

A second disciple comments, 'The inaction of the latter official isn't Good because after murdering his brother, this ruler appoints him as prime minister?'. Confucius reiterates, 'By doing so, this ruler becomes a leader of the regional feudal rulers and brings good order to the whole state that's still benefiting us to this day. Were it not for this prime minister, we'd all be barbarians …'.

Commentary.

Again, virtuous psychotherapists experience that client actions that may initially appear incorrect may sometimes result in positive effects, results and benefits.

18. Text.

An official is promoted by a ruler and has his associate promoted along with him. Confucius hearing of this, says of the official, 'It's for good reason that he's considered to be someone who assists people to attain government positions.'

Commentary.

Virtuous psychotherapists often support, assist and recommend current and former clients when they're applying for and being considered for employment opportunities.

19. Text.

Confucius considers a ruler not be a follower of the Way. An official asks Confucius, 'Why then doesn't he lose the state?'. Confucius replies, 'He has a diplomat to handle foreign envoys, a priest to conduct ancestral ceremonies and a commander-in-chief to lead the army. How can he fail?'.

Commentary.

Virtuous psychotherapists generally assume full responsibility for all aspects of their psychotherapy practice instead of delegating some operational tasks to others and don't experience any difficulties, complications or failures because of doing so.

20. Text.

Confucius says, 'Speak carefully and modestly about Goodness. It may prove to be beyond your power to live up to it and your ability to put it into action'.

Commentary.

Virtuous psychotherapists are attuned to, accorded with, embody and enact the Goodness of the Way/Dao and seldom make it an object of discussion, since it essentially is an ineffable ultimate reality and not simply an abstract mental concept.

21. Text.

A ruler of one state is assassinated and Confucius dutifully responds according to protocol by first informing the ruler of a neighboring state saying, 'I request that the assassin be punished'. The ruler breaks protocol and says, 'Go and inform the heads of the Three Great Families' ... Confucius dutifully but disappointedly informs The Three Greats but they're disinterested and refuse his request.

Commentary.

Except for reporting ethical violations made by trainees, interns and colleagues; virtuous psychotherapists may experience a bureaucratic run-around when obliged to communicate other important information to high-ranking administrative officials who avoid responsibilities by 'kicking the can down the road'.

22. Text.

A disciple asks how to serve a ruler. Confucius says, 'Don't oppose rulers by deception instead of being open, direct and straightforward with them'.

Commentary.

Virtuous psychotherapists confront colleagues and supervisors openly, directly and straightforwardly and don't oppose or undermine them, e.g., through deception and by gossiping.

23. Text.

Confucius says, 'Gentlepersons focus upon what is higher and progress upward. Small persons focus upon what is lower and regress downward'.

Commentary.

Virtuous psychotherapists don't usually judge and rank clients and they focus upon and make progress with client issues that could be judged to be either 'higher' or 'lower' in importance.

24. Text

Confucius says, 'In olden days, human beings study to cultivate learning and self-improvement and nowadays they study to impress and please other people'.

Commentary.

Virtuous psychotherapists study and learn for self-awareness, self-understanding, self-development and self-improvement; to increase their psychotherapy competencies and proficiencies and not to impress students, trainees, interns, colleagues or clients with their knowledge.

25. Text.

Confucius receives a messenger from an official and asks, 'What's your master up to?'. The messenger replies, 'My master's trying to decrease failings but hasn't yet been successful'. After the messenger leaves, Confucius approvingly says, 'What a messenger!. What a message!'.

Commentary.

Virtuous psychotherapists value clients who are working on self-awareness, self-understanding and self-improvement and, in the process, appreciate being provided with information about them according to the protocols and restrictions of confidentiality.

26/27. Texts.

Confucius says, 'Don't discuss policies that aren't commensurate with the responsibilities of your rank and office'. A disciple says, 'Gentlepersons, even in their thoughts, don't depart from what's appropriate to their rank and position'. Confucius adds, 'Gentlepersons don't let their words outrun their actions'.

Commentary.

Virtuous psychotherapists, in their thinking and speaking, only consider and communicate what they know to be true from, and according to, their concrete and direct personal and professional experience. They 'walk their talk', i.e., they speak and act authentically and congruently from first-hand experience.

28. Text.

Confucius says, 'The Way of gentlepersons is three-fold but I haven't fully realized any of them. Gentlepersons who are truly Good, wise and courageous aren't worried, confused or afraid'. A disciple counters, 'But Master, this is your Way of being!'.

Commentary.

Virtuous psychotherapists are modest about any virtues of Goodness, wisdom and courage.

29. Text.

A disciple is continually comparing other disciples. Confucius facetiously says, 'How wise and incomparable is this disciple!. I don't have time for this sort of thing'.

Commentary.

Virtuous psychotherapists value uniqueness and don't waste professional time comparing psychotherapy clients.

30. Text.

Confucius says, 'Gentlepersons don't worry about people not recognizing their abilities, accomplishments and merits. They worry about their own inabilities, failures and shortcomings'.

Commentary.

Virtuous psychotherapists are more concerned about their limitations, shortcomings, inadequacies and inabilities than about not having their abilities, skills, competencies and proficiencies recognized by students, trainees, interns, colleagues and clients.

31. Text.

Confucius says, 'Wise human beings don't expect persons to be false, deceptive and untrustworthy but are the first to recognize when they are'.

Commentary.

Virtuous psychotherapists don't have negative preconceptions about clients or expect them to be inauthentic, dishonest and untrustworthy but recognize if and when they are.

32. Text.

A recluse asks Confucius, 'What's your object in traveling here and there?. Is it just to show off that you're a clever talker and to gain a reputation?'. Confucius replies, 'I've no desire to be a clever talker or to gain a reputation, I just dislike being rigidly stuck in one place'.

Commentary.

Virtuous psychotherapists are flexible and don't attempt to convince clients of, or to have them agree with, their observations, reflections, feedback, interpretations, etc..

33. Text.

Confucius says, 'A good horse isn't famous for its physical strength, abilities and performance but for its inner virtuous nature'.

Commentary.

Virtuous psychotherapists generally value, in themselves and clients; inner qualities of the moral virtue, integrity, energy and power/de of Dao rather than only physical strength, abilities and performance.

34. Text.

A person asks, 'What about the saying, 'Meet hatred with kindness'?'. Confucius says, 'Yes, but then with what do you meet kindness?. Meet kindness with kindness'.

Commentary.

Virtuous psychotherapists address and meet any negative or hateful transference feelings of clients uprightly, kindly and straightforwardly and with the energy and power of their inner virtue/de.

35. Text.

Confucius says, 'No one understands me!'. A disciple asks, 'Why do you say that?'. Confucius replies, 'I don't resent Heaven or blame human beings. I study to learn about what's here below to understand what's high above. Maybe Heaven understands me!'.

Commentary.

Virtuous psychotherapists don't resent or blame the workings of Heaven or the actions of clients and if their Goodness and Rightness aren't understood or recognized down here in the psychotherapy world, it may be in a higher heavenly realm.

36. Text.

A disciple of another master reports to Confucius that an official is slandering one of their disciples saying, 'My master's upset by this but I believe that I can publically expose this official and have him appropriately punished'. Confucius says, 'If it's the will of Heaven that the Way prevails, the Way will prevail. But if it's not, then the Way won't prevail. What can you do to affect the will of Heaven?'.

Commentary.

Virtuous psychotherapists appreciate that higher powers and greater forces than human and personal ones may be operating when the lives of clients are influenced and affected and progress and unfold in the ways that they do.

37. Text.

Confucius says, 'Some human beings withdraw because of a disordered world or because of a disordered state. Others withdraw because of a ruler's discourteous looks or because of people's hostile words. I know seven recluses who do this'.

Commentary.

Virtuous psychotherapists aren't so over-identified with the disorders of the world, government and society that they withdraw from them. Instead, they create the setting, circumstances and conditions that suitably, optimally and effectively support the harmonious order and conduct of their psychotherapy practice.

38. Text.

A disciple spends the night at a frontier and is asked by the gate-keeper, 'Where are you from?' The disciple answers, 'From Confucius'. The gate-keeper comments, 'Oh, he's the one who knows that what he's doing is useless but keeps on doing it, correct?'.

Commentary.

Good gentle psychotherapists don't continue psychotherapy interactions and interventions that are meaningless, pointless, useless, fruitless, ineffective, unproductive and unbeneficial.

39. Text.

Confucius is playing stone-chimes and a passing worker comments, 'How passionately he plays the chimes!'. But when Confucius stops playing, says, ... 'A talent that no one recognizes has nothing left to do but give up!. If water's deep, wade carefully and get wet; if it's shallow, lift up your skirts and move on'. Confucius sarcastically replies, 'Yes, quite right. But that's the easy way out!'.

Commentary.

Virtuous psychotherapists accept the psychotherapy situation as it is and respond to and move within it in whatever ways are appropriate for, and relvant to, the specific nature, circumstances and issues of particular clients.

40. Text.

A disciple says, 'It's said of this ruler that when mourning, he doesn't speak for three years. What does this mean?'. Confucius answers, 'Not just this ruler but all ancient rulers follow this ritual practice. Others don't disturb them and assume their duties for them'.

Commentary.

Virtuous psychotherapists often respectfully honor and mourn the death of clients and the termination of psychotherapy work with them for a long time but don't silence their practice.

41. Text.

Confucius says, 'When rulers love and observe ritual propriety, the people willingly serve them and are easy to govern'.

Commentary.

When virtuous psychotherapists love their psychotherapy work, clients are generally cooperative, collaborative and relatively easy to work with.

42. Text.

A disciple asks about gentlepersons. Confucius says, 'They respectfully and carefully cultivate themselves in order to bring security and peace to the whole populace. Even the ancient great Sage-Rulers find that difficult to do'.

Commentary.

Virtuous psychotherapists cultivate themselves to respect, care for and assist clients and to help them feel safe, secure and at ease in and throughout the psychotherapy relationship process.

43. Text.

A old friend is sitting sprawled out casually awaiting Confucius. Confucius sees this and says, 'When young you've no respect for elders, when older you've nothing to show or to pass on and now you just keep growing older and older without having the courtesy to die like a useless pest'. And then Confucius gently strikes him across the shins with a stick to remind him to correct his posture.

Commentary.

Virtuous psychotherapists are honest and candid (and at times playful?) with long-standing clients and professional colleagues, in spite of their past youthful disrespect of authority, later lack of accomplishments and current unconventional lifestyles and ignorance of social decorum.

44. Text.

A young boy delivers messages to Confucius. A disciple asks, 'Is he improving himself?'. Confucius answers, 'From the way that he inappropriately sits in elder's places and walks beside them; I'd say that he just wants to take a short-cut and to grow up fast instead of learning to improve himself'.

Commentary.

Virtuous psychotherapists are committed to continually improving themselves and their psychotherapy work from just where they currently are in their personal growth, professional development and spiritual evolution rather than being prematurely ahead of and out of synch with themselves.

水

THE ANALECTS
BOOK FIFTEEN
DUKE LING OF WEY

WEI LING GONG

衛靈公

GENTLEPERSONS AND CONDUCT

1. Text.

A ruler asks about military battle formations. Confucius says, 'I've some knowledge about ordering rituals but I've never studied warfare'. The next day Confucius leaves the state.

Commentary.

Virtuous psychotherapists are knowledgeable about techniques, methods and procedures of psychotherapy; are rarely versed in military matters and usually don't associate with human beings who are militaristic, military-minded and pro-war.

2. Text.

Confucius is traveling, supplies are running out and disciples are weak. A disciple angrily says, 'Do gentlepersons suffer such circumstances?'. Confucius says, 'Yes, gentlepersons exerience hardships and firmly withstand them. Only small persons aren't able to'.

Commentary.

Virtuous psychotherapists maintain the structure, safety, solidity, stability and security of the psychotherapy relationship even during difficult interactions, conflicts or power struggles with clients.

3. Text.

Confucius asks a disciple, 'Do you regard me as someone who learns by studying and remembering knowledge. The disciple replies, 'Yes, isn't that so?'. Confucius retorts, ' No!. I learn by having one thread, the Way, upon which to string everything together'.

Commentary.

Virtuous psychotherapists integrate all of their theoretical and methodological knowledge about psychotherapy upon the single reality of Dao, its virtue/de and being a wise, courageous, effective, meaningful and beneficial psychotherapist for clients.

4. Text.

Confucius says to a disciple, 'Few are those human beings who understand and enact the moral virtue/de of the Way/Dao'.

Commentary.

Virtuous psychotherapists are some of the few psychotherapists who understand, internalize, assimilate, practice and live the moral virtue, integrity, energy and power/de of Dao.

5. Text.

Confucius says, 'Legendary Ancient Sage-Rulers govern by wu-wei/effortless action. All that they do is seriously, respectfully and reverently face South'.

Commentary.

Virtuous psychotherapists naturally influence and positively effect the conduct of psychotherapy and the progress of clients by their presence alone and the efficacious resonant energy and power of their virtue/de of Dao.

6. Text.

A disciple asks about getting along with people. Confucius says, 'Be true and faithful to your word and respectful and sincere in your actions and you'll get along well enough, even with barbarians. But if you're untrue and untrustworthy in your speech and disrespectful and insincere in your actions, you won't get along well even with neighbors. See these principles in front of you when you're standing in your place or riding in your carriage and you'll be certain to get along with people'. The disciple writes these words on his sash.

Commentary.

Virtuous psychotherapists are true, loyal, respectful and sincere and are not untrustworthy, disloyal, dispespectful and insincere in their words to, and actions with, clients; who are then more cooperative and collaborative and less prone to making negative transference projections onto them or to having conflicts and power struggles with them.

7. Text.

Confucius says, 'How righteous is this official!. He's straight as an arrow when the Way prevails in the state and when it doesn't. What a gentleperson this other official is!. He takes office when the Way prevails in the state and resigns when it doesn't'.

Commentary.

Virtuous psychotherapists are upright, straight and consistently act wisely and appropriately in psychotherapy in accord with the presence or absence of Dao in their conscious awareness.

8. Text.

Confucius says, 'Not speaking about the Way with human beings who can understand is a waste of human being and speaking about the Way with human beings who can't understand is a waste of words. Wise human beings don't waste human beings or words'.

Commentary.

Virtuous psychotherapists discern which clients they can and can't beneficially speak with about Dao and its virtue/de and their relevance for, and applicability to, psychotherapy practice.

9. Text.

Confucius says, 'Human beings living Goodness with the heart of a real and true human being won't seek life at the cost of the virtue of Goodness. Perhaps because they've already devoted their whole life to Goodness'.

Commentary.

Virtuous psychotherapists who have the heart and qualities of Good human beings don't seek to live their life and to conduct their psychotherapy practice in ways that sacrifice Goodness because they've already devoted their personal and professional life to being Good human beings.

10. Text.

A disciple asks how to become Good. Confucius answers, 'Artisans intending to do good work first sharpen their tools. Wherever you dwell, serve the most worthy officials and befriend the most worthy gentlepersons of Goodness'.

Commentary.

In their intention and commitment to being Good psychotherapists and doing Good psychotherapy work, virtuous psychotherapists are usually educated, trained and supervised by master psychotherapists who themselves are worthy and Good human beings and professionals.

11. Text.

A disciple asks about governing . Confucius says, 'Go by the calendar, use the coaches and wear the ceremonial hats of the three previous dynasties. Only listen to beautiful and peaceful music, ban licentious tunes and avoid glib talkers'.

Commentary.

Virtuous psychotherapists create a Good psychotherapy practice by modeling its approaches, methods and procedures after the practices of Good master psychotherapists and not those pretending to be or posing as such.

12. Text.

Confucius says, 'Human beings who don't worry about what's far off, soon find something worse than worry close by'.

Commentary.

Virtuous psychotherapists are aware of and consider future possibilities, as well as present actualities, of clients and psychotherapy practice and make early and preventative interventions to avoid potentially future negative experiences and outcomes.

13. Text.

Confucius says, 'It's hopeless!. I can't find human beings who love moral virtue more than female beauty'.

Commentary.

On the contrary, virtuous psychotherapists have no preference for, and experience no conflict in, focusing upon and working with issues of both female beauty and sexuality and ethical values and moral virtue.

14. Text.

Confucius says, 'This official is a thief of the positions of others. He knows other officials who are more qualified than he is but doesn't recommend them for positions equal to his'.

Commentary.

Virtuous psychotherapists may have collegial professional relationships with other psychotherapists who are more qualified than they are. They aren't threatened by them, don't compete with them, usurp their authority, co-opt their methods or fail to recommend them for better positions than their own in the field of pychotherapy.

15. Text.

Confucius says, 'Requiring more of oneself and blaming others less is the way to avoid ill-will and resentment'.

Commentary.

Virtuous psychotherapists responsibly and diligently work with themselves and their own issues equally as much or more than they do with those of clients and are not judgmental about or critical of clients and their progress.

16. Text.

Confucius says, 'If human beings don't continully ask themselves, 'What am I to do about this, what am I to do about this?, what am I to do about them, what am I to do about them?''.

Commentary.

Virtuous psychotherapists can do their most effective and successful psychotherapy work with clients who are highly motivated, responsibly self-examining and self-reflective, insightful and undefensive and unresistant to the psychotherapy relationship process.

17. Text.

Confucius says, 'Human beings who spend a whole day together without ever discussing matters of right and wrong yet content themselves with performing petty acts of mercy and justice are hopeless'.

Commentary.

Virtuous psychotherapists conference together to investigate, explore and discuss deeper moral issues underlying their standpoints and work with regard to psychotherapy ethics, psychological and psychopathological conditions, right and wrong client behavior and appropriate and inappropriate treatment approaches, conduct and interventions.

18. Text.

Confucius says, 'Gentlepersons cultivate Goodness and Rightness, use ritual propriety to put them into practice, are modest in speaking and trustworthy in completing actions'.

Commentary.

Virtuous psychotherapists work with what is ethically Good and technically Right in psychotherapy practice, speak modestly and set modest treatment objectives with clients that can be faithfully accomplished by them.

19. Text.

Confucius says, 'Gentlepersons worry about their lack of ability and not by the failure of other persons to understand them or to recognize their accomplishments'.

Commentary.

Virtuous psychotherapists are concerned about any lack of ability, skill, proficiency or competency and continue responsibly working on developing them. They aren't bothered by a lack of professional recognition of their abilities, skills, proficiencies and competencies by clients or colleagues.

20. Text.

Confucius says, 'Many human beings worry about not achieving a memorable reputation by or after the end of their life'.

Commentary

Most virtuous psychotherapists are generally unconcerned about currently or post-humously receiving professional recognition or a meritorious reputation.

21. Text.

Confucius says, 'Gentlepersons make demands upon themselves. Small persons make demands upon others'.

Commentary.

Virtuous psychotherapists make demands upon themselves and may make requests of clients but not demands upon them.

22. Text.

Confucius says, 'Gentlepersons are confident but not aggressive and contentious and ally with individual gentlepersons rather than with parties and movements'.

Commentary.

Virtuous psychotherapists are self-assured and not contentious and ally themselves with individual clients and colleagues rather than with partisan groups or movements.

23. Text.

Confucius says, 'Gentlepersons don't accept persons because of what they're saying nor reject their sayings because of who and how they're being'.

Commentary.

Virtuous psychotherapists don't necessarily accept clients for what they say or necessarily reject what they say because of who and how they're being.

24. Text.

A disciple asks, 'Is there one word that can be used as a guide for living ?'. Confucius replies, 'Reciprocity, 'Don't do to other human beings what you don't want them to do to you' (the 'Silver Rule').

Commentary.

Virtuous psychotherapists are kind, considerate and empathic with clients; have mutual, interdependent, complementary and reciprocal relations with them and practice the 'Golden Rule' of 'Do unto others (clients) as you would have them do unto you' (psychotherapists).

25. Text.

Confucius says, 'I try to refrain from either praising or blaming human beings. But if I've praised someone, there's good reason for it. Human beings of today are the same as those of the three previous dynasties who practice the Good and Right Way.'

Commentary.

Virtuous psychotherapists appreciate the unique individualities and lives of clients and also realize that many of the issues of current clients are universal ones that human beings have been successfully and unsuccessfully working on for a very long time.

26. Text.

Confucius says, 'I remember days when in doubt scribes honestly leave blank spaces (instead of fill them in with interpolations) and when horse owners generously allow strangers to ride them. But that's all over now'.

Commentary.

Virtuous psychotherapists are comfortable with silences and don't fill in any pauses or empty spaces in interactions with clients during psychotherapy meetings. They are appropriately self-disclosing and generously share 'the tools of trade' of psychotherapy with clients.

27. Text

Confucius says, 'Clever talk disrupts the workings of moral virtue/de, just as minor impatience disrupts major projects'.

Commentary.

Virtuous psychotherapists don't use clever words and crafty methods or allow minor concerns to disrupt the efficacy, direction and progress of psychotherapy work with clients.

28. Text.

Confucius says, 'When everyone dislikes a person, careful study is necessary. When everyone likes a person, careful study is necessary'.

Commentary.

Virtuous psychotherapists carefully investigate and compassionately explore the histories, selves, psyches, lives, relationships, actions, etc. of clients; whether or not they are liked and likeable human beings.

29. Text.

Confucius says, 'Human beings are conscious of the Way and the ways of fellow human beings. The Way isn't conscious of the ways of human beings'.

Commentary.

Virtuous psychotherapists can assist clients in being conscious of the Way/Dao and of their own ways of being and realize that there's no way that the Way/Dao is conscious of them.

30. Text.

Confucius says, 'To make mistakes but not correct them is making another and possibly greater mistake'.

Commentary.

Virtuous psychotherapists support and assist clients in consciously exerting the effort it takes to become aware of, change and correct faults, mistakes and errors and to not make more or greater ones by not doing so.

31. Text.

Confucius says, 'I spend a whole day without food and a whole night without sleep in thinking. But it's useless and it'd be better to use the time to study and learn'.

Commentary.

Virtuous psychotherapists experience that thinking and conceptualizing abstractly is not necessarily as productive and useful as studying and learning concretely and experientially.

32. Text.

Confucius says, 'Gentlepersons are more concerned with the Way of life than with making a living. Farming can involve economic shortfalls and learning can bring financial pay but gentlepersons' concern is with progressing in the Way and not with poverty or wealth'.

Commetary.

Virtuous psychotherapists are generally more concerned with progressing in according with Dao/the Way rather than with building a financially lucrative psychotherapy practice by networking referral sources for a large number of high-fee clients.

33. Text.

Confucius says, 'Human beings whose wisdom brings them into power need Goodness to secure that power so as not to lose it. Wise human beings who have their power secured by Goodness need dignity for people so as to be respected. Wise human beings with power secured by Goodness and respect given through dignity who don't handle people according to prescribed ritual are less than Good'.

Commentary.

Virtuous psychotherapists are successful due to their psychological wisdom, fundamental Goodness, dignity and respect for clients and the use of appropriate, relevant, consensually agreed upon and effective psychotherapy techniques, methods, procedures and processes.

34. Text.

Confucius says, 'Gentlepersons aren't valued for minor accomplishments and are entrusted with great responsibilities. Small persons aren't entrusted with great responsibilities and are valued for minor accomplishments'.

Commentary.

Virtuous psychotherpists assume the great human responsibilities involved in conducting psychotherapy and appropriately suit reflections and interpretations and interactions and interventions to the unique abilities of clients and to the specific nature of both their larger and smaller issues being focused upon.

35. Text.

Confucius says, 'Goodness is more vital to human beings than water and fire. I see human beings die walking into water and walking upon fire but never losing their life walking the path of Goodness'.

Commentary.

Virtuous psychotherapists consider that even risk-taking in psychotherapy is safer than deep-diving and fire-walking, especially when swimming and treading the Dao/Way of Goodness.

36. Text.

Confucius says, 'When it comes to practicing and living Goodness, don't defer to anyone, not even your teacher'.

Commentary.

In the greater interests and service of clients cultivating and developing themselves and their Goodness, virtuous psychotherapists have no issue with clients not listening to them, not deferring to them, trying to exceed them in any way or succeeding in doing so.

37. Text.

Confucius says, 'Gentlepersons are consistent and cooperative but neither rigidly unbending and unyielding nor blindly trusting and compliant'.

Commentary.

Virtuous psychotherapists are consistent and cooperative in their relationships with clients and in the conduct of psychotherapy; are aware of issues of authority, power differentials and trust, don't have uncritical belief or blind faith in clients and don't use rigid or inflexible techniques and methods in their treatment.

38. Text.

Confucius says, 'In serving a ruler, be intent upon respectfully and dutifully completing assigned tasks and not bent upon receiving rewards'.

Commentary.

In serving clients, virtuous psychotherapists are respectfully, responsibly and dutifully focused more upon successfully, effectively and beneficially playing their role in, and completing client objectives of, psychotherapy work and less upon receiving rewards for it.

39. Text.

Confucius says, 'With regard to human beings seeking to be taught and to learn, there are no social class distinctions, although the forms of instruction may be different'.

Commentary.

Virtuous psychotherapists work with clients from all different social levels and cultural identities. The different ways of conducting psychotherapy by virtuous psychotherapists are ones of form rather than essence and are suited to unique clients and issues.

40. Text.

Confucius says, 'Don't seek advice or take counsel from those human beings who follow a different Way'.

Commentary.

Virtuous psychotherapists generally believe that their Way of conducting psychotherapy is the most correct, effective, helpful, useful and beneficial for their clients but they're still open to learn from colleagues who use different treatment approaches in order to better empathize and work with clients.

41. Text.

Confucius says, 'In speaking, what matters are words that clearly and fully convey meaning'.

Commentary.

Virtuous psychotherapists recognize the value, importance and effectiveness of clients being able to clearly and fully comprehend the meaning of their verbalizations, observations, reflections, feedback and interpretations.

42. Text.

A blind music master comes to meet with Confucius and Confucius tells him where the steps are when escorting him in, where the mats are when helping him be seated and where the location of everyone present is. Later, a disciple asks Confucius, 'Is this the way to handle a music master?'. Confucius answers, 'Yes, it's the only proper way to handle a music master'.

Commentary.

Virtuous psychotherapists typically adhere to the most appropriate, empathic and effective prescribed ways of considering, relating to and assisting clients and their unique characteristics, needs, circumstances, abilities and issues.

水

THE ANALECTS
BOOK SIXTEEN
CHIEF OF THE JI CLAN

JHI SHI

季 氏

THREE AND NINE THINGS

1. Text.

A ruler is deciding to attack a small neighboring state. Two disciples who are officials in the service of the ruler inform Confucius who says, 'You're responsible for this crime'. ... One disciple explains, 'The ruler desires it, we don't'. Confucius says, ' ... Of what use are you if you see your ruler erring and don't intervene?'... One disciple continues, 'The neighboring state is strongly fortified and if not taken now will give the ruler trouble in the future'. ... Confucius says, 'Your ruler's state is already in trouble and disordered, nothing can save it and now he wants to attack a neighboring state?. The threat to the state isn't from the neighboring one but from inside his own'.

Commentary.

Virtuous psychotherapists do consider early preventative interventions but don't usually make direct pre-emptive strikes on current client issues. They look first within themselves and their treatment methods when working with and intervening with highly defended and resistant clients to understand any difficulties in treating them rather than judging, rejecting or referring them to other practitioners.

2. Text.

Confucius says, 'When the Way prevails in the state, rites and music are ordered by the ruler. When the Way doesn't prevail, such orders are made by lower officials ... and the state usually declines and falls. ... When the Way prevails in the world, the state isn't governed by lower officials and common people'.

Commentary.

Virtuous psychotherapists are committed to according with and embodying the moral virtue and power/de of Dao, are in complete charge of the conducting of their psychotherapy practice and sustain its viability and success by not referring clients to interns or to psychological assistants for treatment.

3. Text.

Confucius says, 'The ruling power of a state is lost for five generations and its government is turned over to officials for four generations. ... No wonder it's declining and failing'.

Commentary.

Again, virtuous psychotherapists maintain successful control of, and responsibility for, the managing and conducting of their psychotherapy practice, sustain its viability and success by continuing to work with their clients by not referring them to interns and psychological assistants for treatment.

4. Text.

Confucius says, 'Three kinds of friendship are beneficial; with upright, trustworthy and well-learned human beings. Three kinds of friendship are harmful; with ingratiating, hypocritical and clever-speaking persons'.

Commentary.

Virtuous psychotherapists typically establish, enjoy and benefit from collegial relationships with other professional psychotherapists who are upright, trustworthy and knowledgeable and who aren't ingratiating, hypocritical and clever-speaking.

5. Text.

Confucius says, 'Three kinds of pleasure are beneficial; harmonius ritual and music, honoring the Goodness of human beings and having worthy friends. Three kinds of pleasure are harmful; arrogance, extravagant entertainment and aimlessly wandering around'.

Commentary.

Virtuous psychotherapists obtain pleasure, satisfaction, gratification, enjoyment, fulfillment and benefit from a well-managed and well-conducted psychotherapy practice, honoring and respecting the Goodness of clients and consulting with professional colleagues and by not being arrogant, extravagant and aimlessly wandering about randomly using techniques and treatment interventions.

6. Text.

Confucius says, 'Three possible mistakes to make with gentlepersons are; speaking before being called upon, forwardness; not speaking when called upon, evasiveness and speaking before gauging their expression, blindness'.

Commentary.

Virtuous psychotherapists maintain professional behavioral and relationship etiquette with clients, are neither too assertive nor unresponsive and carefully and closely observe their body language and expressions.

7. Text.

Confucius says, 'Three things that gentlepersons are on guard about. When young and qi energy is strong and unfocused, lust;

in prime, when qi energy is solidified and unyielding, aggression and in old age, when qi energy is weak and declined, greed'.

Commentary.

Regardless of their age; virtuous psychotherapists are cognizant of and abide by the ethics of not having sexual relationships with clients, not aggressively engaging in competetive power struggles with clients and not exploiting and taking financial advantage of clients.

8. Text.

Confucius says, 'Three things that gentleperson are in awe of are; the will of Heaven, morally great human beings and the words of Divine Sages. The small person doesn't know the will of Heaven, disrespects morally great persons and mocks the words of Divine Sages'.

Commentary.

Virtuous psychotherapists honor, are respectful of and abide by the ethical standards of their professional organizations, of morally great master psychotherapists and of the wisdom teachings of great spiritual masters and sages.

9. Text.

Confucius says, 'The highest human beings are those who are born wise. The next are those who become wise by studying and learning. And the next are those who struggle in acquiring knowledge but still persist. The lowest persons are those who struggle without learning anything'.

Commentary.

Some virtuous psychotherapists are born wise; others become wise through studying and learning and some continually struggle with acquiring knowledge and either acquire it or never seem to acquire it.

10. Text.

Confucius says, 'Gentlepersons have nine concerns:

1) Is my vision clear?. Is my hearing acute?. Is my exression genial?.
2) Is my manner courteous?. Are my words loyal?. Am I respectful?.
3) When doubtful do I seek advice?. When angry do I think of effects?.
4) Do I assess whether it's correct to take the opportunity for gain?'.

Commentary.

Virtuous psychotherapists see and hear clients clearly and distinctly; are friendly, courteous and respectful in demeanor and are faithful in speaking and diligent in psychotherapy work. They consult with colleagues when in doubt, work internally with any angry or other negative countertransference feelings toward clients and do nothing that is unethical, incorrect or exploitive with clients in psychotherapy.

11. Text.

Confucius says, 'When gentlepersons see what's Good, they seize it. When they see what isn't Good, they avoid it. ... Some fulfill aims and realize the Way by secluded living and others by righteous actions. I hear about such persons but don't meet any.'

Commentary.

Virtuous psychotherapists hold onto what is Good and avoid what is not Good in psychotherapy practice. They value both solitiude and right actions that assist them in actualizing personal and professional objectives and realizing the Way/Dao and extending their influence to clients.

12. Text.

Confucius says, 'A wealthy ruler isn't praised for any Good virtues or Right deeds when he dies and two poor legendary brothers die of starvation and are still praised for being virtuous gentlepersons'.

Commentary.

Virtuous psychotherapists aren't usually praised for attaining great reputations or accruing great wealth in the practice of psychotherapy and, rather, are acknowledged for being virtuous gentlepersons and professionals.

13. Text.

A disciple asks the son of Confucius, 'As his son, are you taught special things?'. The son replies, 'No. On two different occasions, he's standing alone, I pass by and he asks, 'Do you study *The Odes* and *The Rites*?. If not, you'll have difficulty speaking and taking your stand'. So, I study *The Odes* and *The Rites*. I did hear these two things from him'. The disciple is delighted, saying, 'I ask about one thing and learn about three; *The Odes*, *The Rites* and that a gentleperson doesn't instruct their own son'.

Commentary.

Virtuous psychotherapists are well versed in psychological theories and psychotherapy techniques for their work with clients but they don't usually teach them to or use them for their own children, although their knowledge and skills inevitably inform and positively influence their parenting.

14. Text.

The wife of the ruler of a state is referred to by a ruler as 'My Lady'. She refers to herself as 'Little Child'. The people of the state refer to her as 'The Lord's Lady'. When in another state, the ruler calls her 'The Little Lord' and the people of that state also call her 'The Lord's Lady'.

Commentary.

Virtuous psychotherapists usually call clients by their first names and in teaching classes and case conferences refer to them generically as 'clients' or use pseudonyms to preserve their anonymity. If married, women are not considered as the 'Mrs. wives' of their husbands. 水

THE ANALECTS
BOOK SEVENTEEN
YANG HUO

YANG HUO

陽 貨

HUMAN NATURE AND SIX LOVES

1. Text.

An official wants to meet with Confucius who refuses to see him ... but later they accidently meet on a road. Alluding to Confucius, the official asks, 'Can one who hides the jewel of his talents in his bosom, allows the country to go astray, longs for office and misses opportunities to serve in affairs be called Good, wise and courageous? Certainly not!. Time slips by'. Confucius reluctantly says, 'Alright, I'll try to take office and serve'.

Commentary.

Virtuous psychotherapists are generally good, wise and courageous human beings who not only serve their clients in psychotherapy practice but usually, in some way, also serve their larger community.

2. Text.

Confucius says, 'Human beings are close together by nature and far apart through development'.

Commentary.

Virtuous psychotherapists feel close to clients by innate human nature and different from them through unique individual human development.

3. Text.

Confucius says, 'Only the most wise and the most unwise human beings don't change'.

Commentary.

Virtuous psychotherapists typically fall somewhere between the most wise and the most unwise of collegial psychotherapists and are constantly changing and transforming in themselves and in their psychotherapeutic work with clients.

4. Text.

Confucius visits a nearby town and hears the sound of stringed instruments and singing. With a wry smile he says, 'One doesn't use an ox-cleaver to kill a chicken'. A disciple says, 'I recall hearing you say, 'Gentlepersons who learn the Way love fellow human beings and common persons who learn the Way are easy to govern'. Confucius says, 'What you say is true. What I just said is a joke'.

Commentary.

Virtuous psychotherapists use psychotherapeutic approaches with clients that are appropriate to and harmonious with their unique human nature and being and to the particular issues with which they are working. They don't 'overkill' with interpretations and interventions. They refrain from asking clients to do more than they're able to do in the way of psychotherapy suggestions, procedures and experiments and they efficiently use a minimum number of techniques to achieve a maximum amount of results.

5. Text.

An official leads a revolt against a ruling family and asks Confucius to join in. One of his disciples disapproves saying, 'After refusing so many other similar requests, why go now?'. Confucius answers, 'In this instance, it's for a good reason and I may have a chance to recreate the Golden Age of the former dynasty'.

Commentary.

Virtuous psychotherapists respond positively to invitations to assist in, and opportunities for, making a significant difference in restoring and carrying forward the best of historical times and events in the professional practice of psychotherapy.

6. Text.

A disciple asks about Goodness. Confucius says, 'Rulers who put the five virtues of respect, sincerity, trustworthiness, diligence and kindness into practice in the state are Good. They're respected, popular, trusted, successful and served by the people'.

Commentary.

Virtuous psychotherapists who value, embody and enact virtues such as respect toward and sincerity with clients; trust and faith in themselves and clients; a strong and solid commitment to psychotherapy work and kindness toward clients are Good. They'll be respected and trusted by clients and won't have to worry about keeping clients or gaining new ones.

7. Text.

An officer leads a revolt and invites Confucius to participate. But a disciple says, 'I recall you saying that, 'A gentleperson won't enter the house of an evil-doer'. This officer is revolting. How can you join him?'. Confucius says, 'The saying is true but it's also said, 'Some things are so hard and so white, no grinding will ever wear them down and no soaking will ever turn them black'. Am I to forever be like a bitter gourd used for decoration and not eaten?'.

Commentary.

Virtuous psychotherapists enjoy the impeccable integrity of their essential nature and character and moral virtue/de and ethical Way of being and desire to be of useful and beneficial service wherever and whenever needed. They are confident that they are strong and courageous enough not to be changed for the worst when dealing with that which is, or those whom are, not Good.

8. Text.

Confucius asks a disciple, 'Have you ever heard about the Six Virtuous Loves and their Six Degenerations?'. The disciple answers, 'No, I haven't'. Confucius says, 'Sit here and I'll tell you and relates;

'1) Loving Goodness without loving learning, the Way degenerates into foolishness,

2) Loving wisdom without loving learning, the Way degenerates into randomness,

3) Loving fidelity without loving learning, the Way degenerates into unfaithfulness,

4) Loving uprightness without loving learning, the Way degenerates into harshness,

5) Loving action without loving learning, the Way degenerates into tumultuousness,

6) Loving courage without loving learning, the Way degenerates into recklessness'.

Commentary.

Virtuous psychotherapists love goodness, wisdom, fidelity, uprightness, action and courage. Because of their simultaneously loving learning the Way/Dao, these loves don't degenerate into their opposite extremes.

9. Text.

Confucius asks disciples, 'Why aren't you studying *The Odes*?. *The Odes* will help you to inspire spirit, sharpen eyes, improve relationships and express feelings. They can be used at home in serving parents or abroad in serving rulers. They'll also teach you the correct names of birds, animals, plants and trees'.

Commentary.

Virtuous psychotherapists often suggest and encourage clients to study inspiring, stimulating and self-improving literature; to learn about Nature, human nature and their own nature and to increase their identification with, empathy for, understanding of and sharing with fellow human beings.

10. Text.

Confucius asks his son, 'Are you studying the first two books of *The Odes* yet?. One who hasn't is like someone standing with their face against a blank wall who sees nothing and can't move forward'.

Commentary.

Virtuous psychotherapists occasionally check in with clients to see what, if any, literature they're reading, enjoying and learning from and seeing whether it contributes to their insights and progress in psychotherapy and in their lives.

11. Text.

Confucius says, 'Ritual, ritual!. Music, music!. They mean so much more than jade and silk, bells and drums!'.

Commentary.

Virtuous psychotherapists don't make interpretations in a routine and stereotyped manner or make interventions in a showy or perfunctory manner. They trust that the suggestions and recommendations that they make to clients and the techniques and methods that they use with clients deeply and meaningfully potentiate their self-awareness, self-acceptance, self-understanding, self-actualization, self-development, self-improvement and self-refinement.

12. Text.

Confucius says, 'Assuming an outward appearance of courage while inwardly trembling is as dishonest as a thief sneaking into a house through a hole in the wall'.

Commentary.

Virtuous psychotherapists encourage, support, facilitate and assist clients in being true to themselves and being genuine, authentic and inwardly and outwardly congruent in their self-presentation, self-expressions and relationships and not opening up a way to sneakily steal virtues by pretending.

13/14. Texts.

Confucius says, 'Self-righteous persons spoil moral virtue/de. Telling on by-ways what's heard on the high-Way abandons moral virtue/de'.

Commentary.

Virtuous psychotherapists don't allow ego-traits, ego-needs and ego-images to impair or abandon their moral virtue, integrity, energy and power/de of Dao or to squander and waste it on extraneous and irrelevant ego-dreams, ego-fantasies and ego-concerns.

15. Text.

Confucius says, 'How can a ruler be served alongside persons who, before getting office, think about nothing but how to get it and who, after getting office, care about nothing but how to keep it. And as soon as they see themselves in the slightest danger of losing office, there's nothing that they won't do to try to keep it'.

Commentary.

Virtuous psychotherapists attend to, but aren't preoccupied with; creating, maintaining, developing or insuring the viability, continuity and security of their psychotherapy practice. They know that it's primarily based upon their Good and Right psychotherapy work with clients.

16. Text.

In ancient times, three kinds of common people at least had three virtues that are now lost and have degenerated;

1) the impetuous were at least upright and now are insubordinate and rebellious.

2) the proud were at least principled and now are overly sensitive and quarrelsome.

3) the foolish were at least straightforward and now are clever, crafty and deceptive.

Commentary.

The clients of virtuous psychotherapists are rarely rebellious, quarrelsome or deceptive and are generally upright, principled and straightforward human beings.

17. Text.

Confucius says, 'Clever talk and a pretentious manner are rarely found in Goodness'.

Commentary.

Virtuous psychotherapists are unpretentious, use few words, choose words carefully and speak the truth when they do.

18. Text.

Confucius says, 'I dislike seeing purple obscuring red, immoral tunes corrupting classical music and glib tongues ruining clans and states'.

Commentary.

Virtuous psychotherapists dislike when admixed and conflated morals, unethical and immoral behavior and clever and glib speech obscure, corrupt and ruin moral virtue/de.

19. Text.

Confucius says, 'I'd rather not speak'. A disciple says, 'If you don't say anything, what would we disciples learn from you and have to pass on?'. Confucius adds, 'Heaven doesn't speak yet the four seasons cycle and the myriad creatures are born. Heaven doesn't say anything!. Heaven doesn't say a thing!'.

Commentary.

Virtuous psychotherapists are comfortable with silence, tend to speak very little and their moral virtue, integrity, energy and power/de of Dao constitute a presence and Goodness that in, of and by themselves are influential, catalytic and potentiating for client's awareness, insight, self-disclosure, change and transformation.

20. Text.

A messenger says that a person wants to meet with Confucius, who refuses with the excuse of ill-health. But as the messenger is leaving, Confucius takes up a zither and sings, making sure that the messenger hears him.

Commentary.

Virtuous psychotherapists may be selective about the clients and colleagues with whom they meet but don't usually make up or flaunt excuses if doing so.

21. Text.

A disciple asks about the three year mourning period and says that one year is long enough. He says, 'If gentlepersons suspend practicing rites and making music for three years they'll decay or die out ...' Confucius asks, 'Would you feel at ease eating fine rice and wearing silk brocade after a year?'. The disciple answers, 'Certainly'. Confucius says, 'Then do so but when true gentlepersons are in mourning, they're not comfortable or enjoy eating tasty food, hearing good music or relaxing at home. That's why they abstain for three years. But if you'd really feel at ease, there's no need to abstain'. After the disciple leaves, Confucius says, 'How inhumane!. A child only leaves its parents' arms after three years. The three year mourning period is a universal custom and practice. Wasn't this disciple too the joy of his father and mother for three whole years?'.

Commentary.

Virtuous psychotherapists don't set an arbitrary time limit for mourning deceased students, trainees, interns, colleagues and clients and appreciate that mourning the loss of loved ones takes as long as it takes and may never really end.

22. Text.

Confucius says, 'Human beings who do nothing but eat all day and never use their minds are hopeless. There are even challenging games to play that are certainly better than doing nothing at all'.

Commentary.

Outside of their psychotherapy practice, virtuous psychotherapists don't idle away and waste their precious lifetime doing nothing and usually engage in some kind of stimulating, meaningful, challenging and absorbing recreational activity.

23. Text.

A disciple asks, 'Is courage valued the most by gentlepersons?'. Confucius says, 'Gentlepersons give first place to moral Goodness and Rightness. If they have courage but not Goodness and Rightness, they become rebels. If small persons have courage but not Goodness and Rightness, they become bandits'.

Commentary.

Virtuous psychotherapists are both courageous and adhere to what is Good and Right in their interactions and interventions with psychotherapy clients.

24. Text.

A disciple asks, 'Do gentlepersons have dislikes'. Confucius replies, 'Yes. They dislike persons who point out what is unlikable in others. They dislike persons who disrespect superiors, whose courage neglects ritual and who are resolute but stubborn. What are your dislikes?'. The disciple says, 'I dislike people who mistake cleverness for wisdom, who mistake insubordination for courage and who mistake story-telling for honesty'.

Commentary.

Virtuous psychotherapists may have some dislikes about themselves, students, trainees, interns, colleagues and clients but they most often constitute the basis and springboards for working out, correcting and improving their self-awareness, self-understanding, self-acceptance, self-actualization and self-development and for understanding, accepting, repairing and healing interpersonal relationships and conflicts with clients.

25. Text.

Confucius says, 'Women and servants are difficult to deal with. If you're friendly, they get out of hand and if you're distant, they resent it'.

Commentary.

Unlike Confucius, virtuous psychotherapists don't misogynistically equate women with servants or experience difficulties in accepting, including, relating to, connecting with and working with women clients as extraordinarily ordinary human beings whom they're not attempting to control or who resent appropriate professional boundaries.

26. Text.

Confucius says, 'Human beings who reach the age of forty and still aren't liked will probably be so until the end of their lives'.

Commentary.

Fortunately, virtuous psychotherapists successfully assist, and continue to successfully assist, many clients over the age of forty in changing habits patterns, life styles, relationships and careers and in becoming Good and authentic human beings who are likeable, liking and well-liked as well as who are love-able, loving and well-loved.

水

THE ANALECTS
BOOK EIGHTEEN
WEI ZI

WEI ZI

微 子

A MADMAN, FARMERS AND RECLUSES

1. Text.

1. The last ruler of an earlier dynasty is a tyrant and alienates, enslaves and assassinates three rulers who are his relatives. Confucius says, 'The dynasty loses three Good and virtuous human beings'.

Commentary.

Virtuous psychotherapists are typically not involved in government or political policies, practices, activities and drama of any kind and abhor corrupt tyrants, fascist leaders, despots, autocrats and dictators who control, dominate, alienate, enslave, imprison, exile and assassinate human beings.

2. Text.

An offical is dismissed three times and someone suggests that he might do better serving elsewhere. He says, 'If I continue serving in honest ways with the Way/Dao, where can I go and not be dismissed. If I serve in dishonest ways without the Way/ Dao, what need is there for me to leave here?'.

Commentary.

Virtuous psychotherapists serve clients and conduct their psychotherapy practice in honest ways according with Dao and there is no one to dismiss them or need to practice elsewhere.

3. Text.

A ruler prepares to receive Confucius and says, 'To treat him as equal to the head of the ruling family is impossible'. He receives Confucius as ranked below the head of the ruling family and says, 'I'm old and don't have any use for you'. Whereupon Confucius leaves the state.

Commentary.

To reserve, conserve, preserve and deserve their moral virtue, integrity, energy and power/de of Dao; virtuous psychotherapists don't usually stay where they aren't needed, wanted, welcome, relevant, useful or beneficial.

4. Text.

The people of a state send a gift of women musicians to a neighboring state in order to distract and delay the government's functioning. The musicians are accepted, no court is held for three days and Confucius leaves the state.

Commentary.

Virtuous psychotherapists don't usually stay in situations that don't mirror or match the vibrational frequency of their moral virtue, integrity, energy and power/de of Dao.

5. Text.

A madman passes by Confucius and sings, ' Oh phoenix, phoenix, how your virtue has degenerated!. The past can't be corrected but the future can still be pursued. Desist, desist!. These days, it's perilous to hold a government office'. Confucius comes down from his carriage to speak with the madman but he has run away.

Commentary.

Virtuous psychotherapists, of course, frequently work with clients suffering from severe chronic mental health issues but they usually stay in their office or treatment setting and can be related and responded to and spoken and worked with.

6. Text.

Two farmers are plowing a field, Confucius happens upon them and directs a disciple to go and ask them where a river can be forded. One of the farmers asks the disciple who is driving the carriage and the disciple says that it's Confucius. The farmer haughtily says, 'Confucius?. He should know where the ford is' and goes back to work. The disciple then asks the other farmer who asks the disciple, 'Who are you?'. The disciple answers and the second farmer cynically says, 'So, you're a follower of Confucius?. He's not going to change all of the turmoil. It's the same everywhere. You'd do better following someone who forgets about individuals and shuns this whole generation' and goes back to work. The disciple tells Confucius about the meetings who regretfully says, 'We can't just live with creatures. If I'm not a human being among fellow human beings, then who am I?. If the Way prevails in the state, I won't have to be trying to change things'.

Commentary.

Amid the prevailing disorder of government and society, virtuous psychotherapists acknowledge, own and accept their professional identity and continue working with the individual clients with whom they are meeting but also work with couples and families and groups and organizations.

7. Text.

A disciple is following Confucius, falls behind, comes across an old man and asks, 'Have you seen my master?'. The old man pointedly asks, 'You who don't toil and sift grains, who is your real 'master'?'. The old man resumes weeding and the disciple respectfully presses his hands together, bows and stands waiting. The old man invites the disciple to spend the night, feeds him supper and introduces him to his two sons. The disciple says about the sons, 'It's not right that they're not serving the country. The laws for youths can't be disregarded and it's not right to set aside duty and subvert the Great Relationship. Gentlepersons take office to put into practice the Goodness and Rightness of that relationship and are aware of the progress being or not being made'. The next day, the disciple finds Confucius and reports to him what happened. Confucius says, 'He's a recluse' and tells the disciple to go back and visit him again but when he does, the old man is gone.

Commentary.

Many virtuous psychotherapists take Dao/the Way as their real 'master' and serve clients according to its moral virtue, integrity, energy and power/de and its Goodness and Rightness operating in their great personally meaningful and professionally intimate psychotherapy relationships.

8. Text.

Confucius says, 'The state loses many good officials who become recluses. Some don't lose their resolve or humiliate themselves and others do. Some speak and act according to proper relationships and others live in seclusion, say nothing and maintain personal integrity. I'm different from any one of these. I don't have any preconceptions about what's okay and not okay or any predetermined rigid dos or don'ts'.

Commentary.

Some psychotherapists speak congruently, act prudently and maintain their purpose and reputation and others don't. Virtuous psychotherapists are ethical; non-dualistic; listen attentively; typically speak little; relate to clients openly, deeply, impartially and flexibly and preserve their personal and professional integrity and the virtue, energy and efficacious power/de of Dao.

9. Text.

The state is in disorder and decline and the Grand Music Master, the band leader, major and minor musicians and the drummers and stone-chime players all leave and go to different states.

Commentary.

Virtuous psychotherapists attend psychotherapy conferences, make presentations, conduct workshops and consult with organizations in various locations throughout the country and the world not because their psychotherapy practice is in disorder or decline but in order to share and transmit knowledge to professional colleagues.

10. Text.

A ruler addresses his son, another ruler, saying, 'Gentlepersons don't neglect close relatives, irritate unheeded officials, dismiss long-time associates or expect one person to do everything'.

Commentary.

Virtuous psychotherapists are generous and fair with regard to their availability and accessibility. They listen attentively to what clients say and they maintain long-standing relationships with colleagues. Virtuous psychotherapists are generally not overly eclectic or jacks-of-all-trades with regard to theories and methods of psychotherapy practice and usually specialize in a few ones that are appropriately suited to being used with particular clients and for specific treatment issues.

11. Text.

This particular state has eight officials who are four sets of twins from the same mother, a rare occurrence that indicates and symbolizes the state's fertility and power.

Commentary.

Virtuous psychotherapists have many ways of demonstrating their personal and professional moral virtue, integrity, energy and power/de of Dao in their psychotherapy practice without begetting four sets of twin children or working with four sets of twin clients.

水

THE ANALECTS
BOOK NINETEEN
ZI ZHANG

ZI ZHANG

子 張

MASTERS, DISCIPLES AND OFFICIALS

1. Text.

A disciple says, 'Gentlpersons when faced with danger, are ready to die; when faced with gain, consider what is Good and Right; are reverent at sacrifices and grieve at funerals'.

Commentary.

Virtuous psychotherapists devote time and energy to psychotherapy practice and worthy causes, don't commit ethical wrongs to earn money in psychotherapy practice or elsewhere and value and express natural, deep and appropriate feelings in psychotherapy relationships with clients and for their ceremonial rites of passage.

2. Text.

A disciple says, 'Human beings who follow the Way but without conviction and who value its moral virtue/de but without sincerity – can't be considered to have anything'.

Commentary.

The greatest possessions of virtuous psychotherapists are Dao/the Way and its moral virtue, integrity, energy and power/de. They accept and work with clients who both follow and don't follow Dao/the Way or both value and don't value its power/de.

3. Text.

Another master's disciple asks a disciple of Confucius about human relationships. The disciple of Confucius asks the other disciple, 'What does your master say?'. The other disciple replies, 'Go with whom it is proper to go and distance from whom it is proper to distance'. The disciple of Confucius says, 'This is different from what I'm taught. Gentlepersons respect the virtuous but include everyone, commend the good and pity the unable. If I'm superior to other persons, I include them. If I'm inferior to other persons, they distance me. So, the question of going with or distancing from doesn't even arise'.

Commentary.

Virtuous psychotherapists don't discriminate between human beings and typically accept, include and respect a wide variety of diverse human beings among their psychotherapy clientele; having commendation for the able and compassion for the unable.

4. Text.

A master says, 'Minor arts have an importance of their own. But if pursued too far, they can become a hindrance. For that reason, gentlepersons usually don't pursue them'.

Commentary.

Virtuous human beings have chosen, pursue, cultivate and practice the important, major and creative art and clientwork of the profession of psychotherapy, unhindered by minor concerns.

5. Text.

A master says, 'Human beings who daily are conscious of what they don't know and learn something new and who monthly remember what they've learned are lovers of learning'.

Commentary.

Virtuous psychotherapists are lovers of learning who continually are conscious of what they don't know, what they need to learn, what they're newly learning and what they've already learned.

6. Text.

A master says, 'Human beings who study broadly and constantly with a definite and dedicated purpose; who question earnestly and acutely and who reflect upon and practice what they learn achieve Goodness'.

Commentary.

Virtuous psychotherapists continue studying psychological theories, the works of master psychotherapists and effective methods of psychotherapy and make up their own minds about what knowledge and techniques are Good, true and fitting to be applied in their psychotherapy work with clients.

7. Text.

A master says, 'Just as apprentices live, learn and work in shops to perfect their crafts, gentlepersons live, learn and practice in the Way to perfect themselves'.

Commentary.

Virtuous psychotherapists are educated in psychotherapy through study, being supervised in practice with clients and being trained in workshops with master psychotherapists and are actualizing their knowledge and abilities in their psychotherapy meetings with clients. They also are learning, cultivating and practicing Dao/the Way and are cultivating, developing, improving and refining themselves, personally, professionally and spiritually.

8. Text.

A master says, 'When small persons go wrong, they rationalize faults, mistakes and errors'.

Commentary.

Virtuous psychotherapists uprightly and straightforwardly acknowledge any personal faults, interpersonal mistakes or technical errors in psychotherapy observations, understandings, explanations, reflections, interpretations and interventions and take appropriate measures to correct them rather than rationalizing them.

9. Text.

A master says, 'Gentlepersons have three different appearances. Seen from a distance, they seem dignified. When approached more closely, they seem mild. When heard speaking, they seem incisive'.

Commentary.

Virtuous psychotherapists have various different demeanors and appearances depending upon the closeness or distance of the relational perspectives of different clients and the nature and requirements of different psychotherapy conditions, circumstances, situations, issues, etc..

10. Text.

A master says, 'Gentlepersons 1) gain the trust and confidence of the people before burdening them, otherwise they'll feel oppressed and 2) gain the trust and confidence of rulers before criticizing them, otherwise they'll feel slandered'.

Commentary.

Virtuous psychotherapists gain the confidence and trust of students, trainees, interns, supervisors, trainers, mentors, colleagues and clients and thus prevent negative feelings from occurring during required processes and/or confrontational interactions.

11. Text.

A master says, 'In major matters of moral virtue, don't 'cross the line'. Allow yourself some latitude in minor moral matters'.

Commentary.

Virtuous psychotherapists don't overstep the ethical limits or cross the moral lines of Goodness, Rightness, properness, integrity, respect, sincerity, loyalty, fidelity, etc. in the conduct of psychotherapy and in relation to client boundaries.

12. Text.

A disciple of Confucius says of disciples of another master, 'They're good when it comes to minor matters like sweeping floors, receiving guests and replying to questions but are at a loss in more important ones'. Their master hears of this and says, 'This disciple is completely mistaken!. In the Way of true gentlepersons, what is less or more important and what comes first and last are clearly distinguished. Disciples are like trees and plants to be treated individually according to their kinds and extent of growth. That's the Way of gentlepersons but only sages unite within themselves both the first and last steps'.

Commentary.

Virtuous psychotherapists decide with clients which of their issues have priority to address and work with. They have a 'first things first' attitude. They don't compare the level of development or degree of progress of their clients with the clients of other psychotherapists. Their timing of insight-promoting reflections, feedback and interpretations are appropriate and effective when each client is related with and treated according to their uniquely individual nature, personality traits, capacities and capabilities and extent of psychological development.

13. Text.

A master says, 'Energy that officials have left after fulfilling official duties can be devoted to studying and energy that they have left after studying can be devoted to official duties'.

Commentary.

The 'official duty' of virtuous psychotherapists is to use their vital energy/de of Dao to study, learn and to fulfill their commitment and responsibiity to serve, understand, assist and benefit clients.

14. Text.

A disciple of Confucius says, 'Mourning ceremonies are carried to the limit that grieving dictates and no further'.

Commentary.

Virtuous psychotherapists are naturally appropriate, moderate and self-limiting in their expression of feelings during psychotherapy meetings with clients and usually modulate the intensity and extensity of their emotional expressions.

15. Text.

A disciple of Confucius says, 'My friend is difficult to match but hasn't yet fully realized Goodness'.

Commentary.

Virtuous psychotherapists realize, understand and appreciate that clients' ability to successfully achieve and accomplish doing things has no necessary relationship with their becoming and being a Good human being.

16. Text.

A master says, 'This disciple is so self-satisfied. It's difficult to practice virtues beside him'.

Commentary.

Virtuous psychotherapists are able to maintain, cultivate, develop and realize their virtuous energy and power/de of Goodness even when working with acting-out, difficult, highly defended, resistant and ego-centric clients.

17. Text.

A master says, 'I hear Confucius say, 'Human beings may not usually express their feelings fully but they are certain to do so when mourning their mother or father''.

Commentary.

Virtuous psychotherapists experience that clients are usually more able to naturally and fully express their emotions when experiencing deep feelings of sorrow and grief when mourning.

18. Text.

A master says, 'I hear Confucius say, 'The filial piety of this official is possible to match in most matters but the way he keeps his deceased father's appointed officials and domestic policies is unequaled''.

Commentary.

The loyalty and fidelity of virtuous psychotherapists is modeled for their clients, some of whom are able to develop and realize their own to a significant degree and equivalent extent.

19. Text.

When a family appoints an official to be chief judge, he comes to a master for advice. The master says, 'High officials lose the Way and common people lose their ways. When you see this in your legal cases, be sad and compassionate instead of being pleased with the discovery'.

Commentary.

Virtuous psychotherapists are displeased with discovering

and seeing evidence of the degeneration of leaders, the disorientation and distress of human beings and the deterioration of society and are appropriately saddened and compassionate.

20. Text.

A disciple of Confucius says, 'I can't believe this tyrant is so immoral!. This is why gentlepersons so love Goodness and so hate dwelling in low positions. They know that's where all that isn't Good accumulates'.

Commentary.

Virtuous psychotherapists 'dwell on the high ground' and 'take the high road' when working with clients and especially with issues of moral corruption and ethically unconscionable acts.

21. Text.

A disciple of Confucius says, 'The faults, mistakes and errors of gentlepersons are like eclipses of the sun and moon. They're seen by everyone and when gentlepersons correct them, they're looked up to'.

Commentary.

Any bad quality or wrong doing of virtuous psychotherapists is quite evident, eclipses the illumination of their usual Goodness and their correction of any faults, mistakes and errors restores it.

22. Text.

An official asks a disciple where Confucius obtains his learning. The disciple replies, 'The Way of legendary Ancient Sage-Rulers hasn't disappeared among present human beings. Those of great learning embody the major principles and practices of this Way and those of lesser learning embody its minor ones. So, there's no one now who doesn't have the Way of Ancient Sage-Rulers within them. Confucius learns from everyone and doesn't have any one particular teacher'.

Commentary.

Virtuous psychotherapists study major texts written by master psychotherapists and participate in training workshops led by them and take continuing education programs in order to learn and master knowledge about psychotherapy theories, techniques, methods and procedures. In their psychotherapy work with clients, they've internalized and assimilated what they've learned, are deeply committed to learning more, relate to the universal innate inner Goodness of clients and, as a result, every client teaches them something.

23. Text.

An official says that one of the disciples of Confucius is superior to him. Another official repeats this to the disciple who says, 'Let's use the walls of a building for comparison. My wall is shoulder-high and it's easy to peer over it and to see the good dwellings on the other side. But Confucius's wall rises many times higher and you can't see the beauty and magnificence of temples and palaces inside unless you're one of the few who finds a gate ... '.

Commentary.

Virtuous psychotherapists may have students, trainees, interns and clients who exceed them in knowlededge, experience and Goodness depending upon who's making the comparative assessment of which areas, from which perspective and using which criteria.

24. Text.

An official speaks disparagingly of Confucius and his disciple says, 'It doesn't matter, Confucius can't be disparaged. Other Good human beings are like hills that can be climbed over but Confucius is insurmountable like the sun and moon. People can disparage the sun and moon but that wouldn't affect either of them. It'd only show the faults and limitations of the disparaging people'.

Commentary.

Virtuous psychotherapists don't usually compare themselves with clients. Suffice to say, without a value judgment, good clients may be like hills and virtuous psychotherapists may be illuminating them from on high.

25. Text.

An official says to a disciple of Confucius, 'This is false modesty. Confucius isn't superior to you'. The disciple says, 'Be careful what you say. One word can reveal truth and wisdom or falsehood and stupidity. It's as difficult to equal Confucius as climbing a ladder to the sky. Had he ever been the ruler of a state or head of a powerful family, it'd be like the saying, 'He raises them and they stand. He guides them and they go. He steadies them and they come. He stirs them and they stay'. His life is truly glorious and his death deeply mourned. How can he be equaled?'.

Commentary.

Virtuous psychotherapists are loved by their gentleclients who regard and respect them highly as unequaled human beings who raise, lead, steady and stir them so that they can stand, go, come and stay as the unique human beings who they essentially are. Virtuous psychotherapists are glorious human beings who, should they die during the time of psychotherapy or before it has naturally terminated, are deeply mourned by their clients for a long time.

水

THE ANALECTS
BOOK TWENTY
YAO SPOKE

YAO YUE

堯 曰

ANCIENT SAGE-RULERS AND LOVELY VIRTUES

1. Text.

A legendary Ancient Divine Sage-Ruler cedes the throne to the next legendary Ancient Divine Sage-Ruler saying, 'Oh. Upon you now rests the Heavenly Succession. Faithfully hold to the middle way. The Four Seas may run dry but this Heavenly gift lasts forever'. The second Divine Sage-Ruler says the same words when ceding the throne to the next legendary Ancient Divine Sage-Ruler and founder of the first Chinese dynasty.

The founder and ruler of the next Chinese dynasty says, 'I make a sacrifice and tell you great Lord that those who are guilty, I'll not spare and your servants, I'll not harm. The decision is in your heart and in accord with your will. If I do any wrong, never let it be visited upon the many people. And if wrong be done by the many people, let it be visited upon me. When this dynasty gives its generosities, it's the Good who are enriched. Although I have my kinsfolk, they are less to me than Good persons. If among my family or the people there's one who does wrong, let the wrong be visited upon me alone'.

Commentary.

Virtuous psychotherapists often regard themselves as successors in a lineage of certain schools of psychotherapy that may even have specific treatment ethics, e.g., having the psychotherapist assume full and complete responsibility for clients and their actions and for the nature, conduct, course and results of psychotherapy when it's not Good, successful, helpful and beneficial.

2. Text.

The ruler of the next dynasty pays strict attention to weights and measures, restores unoccupied offices, reviews statutes and laws and gives political organization to the whole empire. He raises up states that are destroyed, re-establishes lines of succession that are broken, summons lost subjects back to prominence and all of the common people give their hearts to him. What he cares for the most is that the people have food and shelter and that the rites of mourning and sacrifice are fulfilled. A ruler who's inclusive and tolerant and wins the multitude; who keeps his word and is trusted by the people; who's diligent and succeeds in every undertaking and who's equitable, fair and just, is the joy of the people.

Commentary.

Virtuous psychotherapists appreciate their Heavenly gifts and innate talents; care for clients as Good human beings; assume responsibility for any errors in psychotherapy; abide by professional ethical standards; keep their words to clients and agreements with clients; work diligently, effectively and successfully in psychotherapy and are joys who are loved by clients.

3. Text.

A disciple asks Confucius, 'What must a person do to be fit to rule the state properly?'. Confucius says, 'Enact the Five Lovely Virtues and not the Four Ugly Vices. The disciple then asks, 'What are the Five Lovely Virtues?'. Confucius answers, 'Gentlepersons:

1) are bountiful without extravagance, i.e., give advantages that are really advantageous;
2) make people work without creating resentment, i.e., impose only performable tasks;
3) have longings but aren't covetous, i.e., long for and attain the Goodness of the Way;
4) are dignified but aren't proud, i.e., don't disrespect either small or great people;
5) inspire awe but aren't frightening, i.e., are dignified in dress, manner and customs'.

The disciple then asks, 'What are the Four Ugly Vices?'. Confucius answers, 'Gentlepersons don't:

1) put people to death without having taught them what is Right, i.e., being savage;
2) expect the completion of tasks without giving due warning, i.e., being oppressive;
3) be late in giving orders and expecting absolute punctuality, i.e., being tormenting;
4) be reluctantly or grudgingly rewarding people, i.e., being small-minded and petty'.

Commentary.

Virtuous psychotherapists are:

1) generous with clients but not excessive in using techniques.
2) appropriate in assigning homework and achievable processes.
3) desirous of client change and progress but not forcing them.

4)   dignified and not disrespectful of clients and their progress.
5)   energetically catalyzing clients without overwhelming them.

And do not:

1)   terminate or refer clients before they have made sufficient gains and progress.
2)   expect that clients complete psychotherapy assignments without sufficient time.
3)   arrive late for psychotherapy meetings while expecting that clients are punctual.
4)   have or communicate an attitude of small-mindedness when working with clients.

4. Text.

Confucius says,

1)   'Human beings who don't understand Heaven's will can't become gentlepersons.
2)   Human beings who don't understand ritual propriety can't establish their character.
3)   Human beings who don't understand words can't evaluate other people's character'.

Commentary.

Virtuous psychotherapists understand the will of Heaven as the 'locus of control' of psychotherapy, understand the ritual methods of psychotherapy practice and understand the meaning of words that clients speak. Therefore, they affirm the Goodness of clients, are able to assist clients in taking their stand and can accurately evaluate and understand clients.

水

EPILOGUE

After reading, studying, reflecting upon and absorbing this rendition of and commentaries on *The Analects*, I hope that you; 1) have dispelled any preconceptions and misconceptions about Confucius and Confucianism; 2) have come away with a better understanding of Confucius, the human being, and of Confucianism, the philosophical teaching; 3) can see its application to the professional identity of virtuous psychotherapists and to the professional practice of virtuous psychotherapy and 4) can value and appreciate;

1) Confucius as a devoted human being, virtue-ethics moral philosopher and politician;
2) Confucius as an advocate of virtues of benevoloence, righteousness and properness;
3) Confucius as a transmitter of virtues of filial piety, respect, sincerity, reciprocity, etc.;
4) Confucius as identifying cultivating being a gentleperson as the alpha-omega of life;
5) Confucius as a man who has greatly influenced and shaped China's people and culture.
6) Confucianism as a humanistic ideology rooted in ancient Sage-Rulers and ancestors;
7) Confucianism as a belief system surviving a long dynastic history of wars and peace;
8) Confucianism as an ethical philosophy valuing social harmony and governmental order;
9) Confucianism as a philosophy and Way of living that has transformed over many years;
10) Confucianism as a world religion spreading throughout Asian countries and the world.

How can we ignore such a philosopher as Confucius who identifies and transmits a Way of being a better human being living in a better social world governed by better leaders?

How can we ignore such a philosophy as Confucianism that identifes and values creating a Way of individual morality, social harmony and political order through virtuous humanity?

How can we deny that being a real, true, cultured, refined and beautiful human being is not characterized by the life-long and heart-centered love of learning and by the cultivating, improving and refining the virtues of;

Goodness, rightness and properness
Honor, reverence, respect and deference
Humaneness, kindness and gentleness
Understanding, empathy and compassion
Humility, modesty, moderation and balance
Learning, knowledge, insight and wisdom
Genuineness, honesty, integrity and sincerity
Uprightness, straighforwardness and truthfulness
Equality, mutuality, reciprocity and intimacy
Responsibility, dependability and reliability
Loyalty, faithfulness, fairness and justice
Dignity, worthiness and trustworthiness
Devotion, dedication, resolve and diligence
Selflessness, generosity, altruism and charity
Obligation, duty, conformity and compliance
Harmoniousness, peacefulness and happiness
Caring, loving, courageousness and bravery?.

A disciple of Confucius asks, 'In being a real and true self, living a real and true life with real and true fellow human beings is there any more than what Confucius cultivates, teaches and transmits?, i.e.,

1) Cultivating, becoming and being a gentleperson who is loving, caring, kind and friendly.

2) Being and living Goodness and as Good and the best that we can be as human beings.

3) Being and living Rightness and as Right and the best that we can do as human beings.

4) Valuing, cherishing, treasuring, safeguarding, supporting, nourishing and enhancing life.

5) Accepting, appreciating, respecting, cultivating, improving, enjoying and sharing life.

6) Inspiring, encouraging, supporting, teaching, assisting and benefiting fellow human beings.

7) Seeing the reality, truth and beauty of everyone and everything, everywhere and always.

Is there anything more than this?'.

Confucius answers, 'I believe not. It's what I've studied, learned, known, valued, taught and transmitted throughout my whole life'.

Lao Tzu answers, 'Harmoniously attuning to and according, flowing and being One with Ultimate Dao; its uniquely individualized presence, integrity, energy, power and efficacy/De and the ten-thousand myriad things/Wan Wu of human being, existence and experience'.

The Buddha answers, 'Becoming and being awake, enlightened and liberated from suffering by not being an illusional ego-self desiring and being attached to what is impermanent'.[1]

三　教　今　一

San	Jiao	Jin	Yi
Three	Teachings	Now/As	One

Given the choice:
What is so bad about being what is Good?
What is so wrong about doing what is Right?
What is so irregular about doing what is proper?
What is so unnatural about being what is refined?

As a virtuous human being:
Light, love, live and enjoy Dao, Nature,
human life, yourself and each other.

Alas, Alas
This too shall pass
Alas, Alas
All this shall pass

水

APPENDIX ONE
CHINA DYNASTIES

There are a total of 83 Chinese Dynasties during 2,000 years of pre-imperial dynastic rule and over 2,000 years of imperial rule. Below is a partial listing of major dynasties selected from the web site https://wikipedia.org>wiki>Dynasties of China.

Neolithic Cultures ❖ **c. 10,000 – c. 2,000 BCE.** Transition from hunter-gathering to farming-domesticated animal culture. First stage of cultural evolution among prehistoric human beings. Permanent villages in the Yellow and Yangzi River Basins. Yangshao, Longshan, Hongshan, Liangzhu et al Cultures. Millet and rice growing. Silkworm raising. Stone tools, textiles, silk weaving, ceramics, pottery vessels, jade production, tea and alcohol. Burial sites. Some interactions, shared practices and trading between separate cultures. No distinct Chinese civilization but The Yellow Emperor/Huang Di is credited with its later founding and centralizing States and with inventing early writing forms, wooden houses, carts, boats and the bow and arrow. Legendary Sage-Rulers Yao (c. 2324-2255 BCE) and Shun (c. 2255-2205 BCE) are models of worshiping Heaven, filial piety, virtue, benevolence, righteousness and devotion who later inspire Confucius.

The Xia Dynasty ❖ **c. 2100-1600 BCE.** First Dynasty is founded by Yu the Great (2123-2025 BCE). History, myths, tales and oral teachings. Development of irrigation channels, flood control, writing forms, military technology and a calendar system. Only recently is authenticated to have physically existed.

The Shang/Yin Dynasty ❖ 1600-1045 BCE. Earliest recorded history based upon archaeological evidence. First written records of China. Oracle bone script writing and ox scapula and tortoise shell divination. Developments in language, script writing, art, mathematics, astronomy, military technology, chariots, bronzework, iron and pottery. Chopsticks are used instead of spoons.

The Western Zhou Dynasty ❖ 1045-775 BCE. **The Eastern Zhou Dynasty** ❖ 775-221 BCE. The longest dynasty in Chinese history. **The Golden/Axial Age** ❖ 500 BCE. The flourishing development of codified writing and bronze and large seal script, coinage, kites, culture, philosophy and the feudal system. Spring and Autumn (770-475 BCE) and Warring States (475-221 BCE) Periods. Decentralization of individual feudal states and bloody internecine battles for hegemony. Lao Zi/Taoism, Kong Fu Zi and Meng Zi/Confucianism, Sun Zi/Militarism, Mo Zi/Moism, Xun Zi/anti-Confucianism and Han Fei Zi/Legalism and The 100 Schools of Thought; including The School of Names and The School of Yin-Yang et al. Ruling by the Mandate of Heaven that grants the divine right for a ruler to rule justly and if corrupted to withdraw and/or people have the right to rebel and overthrow the ruler.

The Qin Dynasty ❖ 221-206 BCE. Conquers all warring states, unifies the Chinese Empire and centralizes the government. Uniform small seal script writing system, legal code, coinage and currency system. The crossbow is invented. Tyrannical rule and Legalism. Book burning and live burial of Confucian scholars. Roads and bridges are built. Portions of The Great Wall are constructed and connected. The Emperor's Mausoleum and the Terra Cotta Warriors are constructed.

The Western Han Dynasty ❖ 206 BCE-25 CE. The Eastern Han Dynasty ❖ 25-220 CE. Another Golden Age. Strong, stable and prosperous culture and government. Confucianism is the state religion and classics are the basis of civil service examinations. The Yellow Emperor's Canon of Medicine is compiled. Buddhism is introduced to China. The Silk Road is opened for trading. The blast furnace is invented. Iron weapons. Clerical, standard, running and grass script writing; acupuncture, paper and porcelainware. The magnetic compass, seismograph and wheelbarrows are invented. The Chinese people are considered to be the Han people.

The Xin Dynasty ❖ 9-23 CE. Interregnum period of co-existing dynasty between the Western and Eastern Han Dynasties. Central role in Chinese metaphysics, epistemology and ethics.

The Three Kingdoms Period - 220-265 CE/The Six Dynasties Period ❖ 220-589 CE. Wars between States. Later romanticized. Taoism and Buddhism are favored over Confucianism. Developments in astronomy, chemistry, botany, medicine and painting. Coal is used for fuel.

The Western Jin Dynasty ❖ 265-316 CE. The Eastern Jin Dynasty ❖ 317-420 CE. Confucianism. Anti-Taoism and pro-Buddhism. Pottery jars and porcelainware are made.

The Sixteen Kingdoms Period ❖ 303-439 CE. The Northern/Southern Dynasties Period ❖ 386-587 CE. Fragmented, turbulant and bloody time. Foreign rule. Political division and upheaval. Buddhism increases in importance. Well-drilling.

The Sui Dynasty ❖ 581-618 CE. Re-unification. Taoism and Buddhism slightly favored over Confucianism. Largest army in the world. The Great Wall is further connected and extended. The Great Canal is built. Coinage is standardized.

The Tang Dynasty ❖ 618-907 CE. Another Golden Age. The only female monarch/empress (Wu Zetian 624-705 CE). A pinnacle of Chinese culture and civilization. Most peaceful and prosperous time. The largest country in the world. A revival of Confucianism and the civil service examination system but Taoisn is the official State religion. The Turkish invasion. Advances in art, sculpture, silverwork, literature, poetry, wood-block printing, science and technology. The mechanical clock and whiskey are made (to tell the time of 'Happy Hour?').

The Five Dynasties Period ❖ 907-960 CE. **The Ten Kingdoms Period** ❖ 907-979 CE. Fragmented and tumultuous time. Political division and upheaval.

The Liao Dynasty ❖ 916-1125 CE. **The Western Liao Dynasty** ❖ 1125-1218 CE. The first nomadic 'barbarian' tribal rule, e.g., The Liao Dynasty founded and ruled by the Turko-Mongolian Khitan ethnic tribes and the **Western Xia Empire** ❖ 1038-1227 CE founded and ruled by the Sino-Tibetan Tangut ethnic tribes.

The Northern Song Dynasty ❖ 960-1127 CE. **The Southern Song Dynasty** ❖ 1127-1279 CE. Re-unification. Confucianism revitalized through re-establishing the thought of Confucius and Mencius and Neo-Confucianism and is officially adopted and the Classics and Books are required study in schools at all grade levels and are continued for civil service examinations. Gunpowder and rockets are made. Paper money is printed. Movable type printing. Porcelain is made. The Mongol invasion by Genghis Khan.

The Jin Dynasty ❖ 1115-1234 CE. Confucianism, Taoism and Buddhism co-exist. Architectural development. Invasion and conquest by Genghis Khan.

The Yuan Dynasty ❖ 1279-1368 CE. Kublai Khan rules and Mongols adopt Chinese culture and Confucianism. **Northern Yuan Dynasty** ❖ 1368-1635 CE. Famines, plagues, floods and peasant rebellions occur.

The Ming Dynasty ❖ 1368-1644 CE. **Southern Ming Dynasty** ❖ 1644-1662 CE. Huge growth in population, prosperity, culture and the arts. The Great Wall is completed after 2,000 years and 13,171 miles. The Forbidden City/Imperial residence is built. Fine blue and white porcelain china and the bristle toothbrush are made (for and after dinner?).

The Qing Dynasty ❖ 1644-1912 CE. Manchu rule and Chinese culture and Confucianism are again adopted. The civil service examination system is ended in 1905. The last Imperial Dynasty. Pu Yi, a 6 yr. old boy, is the last Chinese emperor. The machine gun is invented. A time of rebellion, revolution and foreign invasion by Japan and Western nations. The Opium Wars. The Wade-Giles Romanized Chinese writing form since 1892.

The Republic of China and Socialist rule ❖ 1912-1949 CE.

The People's Republic of China and Communist rule ❖ **1949-Present**. Simplified form of Chinese writing since 1949 and Han Yu Pin Yin form since 1958.

水

CHRONOLOGY OF CONFUCIUS*

BCE

551 ❖ Born in the Chinese State of Lu to mother, Yan Zheng Zai, and father, Kong Shu Liang He, a military officer of distant royal descent but with no current hereditary entitlements or privileges and with nine daughters and one disabled son. Confucius is named Qiu and Zhong Ni, being the middle son born near Mt. Ni. The Kong family had been forced to flee from the State of Song to the State of Lu and to live in relative poverty.

549 ❖ Father dies when 3.

546 ❖ Loves learning and plays make-believe ceremony games when 6.

541 ❖ Begins doing menial work when 11.

537 ❖ Sets mind to self-studying and learning when 15.

536 ❖ Mother dies at age 33 when 16.

535 ❖ Refused for admission to a banquet for scholars when 17.

533 ❖ Marries Lady Qi Guan when 19.

532 ❖ Son named Li/Bo Yi is born when 20.

531 ❖ Employed as a clerk at a sheep farm when 21.

530 ❖ Employed as a clerk at a warehouse when 22.

522 ❖ Is established as an authority on moral conduct and ritual when 30.

517 ❖ Backed a defeated rebel ruler and is exiled to Qi State when 35.

516 ❖ Absorbed in peace music in Qi when 36.

   ❖ Rejected for court membership in Qi when 36.

515 ❖ Death threats in Qi and returns to Lu when 37.

512 ❖ Declines services sought by a Lu administrator when 40.

509 ❖ Police Commissioner of Lu when 43.

505 ❖ Services sought by another Lu administrator when 47.

502 ❖ Declines services solicited by another Lu administrator when 50.

501 ❖ Enters government service and politics in Lu as a magistrate when 51.

500 ❖ Appointed as Minister of Public Works and Justice in Lu when 52.

   ❖ Reportedly consults with Lao Zi regarding matters of governance when 52.

499 ❖ Elevated to a prestigious position at Qi-Lu State meeting when 53.

497 ❖ Distrusted after initiating plans to demolish fiefdom walls when 55.

   ❖ Advises and has a falling out with the ruler of Lu and goes into self-exile when 55.

   ❖ Leaves Lu to travel for fourteen years (498-484 BCE) to neighboring states to consult with rulers and government officials and to seek government office when 55.

496 ❖ Made a court member in Wei State but is seldom consulted when 56.

   ❖ Leaves Wei after ten months and disparaging remarks to the ruler when 56.

   ❖ Besieged en route to Chen State for five days when 56.

   ❖ Forced to return to Wei and is welcomed back by the ruler when 56.

494 ❖ Talked out of accepting an offer in Jin State by a disciple when 58.

493 ❖ Leaves Wei after being asked about military strategies when 59.

   ❖ On the way to Chen State is unreceived by rulers of Cao and Song States when 59.

❖ Narrowly escapes an assassination attempt in Song when 59.

❖ En route to Chen passes through Zheng State and is not received when 59.

492 ❖ Arrives in Chen. The Prime Minister of Lu dies and he is invited back to Lu when 60.

490 ❖ Expresses his desire to return to Lu solely to teach when 62.

489 ❖ Chen is invaded forcing departure to Chu State when 63.

❖ Stranded and runs out of food en route and disciples become ill when 63.

❖ In Chu, discusses governance and filiality with a minister when 63.

❖ Wei stabilizes, some disciples are ministers and returns to Wei when 63.

485 ❖ Wife dies when 67.

484 ❖ Qi invades Lu. Invited back to Lu by the current ruler and returns when 68.

483 ❖ Declines to concur with, and is angered over, Lu's tax increases when 69.

❖ Leaves official positions and commits to teaching full-time when 69.

482 ❖ Edits several major Chinese Classics and Books when 70.

❖ Son dies at age 50 when 70. Birth of grandson Zi Si.

481 ❖ Favorite disciple, Yan Hui, dies at age 42 when 71.

480 ❖ An outstanding disciple, Zi Lu, dies at age 63 when 72.

479 ❖ Dies when 73 and is mourned for three years and for six years by disciple Zi Gong.

* Based upon passages in chapters of the 20 Books of *The Analects* and cited on pages 20-21 and 242-246 of the Li reference and pages 36-38 of the Huang reference of this rendition.

水

APPENDIX THREE
DYNASTIC CONFUCIANISM

Confucianism undergoes alternating periods of 'popularity' throughout its over 2,500 year history in major Chinese Dynasties that correspond with their alternating periods of peace and war. This complementary dancing of yin-yang qi energy is succinctly captured in The Romance of the Three Kingdoms (1330-1400 CE) expression; 'The Empire long divided must unite; long united, must divide'. The following listing notes some of these fluctuations:

Eastern Zhou Dynasty ❖ 775-221 BCE. Confucius transmits the cultural values and practices of the legendary Sage-Rulers of the preceding Xia, Shang/Yin and Western Zhou Dynasties to the rulers of numerous states of his Eastern Zhou Dynasty with great difficulty and limited success.

Qin Dynasty ❖ 221-206 BCE. Legalism is preferred. Confucianism is repressed, texts are burned and scholars are buried alive.

Han Dynasty ❖ 206 BCE-200 CE. Confucianism is revived, replaces Legalism, becomes 'Confucianism' as the official state ideology and is required to be mastered in order to pass civil service examinations and to be eligible to hold public office. Confucianism is a syncretic outgrowth of Taoism and Buddhism.

3 Kingdoms / 6 Dynasties Period ❖ 220-581 CE.
Confucianism is less favored than Taoism and Buddhism.

Jin Dynasty ❖ 265-420 CE. Confucianism regains some popularity.

Sui Dynasty ❖ 581-618 CE. Confucianism declines in popularity and is eclipsed by Buddhism.

Tang Dynasty ❖ 618-907 CE. There is a revival of Confucianism and a synthesis with Taoism and Buddhism but Taoism is the official state religion.

The Five Dynasties and Ten Kingdom Period ❖ 907-960 CE. A period of intense struggle and conflict. Confucianism is side-lined and is found in the underground devotion of the people.

Song Dynasty ❖ 960-1279 CE. Confucianism is again revived, officially adopted and required study in schools at all levels and for civil service examinations. Neo-Confucianism emerges as a reaction to, and synthesis of, Taoism and Buddhism made by Zhu Xi (1130-1200 CE).

Jin Dynasty ❖ 1115-1234 CE. Confucianism is integrated with Taoism and Buddhism.

Yuan Dynasty ❖ 1279-1368 CE. Confucianism and Neo-Confucianism are part of the government and are used by Mongols to 'Chineseify' their culture. The teachings of Neo-Confucianist, Zhu Xi (1130-1200 CE) are considered orthodox in 1313 CE and Confucian Classics and Books are required for State civil service examinations until they are discontinued in 1910 CE.

Ming Dynasty ❖ 1368-1644 CE. Neo-Confucianism prevails. The Heart School is a branch of Confucianism focused upon the inner search for the True Self.

Qing Dynasty ❖ 1644-1912 CE. The last dynasty. Manchu rule. Confucianism is again adopted as the State religion and is the apex of rulership and governance. Confucianism is unfortunately used to reinforce traditional gender roles by which women are discriminated against and subjugated to dominant male authoritarianism.

水

APPENDIX FOUR
SOME ANALECTS BOOK TITLES

Most translators of *The Analects* title each of the 20 Books by its book number from 1 to 20. Some translators use titles and their Chinese characters. Other translators use English titles that begin each book or that name the general subject content of each book. A few translations don't use individual book titles at all. Also, the individual sayings in the 20 Books of *The Analects* are numbered slightly differently in different translations. The following lists the titles of some texts cited in the References:

Giles: Divides and organizes the content of the individual books of *The Analects* into chapters of his translation titled: 1– Government and Public Affairs. 2– Individual Virtues. 3– Confucius's Estimate of Others. 4– Confucius on Himself. 5– Miscellaneous Sayings. 6– Personalia. 7– Confucius as Seen by Others. 8– Sayings of the Disciples.

Huang: 1– Xue Er/To Learn Something. 2– Wei Zheng/He Who Conducts Government. 3– Ba Yi/Eight Rows of Dancers. 4– Li Ren/To Live Among Humane Men. 5– Gong Ye Chang. 6– Yong Ye (Yong). 7– Shu Er/I Transmit. 8– Tai Bo. 9– Zi Han/The Master Seldom. 10– Xiang Dang/In His Native Place. 11– Xian Jin/Those Who First Entered. 12– Yan Yuan. 13– Zi Lu. 14– Xian Wen/Xian Asked. 15– Wei Ling Gong/Duke Ling of Wei. 16– Ji Shi. 17– Yang Huo. 18– Wei Zi/The Viscount of Wei. 19– Zi Zhang. 20– Yao Yue/Yao Said.

Legge: 1– Studying. 2– Practice of Government. 3– Eight Rows of Dancers. 4– Benevolent Unity. 5– Gongye Chan, Son-In-Law. 6– Ran Yong, Student of Confucius. 7– Transmission. 8– Wu Taibo, Founder of the State of Wu. 9– The Master Shunned. 10– The Xiang and Dang Clans. 11– Former Generations. 12– Yan Yuan, Disciple of Confucius. 13– Zi Lu, Student of Confucius. 14– Yuan Xian, Student of Confucius. 15– Duke Ling of Wei. 16– Chief of the Ji Clan. 17– Yang Huo, Official of the Ji Clan. 18– Wei Zi, Founder of the Song State, 19– Zi Zhang, Student of Confucius. 20– Yao Spoke.

Li: 1– The Joy of Learning. 2– The Art of Governance. 3–The Supremacy of Conduct. 4– The Aquisition of Nobleness. 5– The Assessment of Disciples. 6– The Assessment of Disciples II. 7– The Pursuit of Scholarship. 8– The Conduct of Governance. 9– The Courage of Conviction. 10– The Application of Etiquette. 11– The Assessment of Disciples III. 12– The Observance of Conduct. 13– The Exemplification of Governance. 14– The Contributions of Ministers. 15– The Obligation of Gentlemen. 16– The Power of History. 17– The Challenge of Administrators. 18– The Nobleness of Recluses. 19– The Wisdom of Disciples. 20– The Legacy of Past Kings.

Rosemont: 1– Some Basic Concepts/Terms. 2– Xiao (Family Reverence), Governance. 3– Li (Rituals & Ritual Propriety). 4– Ren (Consummate Person/Conduct). 5– The Master's Comments on Students. 6– The Master's Comments on Students. 7– Autobiographical; Transmitting the Past. 8– Steadfast Commitment to Dao (Way). 9– Contextless Sayings of Confucius. 10– Formal Behavior of Confucius. 11– The Master's Comments on Students. 12– On Governance. 13– On Governance. 14– Evaluations of Historical Personages. 15– More Contextless Sayings of Confucius. 16– Miscellany.

17– Miscellany. 18– Unusual People, Recluses, etc.. 19– Sayings of Students. 20– Miscellany.

The Analects original received text: 1– Studying and Practicing/Xue Er. 2– The Practice of Government/Wei Zheng. 3– Eight Lines of Eight Dancers/ Ba Yi. 4– Living in Brotherliness/ Li Ren. 5– Gongye Chang/Gong Ye Chang. 6– There is Yong/Yong Ye. 7– Transmission/Shu Er. 8– Taibo/Tai Bo. 9– The Master Shunned/Zi Han. 10– Among the Xian and Dang/Xiang Dang. 11– Those of Former Eras/Xian Jin. 12– Yanyuan/Yan Yuan. 13– Zilu/Zi Lu. 14– Xian asked/Xian Wen. 15– Duke Ling of Wei/Wei Ling Gong. 16– Chief of the Ji Clan/ Ji Shi. 17– Yanghuo/Yang Huo. 18–Weizi/Wei Zi. 19– Zizhang/ Zi Zhang. 20– Yao Spoke/Yao Yue.

Vespe: 1– Virtues and Conduct. 2– Filial Relationships and Learning. 3– Ritual and Propriety. 4– Goodness and Gentlepersons. 5– Self and Relationships. 6– Disciples and Questions. 7– Confucius and Sayings. 8– Confucius and Sayings. 9– Qualities of Confucius. 10– Confucius and Rituals. 11– Confucius and Disciples. 12– Confucius and Disciples. 13– Governing and Gentlepersons. 14– Human Beings and Conduct. 15– Gentlepersons and Conduct. 16– Three and Nine Kinds of Things. 17– Human Nature and Six Loves. 18– A Madman, Farmers and Recluses. 19– Masters, Disciples and Officials. 20– Ancient Sage-Rulers and Lovely Virtues.

水

APPENDIX FIVE
RELATIONSHIP AND RECIPROCITY

The word 'reciprocity'/Shu – 'empathy, understanding, consideration and forgiveness' only appears twice and the word 'relationship'/Lun – 'natural relationships' only appears once in books of *The Analects*. This is perhaps because reciprocal relationships are so integral and central to the individual identity of the Chinese people that they aren't objectified and separated into oneself and other human beings. The 'I' is a 'we', I-Thou and self-other unity rather than an 'I or me and you' and 'self and other' duality. Reciprocal relationship is a 'given'.

Metaphorically, in the 'coin' of human reciprocal relationships, 'heads' or 'tails' matter when coins are flipped to see who 'goes first' or 'wins' and in the coin method of I Ching divination by creating the yang and yin lines of trigrams. But when coins are used for purchases, whichever side faces up doesn't affect their monetary value or buying power.

That being the case, and because reciprocal relationships are the foundation and heart of virtuous psychotherapy, it's good to include the Chinese characters and their etymologies for the words 'relationship' and 'reciprocity'.

A disciple asks for one word that guides human conduct throughout life and Confucius replies, 'Reciprocity', the consideration of the Golden Rule. 15-24.

A disciple says that the single thread of Confucius's way is loyalty to our moral nature and reciprocity toward fellow human beings. 4-15.

The important Five Great Relationships are not to be violated or discarded. 18-7.

$$\text{伶} = \text{亻} + \text{侖} = \text{人} + \text{冊}$$

1a. Lun - natural relationships = Tzu/Zi - human being + Ch'ai/Chai - book + Lun/Lun - arrange, put in order.

$$\text{恕} = \text{心} + \text{如} = \text{女} + \text{口}$$

1b. Shu - reciprocity, empathy, understanding, forgiveness = Hsin/Xin - heart + Ju/Ru - like, go to, follow, as good as, equal to, according to + Nu/Nu - woman + K'ou/Kou - mouth.

Reciprocal relationships are harmonious, understanding, empathic, forgiving, heart- centered, human-hearted and heart-felt between human beings who are equal to, as good as each other and in accord and who speak together with feminine and womanly grace, intimacy, wisdom and compassion.

$$\text{關} = \text{門} + \text{絲} = \text{幺} + \text{絲}$$

2a. Kuan/Guan - gate, connect, involve = Men/Men - gate, door, sect, school + Kuan/Guan - run threads thru a web + Yao/Yao - coil, tender, a coil of silk thread + Yu/You - small. 17

$$\text{係} = \text{亻} + \text{系} = \text{幺} + \text{小}$$

2b. Hsi/Xi - be related, connected, tie, link, succession, geneology, to be = Jen/Ren - human being + Hsi/Xi - to tie + Yao/Yao - coil, tender, a coil of silk thread + Hsiao/Xiao - small. 17

Reciprocal relationships are finely interwoven wholes of interrelated, interconnected and mutually involved human beings and gateways and openings to the shared virtues of respect, honesty, loyalty, fidelity, trust and intimacy,

$$對 = 丵 + 干 + 寸$$

3a. Tui/Dui - reciprocity, equality. Tui/Dui - correspond, match, agree, fit, suit, right, make a pair = Tsao/Zao - luxuriant vegetation, emanation + Shih/Shi - scholar, gentleman + Ts'un/ Cun - small. 17

$$等 = 竹 + 寺 = 土 + 寸$$

3b. Teng/Deng - compare, be equal to, alike = Chu/Zhu - bamboo + Szu/Si - temples and monasteries where laws of virtuous conduct are modeled, taught, learned, cultivated and lived + T'u/Tu -earth + Ts'un/Cun - small. 17

Reciprocal relationships are virtuous, corresponding and abundantly growthful ones that are fitting, suitable and right between individual human beings who are equal, alike, matching, united and paired.

$$互 = 二 + 吾 = 五 + 口$$

4a. Hu/Hu -reciprocal, mutual, mutually beneficial, interlocking, each other = Erh/Er - two + Wu/Wu - I, me + Wu/Wu - five, between heaven and earth, the dual powers of yin-yang creating the five elements, Wu Hsing + K'ou/Kou - mouth, opening, aperture, portal.

惠 = 心 + 叀

4b. HUI/HUI - willingly kind, gracious, accord with, obey, comply, heart-winning benevolence = HSIN/XIN - heart + CH'UAN/CHUAN - straps of an ox harness used for drawing objects.

Reciprocal relationships are natural, heavenly and earthly; energetically complementary, harmonious and creative and mutually beneficial ones that are opening up within us kindness, graciousness, benevolence and all of the other human virtues that are winning and drawing our hearts.

水

APPENDIX SIX
TEACHING AND LEARNING CHARACTERS

傅

傳

FU/FU - teach, teacher = JEN/REN - human being + FU/FU - spread + FU/FU - begin, just now, great + TS'UN/CUN - inch, small, thumb (used for hand in writing).

CH'UAN/CHUAN - transmit, pass on = JEN/REN - human being + CHUAN/ZHUAN - single, solely, particular, specially care, engrossed with + TS'UN/CUN - inch, small, thumb (used for hand in composition).

教 孝

CHIAO/JIAO - teach, instruct, learn = HSIAO/XIAO - learn, (not filial piety) + LAO/LAO - old, venerable, skilled + TZU/ZI - child + P'U/PU -tap, rap, knock (use the teaching rod).

念

NIEN/NIAN - study, learn =
CHIN/JIN - present + Hsin/Xin - heart.
(what is in the heart and mind).

學

HSUEH/XUE - study, learn =
TZU/ZI - child + Hsiao/Xiao - study, learn.
(a student holding a book).

水

CHINA AND CHINESE CHARACTERS

中

國

CHUNG/ZHONG - center, middle, inside , within, among, hit the center exactly, fit perfectly, all right, in progress.

KUO/GUO - country, nation, kingdom state, dynasty = WEI/WEI - surround, enclosure + KO/GE - spear, lance + K'OU/KOU - opening + I/YI - one.

China is ZHONG GUO, The Middle Kingdom.

中

華

CHUNG/ZHONG - center, middle, inside, within, among, hit the center exactly, fit perfectly, all right, in progress.

HUA/HUA - flowers, splendor, glory, China, magnificent, flourishing, prosperous = TS'AO/CAO - grass, luxuriant vegetation + TSAO/ZAO - early, first sun, morning, soon, former, previous, long ago.

CHINA IS ZHONG HUA, The Central Flourishing Magnificence.

264 / CONFUCIUS *THE ANALECTS*

漢　人

HAN/HAN JEN/REN - the Han people,
the Chinese race, nationality, people,
belonging to China = SHUI/SHUI - water +
CHIEN/JIAN - difficult (originally a human
being with hands held behind the back) +
JEN/REN - persons, human beings.

水

Notes

1. The Three Vinegar Tasters is a popular Chinese allegory and Japanese painting depicting the expressions of Lao Tzu, Confucius and the Buddha when tasting vinegar from a large vat.

Confucius – Scowling over the sour taste. Society, government and the world are disordered and have declined from the morality, goodness, rightness and rituals of the legendary Ancient Sage-Rulers and the Way of Heaven and are in critical need of learning and rectifying.

The Buddha – Frowning over the bitter taste. Human life is suffering due to illusional and deluded ego-selves desiring and becoming attached to what is impermanent and many human beings have not followed a path of awakening, enlightenment and liberation.

Lao Tzu – Smiling over the natural taste. Life experiences are spontaneous, harmonious and perfect in their natural Tao-state, just what they are as they are, and are to be appreciated, accepted, enjoyed and shared as such in the present here-now moment.

The allegory reflects the syncretic reality of integrating the three wisdom traditions in a complementary and harmonious manner in everyday living and ordinary experiencing and resulting in being and living morally, consciously and naturally and peacefully, freely, intimately and happily.

Confucianism	Buddhism	Taoism
The Way of Ancients	The Way of Dharma	The Way of Nature
Ethical Principles	The Eightfold Path	Natural Laws
Moral Virtues	Emptiness	Energy Flow
Social Rituals	Suchness	Accord with Dao
Order	Awakening	Harmony
Human Nature	Buddha/True Nature	Dao Nature
Social consequences	Karmic retribution	Yin-Yang reversing
Ancestral	Transformational	Natural
Cultural	Enlightenment	Spiritual
Ethical	Non-Ego	Vital
Moral	Impermanence	Instinctual
Social	Non-Attachment	Individual
Political	Liberation	Presence
Personal	Personal	Personal
Interpersonal	Non-Personal	Transpersonal
The Gentleperson	The Monk	The Sage
551-479 BCE	563-483 BCE	6th Century BCE
Kong Qiu	Siddhartha Gautama	Li Er
Zhong Ni	Shakyamuni	Lao Dan
Kong Fu Zi	The Buddha	Lao Zi
Confucius	The Awakened One	The Old Boy
Cultured Human Being	Enlightened Human Being	Natural Human Being

4,010,678 Followers   251,876,213 Followers   5,510,658 Followers
(Atheist = 805,465,234; Folk = 264,065,876; Christian = 60,667,567; Islam = 19,012,567).

The realities and truths of the three spiritual traditions of Confucianism, Buddhism and Taoism harmoniously co-exist within and as our own consciousness, being and living and our heart, mind and Soul. Our real and true human nature is 1) fundamentally and culturally ethical, moral and virtuous; 2) personally and peacefully awake, free and open and 3) happily, intimately and infinitely one with Mother Nature, all creation and fellow human beings.

2. For the commentaries, I originally designated psychotherapists as 'Good gentle psychotherapists' in line with the principal Confucian virtue of 'Goodness' as embodied and personified in the 'Gentleperson'. Continually using the name 'good gentle psychotherapists' became awkward, cumbersome and tedious and 'good' and 'gentle' suggest 'bad' and 'rough' and not the Confucian meanings of Goodness and Gentlepersons.

I thought of using the name 'exemplary psychotherapists' and liked the denotation of the psychotherapist; 1) being an 'example' (L. - ex- + -emere - to take out) and 'teaching by example'; 2) being 'exemplary' - 'commendable', 'outstanding', 'excellent', 'distinguished' and 3) being an 'exemplar' - 'a model, pattern, example and illustration deserving to be imitated'; certainly comparable qualities of the truly Good gentlepersons of Confucian virtues.

The word 'virtue' triggered the realizing of Confucianism's 'virtue ethics' as a central teaching and I settled on designating the psychotherapist as 'the virtuous psychotherapist', which includes 'virtue' (L. virtus - strength), 'virtuous' - 'moral excellence' and 'efficacious potency', 'virtuoso/a' - 'one who excels in the technique of an art' and 'virtuosity' - 'great technical skill in the practice of a fine art'.

3. Some basic and advanced counseling skills that psychology graduate school students, trainees and interns are instructed and trained in are:

Attending and listening	Exploring and suggesting
Clarifying and inquiring	Explaining and amplifying
Repeating and paraphrasing	Analyzing and interpreting
Reflecting and summarizing	Reframing content
Acknowledging and joining	Confronting and challenging
Mirroring and imitating	Probing and deepening
Giving Feedback	Self-disclosing and sharing

Et Al

Such counseling skill-sets are designed and implemented; 1) to assist counselors and psychotherapists in being open to, accepting of, interested in and engaged, connected, involved, interacting and effective with clients and patients and 2) to provide clients and patients with a sense of reality, relatedness, meaningfulness, purposefulness and progress in their counseling and psychotherapy.

4. Confucius and his three most accomplished disciples; probably Yan Hui, Zi Gong and Zi Lu; travel for fourteen years from their Lu State to the neighboring Zhou Dynasty principality states of Cai, Cao, Chen, Chu, Jin/Yi, Qi, Qin, Song, Wei, Wu, Yan, Yue and Zheng. Confucius consults with state rulers and seeks governmental official positions to no successful end.

5. Confucian Symbols.

水	囍	儒	☯
Water	**Confucius**	**Scholar**	**Bipolar Unity**
SHUI	KONG ZI	RU	YIN-YANG

6. The classic Confucian hierarchical social classes that are designed and formulated to insure social order and harmony are the following:

1. SHI - Scholars, government officials and public servants. Maintaining essential social order.

2. NONG - Farmers, landowners and peasants. Growing and providing essential food.

3. GONG - Artisans and craftspersons. Creating and producing essential goods.

4. SHANG - Merchants and tradespersons. Selling and transporting essential goods.

These social classes are an occupation-based hierarchy, are

not based upon heredity or socio- economic status and change their order in different dynasties that gave the occupations relatively greater or lesser value and importance. Confucius emphasizes and advocates for the 'rectification of names, titles and roles' that results in social order and harmony, e.g., when a farmer is a farmer only, a scholar is a scholar only, an artist is an artist only, an official is an official only, etc..

7. Confucianism was originally referred to as Ruism and defined as 'A vast interconnected system of philosophies, ideas, rituals and practices of the heart'; 'A tradition of philosophy, religion, rationalism and humanism and a way of governing and living' and 'A class of specialists concerned with preserving and transmitting traditional texts and rituals of the Zhou Dynasty'.

Ru is the Chinese term for 'scholar'/'learned' and Ru Jia is 'the school of the learned'. Etymologically, the Chinese character Ru is a combination of the two characters, Ren - human being, humanity and Xu - need, require, necessary, essential, indispensable, bent on doing, duty, obligation. The term Ruism is preferred because it accurately reflects the essential centrality and obligatory necessity of learning rather than does the Latinized word Confucianism.

8. The first recorded introduction of Christianity to China reportedly occurs in 635 CE as discovered in the 1620s in Xian, the capital of China on a large excavated stone stela carved by a Christian monk in 781 CE and probably buried in 845 CE. Reportedly, a heretical form of Nestorian Christianity of The Church of the East centered in Persia separates from Byzantine Christianity after 431 CE and is later brought to China by a Nestorian monk, Aluoben/Alopen and Syrian missionaries via the Silk Road in 635 CE during the Tang Dynasty (618-907 CE).

Nestorian Christianity holds the heretical beliefs 1) that Jesus Christ is not a one God-man and both a human being and the Son of God, that His two human and Divine natures are separate and that He is a God-inspired human being by virtue rather than the Son of God by nature and 2) that Mary, therefore, is not the Mother of God. During this time, The Holy Bible is translated into the Chinese language and Nestorian Christianity survives for some two-hundred years in China before being persecuted and finally banned in 845 CE, along with all 'foreign' religion, by imperial edict and disappears in 907 CE at the end of the Tang Dynasty.

9. *The Five Confucian Classics.* Wu Jing.

The Classic of Changes. Yi Jing. A divination oracle and system of yin-yang relationships.

The Classic of Odes. Shi Jing. A collection of various ancient poems, songs and hymns.

The Classic of Documents. Shu Jing. History of Ancient China/Sage-Rulers Yao and Shun.

The Classic of Rites. Li Jing. Social norms, moral conduct and ritual practices of Zhou Dynasty.

The Spring and Autumn Annals. Chun Qiu. An historical chronicle of the State of Lu.

(The *Classics of Music* and *Agriculture* are not included or are lost).

The Four Confucian Books. Si Shu.

The Great Learning. Da Xue. Rites and guides for pursuing learning and self-cultivation.

The Doctrine of the Mean. Zhong Yong. Good rulers maintain moderation and balance.

The Mencius. Meng Zi. Dialogues of Mencius. Natural goodness and virtuous rulership.

The Analects. Lun Yu. A collection of Confucius's teachings and dialogues with disciples.

10. *The Five Cardinal Relationships.* Wu Lun.
   1) Father-Son (Mother-daughter/son?. Father-daughter?). Respect, obedience, care.
   2) Ruler-Subject. Govern by benevolence and righteousness. Loyalty, obedience, duty.
   3) Husband-Wife. Respect, love, fidelity.
   4) Older-Younger Brother (Sisters?). Respect, obedience.
   5) Older-Younger Friend. Mutual understanding, sincerity, trust, loyalty, support.

11. The Five Virtues
   Benevolence – REN
   Righteousness – YI
   Propriety – LI
   Sincerity – XIN
   Wisdom – ZHI

12. The Six Arts
   Rites
   Music
   Calligraphy
   Mathematics
   Archery
   Charioteering

13. The 4 Eastern Zhou Dynasty Rulers during the time of Confucius – 551-479 BCE
   King Ling – 571-545 BCE – weakened relations.
   King Jing – 544-521 BCE – caused rebellions.
   King Dao – 520-519 BCE – brother assassinates.
   King Jing – 519-476 BCE – exiled during revolt.

14. The English language word 'gentle' (L. gentilis - of the same clan/nation) is defined as:

1. belonging to a family of high social station, honorable, distinguished, chivalrous,

2. of or relating to a gentleman, a man of noble or gentle birth and rank,

3. moderate, kind, amiable, tractable, docile, soft, delicate, not rough or harsh,

4. free from sternness, harshness, unethical and immoral behavior and violence,

5. conduct conforming to a high standard of propriety and good and right behavior.

15. The ritual practices of Chinese culture may be more explicit and obvious than those of American ones, however it's worth noting some 'rituals' that are common to both cultures as well as being uniquely different. Rituals, rites and ceremonies create personal order, social harmony and cultural stability and reflect the mores, activities, behaviors and practices of socialized, acculturated and cultured and civil human beings. Some rituals that are both prescribed and formal and spontaneous and informal that are often ignored as such and that can be appreciated as such are the following ones:

Personal.

1. Eating times, self-care and regular personal habits and daily routines.

2. Exercise routines; meditation times, yoga postures and sexual positions.

3. Times of favorite video programs and playing music, sports and games.

4. Times made for hobbies, entertainment activities and attending events.

5. Regular scheduling of medications, bill paying, pet feeding and dog walking.
6. Regular times set aside for diary entries, journaling and bedtime prayers.
7. Scheduling doctor's appointments and auto and appliance maintenance.
8. Washing dishes, doing laundry, ironing clothes, cleaning and watering plants.
9. Dressing appropriately for various activities, events, affairs and occasions.
10. Putting up commemorative banners and flags and flying flags at half-mast.
11. Clapping hands and giving fanfares and standing ovations at performances.
12. Complying with proper behavior at weddings, graduations and funerals.
13. Complying with proper behavior in churches, schools, hospitals and stores.
14. Complying with proper behavior at ceremonies, celebrations and festivities.
15. Adhering to any and all laws, rules, regulations, protocols and instructions.
16. Planting garden vegetables and flowers seasonally, pruning and fertilizing.
17. Observing the four seasons, solstices, equinoxes, lunar phases and eclipses.
18. Checking car tires and warning lights and buckling seatbelts before driving.

Social.

1. Saying good morning, hello, goodbye, good night, thank you and you're welcome.
2. Giving smiles, handshakes and hugs; clasping hands, nodding and bowing.

3. Making apologies, saying 'sorry', 'excuse me', 'may I?', 'please' and 'could you?'.

4. Listening to, attending, caring for, supporting, helping, aiding and assisting others.

5. Not neglecting, harming, injuring, abusing, cheating, robbing and betraying others.

6. Having dignity and respect; being civil, courteous, kind and gentle with others.

7. Being understanding, compassionate, empathic and considerate with others.

8. Acting in ways that are accepting, inclusive, non-judgmental, friendly and warm.

9. Celebrating births, weddings, funerals, holidays and various rites of passage.

10. Sending birthday, anniversary, sympathy, get well and holiday greeting cards.

11. Observing religious and national holidays and the birthdays of famous people.

12. Giving presents, flowers, jewelry, books, games, toys and trinkets to others.

13. Table setting, seating places, saying grace, making toasts and clinking glasses.

14. Serving elders, women, children first; attentively listening to conversations.

15. Letting others go ahead in store lines. Opening the car door for passengers.

16. Assisting elderly and disabled people, pregnant women and young children.

17. Picking up things and giving them to people who accidently dropped them.

18. If driving, obeying the 'rules of the road' and giving others the 'right of way'.

16. While much understanding of the literature and cultural tradition and legacy of China and its rulers and people can be obtained from archaeological evidence, I personally object to the disrespectful desecrating of sacred burial sites that amounts to government sanctioned and sponsored tomb raiding and grave robbing. I'm surprised, dismayed and confused by why and how it's allowed, in spite of quasi-legitimate professed scientific and scholarly reasons to understand and appreciate the nature, cultural legacy and evolution of our human existence.

17. In Appendix Five, parts 2a, 2b, 3a and 3b, the use of three different characters for 'small' (also meaning 'inch' and 'a little') are puzzling and perhaps connote the virtues of 'humility' and 'humbleness', 'moderation' and 'moderateness' and 'deference' that constitute virtuous, mutual, equal, complementary and reciprocal human relationships.

水

THE VIRTUE POEM

Goodness and the Right,
not hypocritical or trite,
shining clear and bright.

Ritual and ceremony,
not rigid or stony,
perfunctory or phony.

Filial respect and piety,
duty and propriety
in their infinite variety.

Courtesy and gentility,
an absence of hostility,
the conduct of civility.

Integrity and sincerity,
well-founded in verity,
not an exceptional rarity.

Dedication and fidelity,
devotion and loyalty,
not simply for royalty.

Learning and knowledge,
self-improver's pledge,
true wisdom to dredge.

Equality and reciprocity,
preventing any atrocity,
insuring peaceful felicity.

With the ideal gentleperson;
sibling, daughter and son,
humanity will not worsen.

Virtue/De and Dao/the Way,
ever present night and day,
ever creating work and play.

水

FINAL BLESSING

福

FU - blessing, happiness, felicity, good fortune and prosperity.

ネ   or   示

SHI - proclaim, reveal, exhibit, see, teach, signs from heaven revealing transcendent things, the influx from heaven, the will and power of heaven known to human beings.

尣

SHANG - heaven above, high and superior and sun, moon and stars shining down.

畐

FU - land heaped high, goods of earth, abundance, fullness, wealth and riches.

一

YI - one, first, like, same as, unity, whole and all.

田

TIAN - cultivated and furrowed field and land.

口

KOU - mouth, opening, aperture, entrance, speech and talk.

May you experience the blessed bestowal
of your most precious life.

May you experience heaven's inflowing revelation
of transcendent reality.

May you discover, actualize and contribute
your unique purpose in your life.

May you enjoy the good fortune, prosperity,
abundance and richness of your life.

May you treasure the sacredness, peacefulness
and happiness of your life.

May you have a safe, secure, healthy, creative,
intimate and meaningful life.

May you have an absolutely beautiful and a
completely fulfilling long life.

May you have an ethical consciousness
and moral conscience guiding your life.

May you be committed to learning as self-cultivation,
self-refinement and self-improvement.

May you cultivate the goodness, rightness, oneness,
and wholeness of your life.

May you be wise, ethical, moral, responsible,
dependable, accountable and trustworthy.

May you be authentic, honest, sincere,
faithful, loyal and courageous.

May you be dignified, cultured, egoless, humble,
friendly, trusting, caring and loving.

May you awaken to pure clear consciousness
of the reality and truth of your unique being.

May you be kind, courteous, civil, compassionate,
empathic, fair, just and forgiving.

May you be gentle, understanding, tolerant,
patient, generous and grateful.

May you be supportive, helpful, encouraging,
reinforcing, inspiring and elevating.

May you be devoted, dedicated, committed,
resolved, dutiful and diligent.

May you venerate ancestors and respect parents,
women, children and elders.

May you be grateful for your family, friends,
neighbors, peers and strangers.

May you be intimately connected with Nature
and all fellow human beings.

May you have reciprocal personal, interpersonal,
and transpersonal relationships.

May you bring light, life, love, freedom, peace
and happiness to all you meet.

May you intimately share your reality, truth
and beauty with fellow human beings.

May you realize that there is no question or
choice about being a humane being.

May you realize that there is no alternative to
or option for being a humane being.

水

GLOSSARY

Ai - to love
Axial Age - ~500 BCE
Bian - change
Cheng - honesty
Chi - shame
Chung Yung - Middle Way between extremes
      - moderation, compromise
Da Xue - Great Learning
Dao - the moral Way of Ancients, social order
  - the Way of Heaven, the way human beings go
De - individual moral virtue, integrity, energy, power
    - inner character, excellence, social ethics/morality
    - moral worthiness, moral kindness
    - endowment of virtue from Heaven
Di - emperor
Di - sacrificial ritual
Duke of Zhou - 1045-1035 BCE reign
Eastern Zhou Dynasty - 770-221 CE
Fu Xi - legendary Neolithic Ruler - 2852-2737 BCE
Gong - respect, courtesy
Guan - official
Gui - ghost, spirit
Guo - country, kingdom, state, nation
Han Dynasty - 206 BCE-220 CE
Hao Xue - love of learning
He - harmony
Hua - transform
Hui - benevolence
Hui - teach, impart light

Jia - family, home

Jiao - teachings

Jie - self-restraint

Jin Dynasty 265-420 CE

Jing - classsic text

Jing - respect, reverence

Jun - ruler

Jun Zi - ruler's son, gentleperson

     - highest cultivated/refined moral character

     - highest moral self-development

     - disciplined/educated/cultured human being

     - superior/noble/exemplary human being

Jung - center, heart

King Wu of Zhou - 1046-1043 BCE reign

Kong Fu Zi - Confucius - 551-479 BCE

Kong Shu Liang He - Confucius's father

Kong Jiao - Confucius's daughter

Kong Li/Bo Yu - Confucius's son -532-482 BCE

Kong Qiu - Confucius's birth name

Kung - respectfulness

Lady Qi Guan - Confucius's wife

Lao Zi - Dao De Jing author. 6th C. BCE

Le - happiness, joy (same character as Yue - music)

Li - physical force as opposed to moral force

Li - propriety, etiquette, social mores, manners

   - rituals, rites, moral practice, observances

   - ceremonies, offerings, sacrifices

   - body of rules of conduct in all of life

   - whatever is done for self-cultivation

   - centering of heaven, earth, human being

   - harmonious acting in accord with Goodness

Lian - loyalty

Liao Dynasty - 916-1125 CE

Li Xue - Neo-Confucianism

Lu - Confucius's State
Lun Yu - *The Analects*
Meng Zi/Mencius - 372-289 BCE - Confucianist
Min - common people
Ming - destiny, fate, mandate, decree, command
Ming Dynasty - 1368-1644 CE
Ming - light, brightness
Mo Zi - 470-391 BCE
Ning - glib
Po - elder
Qi - material force, energy
Qian - humility
Qin Dynasty/First Imperial Dynasty - 221-206 BCE
Qing/Last Dynasty - 1644-1912 CE
Qu Fu - Confucius's hometown
Rang - modesty, deference
Ran Yu - disciple of Confucius - 522-? BCE
Ren - benevolence, Goodness, humaneness
    - human heartedness, love of humanity
    - respect, empathy, compassion
    - kindness, gentleness, charity, altruism
    - Heaven endowed essence of human being
    - internalized Way/form of Heaven
    - highest virtue possessed
    - source of moral virtue/conduct, social good
Ren - freemen, tribal members
Ren - human being, humankind, fellow human beings
Ru - Confucian scholars, literati, teachers
    - devoted to learning/peaceful arts
    - traditional ritual specialists
Ruism - Confucianism
Ru Jia - school of Confucianism
Ru Jiao - religion of Confucianism
Shan - Good, Goodness, useful, able

Shan Ren - excellent person
Shao - peace music of Shun
Shang Di - highest deity
Shang Dynasty - 1600-1045 BCE
Shen Gui - gods and spirits
Sheng Ren - sage
Shang Sheng - Divine Sage
Sheng Wang - Sage King
Shi - Military Knight of the Way
Shi - odes, poems, poetry
Shi - scholar, educated person
Shi - social class between aristocrats/commoners
   - lowest social level of aristocracy
   - public servant
Shi - timeliness
Si - thinking, concentrating
Sima Qian - 1st C. BCE Han Dynasty historian
        - first biographer of Confucius
Shou - water
Shu - reciprocity, mutuality, equitability
   - kindness, forgiveness, mercy
   - empathic understanding
   - harmony in social relationships
   - practicing of the Golden Rule
Shui - water
Shun - legendary Neolithic Sage-Ruler - 2255-2205 BCE
Si - think, reflect
Si Shu - The Four Books
Song Dynasty - 960-1279 CE
Spring & Autumn Period/Chun & Qiu - 770-475 BCE
Ssu - thinking, attention, observation
Sui Dynasty - 581-618 CE
Sun Zi - Art of War author - c.544-c.496 BCE
Tang Dynasty - 618-907 CE

Ti - respect for elders

Tian - sky, heavens, Heaven, Providence, Nature
- supreme moral force deciding human destiny

Tian Dao - The Way of Heaven, order of the world

Tian Ming - The Mandate/Decree of Heaven

Tu - disciple, apprentice

Wang - king

Wang Yang Ming - Neo-Confucianist - 1472-1529 CE

Warring States/Zhang Guo Period - 475-221 BCE

Wen - refinement, culture, literature
- arts of peace as opposed to art of war
- music, dance, poetry

Wen - gentleness

Wen - mighty

Wen Yan - Chinese imperial language

Western Zhou Dynasty - 1045-770 BCE

Wu - war music of King Wu

Wu - warrior

Wu Ching - the Five Classics

Wu Lun - the Five Relationships
- centered in love

Wu-Wei - non-'doing', effortless action

Xi - practice

Xia/First Dynasty - 2100-1600 BCE

Xian - worthy, worthiness

Xian Shi - Confucius as 'first teacher'

Xiao - filial piety, family reverence
- dutiful honoring, respecting, devotion
- serving, caring for parents/elders

Xiao Ren - smaller/lesser/petty/common persons

Xin - heart, heart-mind, center

Xin - sincerity, honesty, integrity, fidelity
- truthfulness, faithfulness, trustworthiness
- reliability in word, promise keeping

Xing - deed, action, conduct

Xing - human nature

Xue - life-long learning/study, self-cultivation
- self-improvement, moral development

Xun Zi - 310-238 BCE - Confucianist (critic?)

Yan - words, speech, to speak

Yan Hui - Confucius's favorite disciple - 522-481 BCE

Yan Zeng Zai - Confucius's mother

Yao - joy, happiness

Yao - legendary Neolithic Sage-Ruler - 2324-2255 BCE

Yellow Emperor - 2698-2598 BCE

Yi - Righteousness, correctness, appropriateness
- moral integrity, uprightness, honesty, fairness
- ethical conduct, responsibilty, duty, justice

Yi Jing - Classic of Changes

Yong - courage, bravery

Yu the Great - legendary Xia Sage-Ruler - 2123-2025 BCE

Yuan Dynasty - 1279-1368 CE

Yue - music (same character as Le -happiness, joy, pleasure)

Zeng Zi/Master Zeng/Zi Yu - disciple of Confucius - 505-435 BCE

Zheng - govern, rule, government

Zheng - correct, upright, rectify

Zheng Ming - rectification of names/titles
- congruence with reality

Zhi - upright, uprightness, straightness

Zhi - will, intention

Zhi - wisdom, knowledge, understanding
- realization, acknowledgement
- reflection, insight, self-cultivation

Zhong - center

Zhong - duty, loyalty, obedience
- to do one's best

Zhong Ni - Confucius's honorific title

Zhong Yong - Doctrine of the Mean
         - The MiddleWay, moderation
         - everpresent middle ground
         - compromise, not extremes
Zhou - state
Zhou Dynasty - 1045-221 BCE
Zhu Xi - Neo-Confucianist - 1130-1200 CE
Zi Gong - disciple of Confucius - 520-456 BCE
Zi Lu - disciple of Confucius - 542-480 BCE
Zi Si - grandson of Confucius - 481-402 BCE
Zi Xia - disciple of Confucius - 507-400 BCE
Zi Yue - the Master says
Zi Zhang - disciple of Confucius - 503-? BCE
Zong Ni - Confucius's honorific title

水

REFERENCES

Ames, Roger T. and Rosemont, Henry Jr. (Trs.). *The Analects of Confucius: A Philosophical Translation.* New York: Ballantine Books. 1998.

Chin, Annping. *The Authentic Confucius: A Life of Thought and Politics.* New York: Scribner. 2007.

Chin, Annping (Tr.). *Confucius: The Analects (Lunyu).* New York: Penguin Books. 2014.

Dawson, Raymond (Tr.) *The Analects.* Oxford: Oxford University Press. 1993.

Fenn, C.H.. *The Five Thousand Dictionary: Chinese-English.* Cambridge, Massachusetts: Harvard University Press. 1976.

Fingarette, Herbert. Confucius: *The Secular as Sacred.* New York: Harper & Row. 1972.

Giles Lionel (Tr.). *The Analects of Confucius.* Ottawa, Canada: East India Publishing Company. 2022.

https:wikipedia.org>wiki>Analects

https:wikipedia.org>wiki>Confucianism

https:wikipedia.org>wiki>Confucius

https:en.wikipedia.org>wiki>Confuciuspolitics

Huang, Chichung (Tr.). *The Analects of Confucius.* New York: Oxford University Press. 1997.

Lau, D.C. (Tr.). *Confucius. The Analects.* New York: Penguin Books. 1979.

Lau, D.C. (Tr.). *Confucius. The Analects: Bilingual Edition.* Hong Kong: The Chinese University Press. 2014.

Legge, James. *The Analects of Confucius: Bilingual Edition.* North Haven, Connecticut: Dragon Reader. 2016.

Leys, Simon (Tr.). *The Analects of Confucius.* New York: W.W. Norton. 1997.

Li, David H. (Tr.). *The Analects of Confucius: A New-Millenium Translation* (With Chinese Text and Annotation). Bethesda, Maryland: Premier Publishing Co. 1999.

Li Dong. *Concise Chinese Dictionary: Chinese-English/English-Chinese.* Rutland, Vermont: Tuttle Publishing. 2015.

Mathews, R.H.. *Chinese-English Dictionary.* Cambridge, Massachusetts: Harvard University Press. 1943.

Ministry of Foreign Affairs. *Republic of China (Taiwan). Taiwan Today. Travels of Confucius.* Posted 5/27/2024. https://taiwantoday.tw>news

McNaughton, William and Lee Ying. *Reading and Writing Chinese Characters:* Traditional Character Edition. Rutland, Vermont. 1999.

Quanyu Huang, Tong Chen and Kuangyan Huang. *McGraw-Hill's Chinese Dictionary and Guide to 20,000 Essential Words.* New York: McGraw-Hill. 2010.

Rosemont, Henry Jr.. *A Reader's Companion to the Confucian Analects.* Honolulu: University of Hawaii Press 2012.

Slingerland, Edward (Tr.). *Confucius Analects with Selections from Traditional Commentaries.* Indianapolis: Hackett Publishing Company, Inc.. 2013.

Van Norden, Bryan W.. *Confucius and the Analects: New Essays.* New York: Oxford University Press. 2002.

Waley, Arthur (Tr.). *Confucianism: The Analects. Sacred Writings. Confucianism: The Analects of Confucius.* Jeroslav Pelikan (Ed.). New York: Quality Paperback Book Club. 1992.

Watson, Burton (Tr.). *The Analects of Confucius.* New York: Columbia University Press. 2007.

Webster's New Collegiate Dictionary. Springfield, Massachusetts: G. & C. Merriam Company. 1979.

Wieger, L.. *Chinese Characters: Their Origin, Etymology, History, Classification and Signification.* L. Davrout (Tr.). New York: Dover Publications.

Wilder, G.D. and Ingram, J.H.. *Analysis of Chinese Characters.* New York: Dover Publications. 1974.

Readers desiring to learn more about Confucius, Confucianism and *The Analects* are encouraged to make Google searches and to watch relevant You Tube video presentations.

水

About The Author

I am a former Associate Professor of Integral Counseling Psychology and a retired Licensed Marriage Family Therapist after; 1) enjoying a fifty year long professional career educating, training, supervising and mentoring graduate school counseling trainees and psychology interns and 2) conducting an individual psychotherapy and counseling private practice for children, adolescents and adults and individuals, couples and families.

I have studied with prominent philosophy and psychology educators and trained with master psychotherapists and counselors in the fields of Phenomenology and Existential, Humanistic and Transpersonal Psychology and Psychotherapy. I have worked as a clinical psychologist in a wide variety of inpatient hospitals, outpatient clinics and group and individual private practices and have held clinical directorship positions in several community counseling centers and substance abuse treatment centers.

I have experienced principal teachers, teachings, Masters and meditation practices in the spiritual traditions of Hinduism; Theravada, Mahayana, Vajrayana, Ekayana, Ch'an and Zen Buddhism; Taoism and Zen. I have participated in small group shamanic medicine circles and experienced consciousness awakenings and openings and the transformative healing power of various natural plants and psychotropic substances.

I have written six other books integrating the spiritual and practical wisdom of Taoism and Zen:

1) A rendition of Lao Tzu's *Tao Te Ching* with psychotherapeutic commentary.

2) A rendition of Chuang Tzu's *Seven Interior Records* with psychotherapeutic commentary.

3) A rendition of Lieh Tzu's *The Nature of Real Living* with psychotherapeutic commentary.

4) A rendition of Lao Tzu's *Tao Te Ching* with soul-journeying commentary.

5) A rendition of *The Ten Ox-Herding Pictures* with psychospiritual commentary.

6) A rendition of Sun Tzu's *The Art of War* with psychosocial commentary.

My former early life was enjoyed in intimate relationship with Great Mother Nature and Her creatures and living close to river, forest and lake natural settings. My current later life is being enjoyed living in a wooded natural setting beside a seasonal creek and close to the Pacific Ocean. Thus, a full circle of being and living is coming to completion.

水

OUR CHOICES

Regardless of our circumstances
in any and every given situation
and at any particular given time,
we all and always have the choice
in relations with fellow human beings
to either be or to not be
accepting and inclusive,
acknowledging and appreciative,
respectful and courteous,
friendly and considerate,
good, right and proper,
available and accessible,
real and authentic,
true and genuine,
honest and sincere,
interested and attentive,
empathic and compassionate,
inspiring and encouraging,
uplifting and elevating,
nourishing and beneficial,
supportive and helpful,
faithful and trustworthy,
loyal and devoted,
giving and generous,
equalitarian and fair,
kind, tender and gentle,
tolerant and patient,
loving and caring,
grateful and forgiving.

水

www.ingramcontent.com/pod-product-compliance
Lightning Source LLC
Chambersburg PA
CBHW051712020426
42333CB00014B/948